Praise for *The Complete Cat's Meow*

This is a book to be treasured by every cat lover—and we are legion. I learned a lot and enjoyed every minute.

> —Betty White, actress and author

"Darlene Arden's work has always been top-notch, and like most pet writers' work, mostly focuses on dogs. This is the most complete, on-target cat book I've read in a very long time. Truly everything you need to know about having a cat is here; in fact, Darlene does everything except adopt the cat for you. And along the way she dispels myths and mistaken notions about cats, too. With this book, Darlene instantly CATapults herself into a select group of top cat experts in the country."

> —Steve Dale, CABC, contributing editor *USA Weekend*, syndicated Tri-
> bune Media Services columnist, host of *Steve Dale's Pet World* national
> radio shows, and board member of the American Humane Associa-
> tion, Winn Feline Foundation, and CATalyst Council board of directors

"Darlene Arden puts her usual writing flair into *The Complete Cat's Meow*. Accurate, well-researched, and full of useful and fascinating facts, this book provides what the title promises: complete information. Think cats can't be trained? Think again. This book will teach you a great deal, whether you're a beginner or have been cat-owned for many years. Although all sections of this book are accurate and well written, I was particularly impressed with the section on handling and social-izing kittens, as this is vital to their growing into well-behaved and loving adults. The section on understanding cat behavior is equally noteworthy, since so many problems can be avoided if one understands how cats relate to their world. The section on popular cat breeds is spot-on accurate, for those of you who wish to share your life with a pedi-greed feline. A must-have for any cat lover!"

> —J. Anne Helgren, author of six cat books, including *Barron's Encyclope-*
> *dia of Cat Breeds* and *Communicating with Your Cat,* as well as hun-
> dreds of articles on cats and cat breeds

"In thirty-plus years of living and working with cats as a veterinarian, I believe people become cat lovers by finding the specific cat that fits their personality. *The Complete Cat's Meow* is full of information enhancing the human-cat bond and ensures loving cats is a lifelong pleasure."

—Vicki Thayer DVM, DABVP (feline); president-elect, Winn Feline Foundation; past president, American Association of Feline Practitioners

THE COMPLETE
CAT'S MEOW

THE COMPLETE CAT'S MEOW

Everything You Need to Know about Caring for Your Cat

DARLENE ARDEN

WILEY

Wiley Publishing, Inc.

Library of Congress Control Number: 2011922017

ISBN 978-0-470-64167-5 (paper: alk. paper)

ISBN 978-1-118-02456-0 (ebk.)

Printed in the United States of America

10 9 8 7 6 5 4 3 2 1

Book design by Lissa Auciello-Brogan
Cover design by Wendy Mount
Book production by Wiley Publishing, Inc., Composition Services

To the memory of my mother and her first cat, Susie; to my little muse and her last cat, Aimee (GP Sinaye's Plaisir d'Amour of Ajolie); to the late Barbara Royer, who insisted I should write a cat book as useful as my small dog book; to Dru Milligan and Jolie Stratton for entrusting me with Aimee; and to the memory of my friend Kari Winters, taken from us far too soon under mysterious circumstances, who rescued and rehabilitated more cats than anyone will ever know. This book is dedicated to each of you with my love and grateful thanks.

CONTENTS

ACKNOWLEDGMENTS

There are people who deserve a big thank you for sharing their knowledge, for cheerleading, for caring so much about this book. In alphabetical order:

Jill Archibald; Linda Aronson, DVM, Pet Shrink, Berlin, Massachusetts; Joan Bernstein; Jane E. Brunt, DVM, executive director, CATalyst Council; Carol Carberry, DVM, DACVS, Oradell Animal Hospital, Paramus, New Jersey; Shawn Finch, DVM; Vickie Fisher; Sue Janson; Pam Johnson-Bennett, CCBC; Dottie LaFlamme, DVM, PhD, DACVN, Nestle Purina Pet Care Research; Dru Milligan; Jolie Milligan-Stratton; Jacqueline Mason Munera, BA, CCBC, ProCBC, CAP2; Karen Overall, MA, VMD, PhD, DACVB, ABS; Phil Padrid, DVM, associate professor of molecular medicine (adjunct), University of Chicago Pritzker School of Medicine, associate professor of small animal medicine (adjunct), the Ohio State University School of Veterinary Medicine, regional medical director VCA, NM, AZ, NV, UT, NB; Mary Rathbun; Raymond Russo, DVM, president, Kingston Animal Hospital, Kingston, MA; Lucy Schroth, DVM; Vicki L. Thayer, DVM, DABVP (feline), Purrfect Practice PC, Lebanon, Oregon, Winn Feline Foundation board member, American Association of Feline Practitioners president; Alice Villalobos, DVM, DPNAP, director of Pawspice of Hermosa Beach, California, director of Animal Oncology Consultation Service of Woodland, Society for Veterinary Medical Ethics president.

Also Pam Mourouzis, acquisitions editor at Howell Book House; and my editor and friend Beth Adelman, who gracefully wears both hats, as well as that of a fellow cat behavior consultant.

INTRODUCTION

Cats. They are glorious, elegant, sweet, dear companions—loved, adored, and, yes, worshipped. In the United States, they outnumber dogs as household pets. And yet, for entirely too long they have been misunderstood. Perhaps *that* is the true mystery surrounding cats.

They are considered aloof, independent, solitary. That is so far from the truth that it would be laughable if it didn't end up being harmful to these wonderful animals. Cats are solitary *hunters*, not solitary animals. Indeed, if you look at unowned and feral cats, you will see them living together in groups. (In case you're wondering about the difference, unowned cats are those who were once owned by a family but were thrown away to live on their own, while feral cats have never had a home with people.) And unowned cats often seek out human companionship—no food involved—just because they miss it.

A group of cats is called a clowder. They will cuddle together to sleep, to find warmth and companionship. At home, we become their clowder. We provide warmth, food, love, and companionship. And, of course, proper medical care.

Those who think cats are not affectionate are in for a big surprise. Still, as affectionate as cats are, some cat owners think their cat's loving behaviors are unusual. They'll say their cat is "doglike" when the cat is simply being himself. Affectionate cats are not behaving like dogs, they are behaving like themselves—which anyone will discover once they give a cat a chance to show his true personality.

As with anything else, you get out what you put in. Cats respond to your affection with more of the same. But the type of body language

As you can see on this Scottish Fold, cats have the largest eyes in proportion to their body size of all mammals.

they appreciate is different from the type a dog prefers. Many dogs want immediate attention, while most cats prefer attention on their own terms. These kinds of misunderstandings lead to the *aloof* label. It may seem obvious, but it's so important to remember that it bears repeating: A cat is not a little dog.

Even the medical community used to treat cats as if they were little dogs. But cats are another species, with their own special needs and considerations. Their nutritional needs are different, as are their medical needs. Thankfully, this has finally been recognized, and cats can get better health care today than at any other time.

We'll be talking about this and so much more. For those who know cats for the wonderful family members they are, I think you'll find this book helpful in many ways. For those who are about to get their first cat or kitten, or who have suddenly found themselves with a cat and aren't quite sure how that happened, well, you have some happy surprises in store.

People who rescue cats and often find themselves raising a litter will find it helpful to read the sections I've included about how cat breeders raise their kittens to be well-adjusted pets. These tips can easily be applied to every kitten to help him fulfill his destiny to be a wonderful companion.

I have had dogs throughout most of my life but have always liked and admired cats, learned as much about them as I could, and spent time with friends' cats. And then Aimee came into my life and stole my heart. A retired show cat, I got her for my mother because a dog would have been far more work when I was already working full time and caregiving full time. Neither my mother's cane nor her walker was a problem for Aimee. She took everything in stride—any pun intended.

I'll forever be grateful to Aimee's breeder and to her subsequent owners, Dru Milligan and Jolie Milligan-Stratton, for allowing me to have this wonderful, amazing girl, and to Susan Conant for introducing me to them when I was looking for a cat. Aimee brought light and happiness into my mother's life. And when my mother died, it was Aimee who was there watching over me, sitting near me, comforting, headbutting, purring, kissing, loving.

I was utterly captivated by how easily cats could be trained to do things, even when I wasn't particularly trying. Aimee learned to weave and spin on cue, and do things that are usually reserved for dogs. I began to see how much more fulfilling life is with a cat than most people would imagine. As an added bonus, her deliberate cuddling and purring with me when I have a migraine helps ease the pain. A little miracle worker on four paws.

I know that having a cat in my life has greatly enriched it. You don't have to be just a dog person or just a cat person. I prefer to call myself "multicultural," because I love dogs *and* cats. My journey through life would be much poorer without all my four-legged companions.

For all they do for us, cats ask so little in return. *The Complete Cat's Meow* will help you choose a cat—if one hasn't already chosen you— enrich your relationship with your cat, and help your feline companions live longer, healthier, happier lives. In return, you will reap a boundless bounty of love and affection.

CHAPTER 1

THE NEWBORN KITTEN

Tthere's something positively angelic about a kitten—any kitten. Every kitten's life is special, but to understand more about the early life of a cat and the best way to bring a kitten into the world, there's no better example than responsible pedigreed cat breeders.

Of course, when you decide to add a kitten or cat to your home, you have options. Your feline friend can come from a variety of backgrounds. Perhaps you want a pedigreed kitten; the best place to find one is a responsible breeder who raises their kittens the way I'll describe in this chapter. There are shelter pets who may have been found on the streets or given up by their owners. That doesn't mean they're bad cats; it means they've had bad luck and need a second chance in life.

Sometimes a cat finds you. Stray cats might have been dumped by their irresponsible owners, or they might be feral (born in the wild). You'll know the difference, because feral cats can be more difficult to approach, while strays often come to you looking for food and companionship. Feral cats can be more challenging as pets, although gaining the trust of a feral is incredibly rewarding. If a feral kitten can be captured and handled by people, learning that humans are kind and good, she can certainly become a wonderful pet.

Rescue groups for various cat breeds can also be excellent sources for finding a new feline companion. As with shelter cats, sometimes pedigreed cats lose their homes because their owner has died and no family member will take the cat, or the family is moving and refuses to take the cat, or a child is horribly allergic to cats. Their castoff can be your most wonderful treasure. You might also have an opportunity to adopt a retired show cat who will enjoy the special attention of being in a loving home where she's not one of many cats in a cattery. Usually this happens after the cat's show and breeding careers have ended.

Pedigreed cats are shown to get expert opinions about whether they are outstanding examples of the breed. Only the cats who are good examples are bred. Of course, cat breeding is not for everyone, and there's really no reason to breed a cat who is not part of a carefully planned line of pedigreed cats. That's why responsible pet owners spay and neuter their cats. But looking at what the good breeders do illustrates the best way to start every kitten out in life. It also gives you a very good idea of what to look for when you're searching for your special companion. If you end up adopting the kittens produced by a friend's cat, this information is still valuable to help you (and your friend!) understand what sort of socialization and care is important for all kittens.

Before the Kittens Are Born

Before a responsible breeder decides to mate two cats, health checks are done on both the male and the female. Some breeds are prone to particular health problems, such as skeletal problems or heart defects. Breeders know what the problems are in their breed, and they test all their breeding cats to avoid passing these problems on to the kittens they breed. Cats who have these genetic problems shouldn't be bred.

All cats are checked for parasites, inside and out. Their vaccinations are kept up to date—although it's important not to overvaccinate. The cats are checked for disease that can be transmitted by sexual contact, and also for any illnesses that might affect the healthy development of the kittens. Breeders also check the male's and the female's blood types, because they must take special measures at birth if the parents have different blood types. A cheek swab can be used for a genetic profile that includes blood typing.

Sometimes a breeder will keep several breeding females, called queens, but may not keep a breeding male. Intact males are difficult to keep because they frequently spray a foul-smelling urine to mark territory. Their behavior is also focused on mating. Even if the breeder has an intact male, they may want to mate one of their females with someone else's male. In both cases, the queen is sent to meet her mate.

The breeder must absolutely trust whoever will be keeping their girl for breeding. Many diseases are contagious among cats—even cats who have been vaccinated. Cleanliness and health are of the utmost importance when a queen is to be bred, because any germs or parasites she is exposed to will also affect her kittens.

Introducing the male and the female can be tricky. The queen will be wary because she is not at home. And she will only mate at a specific time in her heat cycle. Meanwhile, any other males in the cattery will want to be with her, so the mating pair must be kept separate and safe at all times. There must be good cattery management practices to take care of all of that.

Every breeding is planned, and that means the breeder must look ahead to see what's going to be happening in their own life when kittens are due to be born. A good breeder wants to be at home, with no major commitments. While most cats give birth without a problem, not all do. The queen can have all sorts of problems, and so can her kittens. Pedigreed kittens have the best possible welcome to this world with the breeder right there to look after them.

The breeder sets up a special, safe place for the birth of the kittens. This may be the bedroom or bathroom or another room set aside for whelping. They also have IV fluids and tubes for tube feeding on hand in case any of the kittens or the mother needs help. The whelping room has been kitten-proofed in anticipation of the time when the babies will be tumbling around the room as they begin to explore their surroundings. Sometimes the breeder constructs a large whelping pen or enclosure so the kittens don't roll out or fall anywhere. Sometimes they clear out a floor-level cabinet because queens like to give birth in enclosed, hidden spaces. It's not unusual for kittens to be born in a closet or in a laundry basket, despite the breeder's best efforts.

Exactly when the kittens are born, of course, depends upon the mother cat. It's not unusual for a responsible breeder to camp out in the whelping room (whichever room that turns out to be) while the queen is having her babies. This way, the breeder can stay close to the mother to make sure she won't look for someplace dark to hide and have her kittens.

After the Kittens Are Born

Kittens are born with their eyes and ears closed. They use heat detectors on their tiny faces to find their way to their mother and their littermates. The breeder keeps their bedding clean and dry, and makes sure they have a place to warm up and a place to cool down. Even if the kittens have been born in an inconvenient place, the breeder won't move them for forty-eight to sixty hours because it upsets the queen.

If the queen dies during the birthing process, the kittens must be either hand-raised or adopted by another queen with kittens born around the same time, who will raise them with her own. Introductions must be made very carefully. A towel is rubbed on the kitten and the queen so the smell of each is familiar to the other. Then the baby is offered to the queen. If an accommodating queen can't be found, it will be an exhausting and full-time project to feed the kittens every four hours—or more often if they'll eat that much—and then stimulate them to eliminate by using a warm cotton ball to gently wipe the baby's private parts.

Sometimes, a litter or a single kitten will be adopted by a female of another species who is happy to nurture babies no matter what the species. Most commonly, we've seen dogs who have allowed kittens to be placed with them and have accepted them gracefully. (Of course, a human caretaker will still need to feed the kittens round the clock with a feline milk replacer.)

If kittens are introduced to another species at a young age, they recognize that species as a friend.

If only one kitten is born, or only one survives, it's important to try to find other kittens close in age for her to play with. Kittens learn important social lessons from their littermates, and they also learn how to bond with other cats. The ones who are raised solely by humans tend to be less friendly with other cats. They also tend to be nippy, because they lack littermates who would teach them not to play roughly.

The kittens stay in their clean whelping box until they start wobbling about and need more space. As soon as they start to climb out, at about 2 weeks of age, it's especially important to ensure their safety and not allow them the run of the house. So the breeder moves them to an enclosure where their mom can easily get in and out but the babies can't. Bedding from their whelping box is used to line the enclosure, so it smells familiar. Sometimes, the whelping box itself is put inside the enclosure as a bed for the kittens.

As the kittens gain mobility, the breeder keeps enlarging their living area. This keeps the kittens safe until the breeder is comfortable letting them out—into a kitten-proofed room—when they're anywhere from 3 to 5 weeks old.

Litter Box Lessons

These first five weeks are when the kittens learn to use a litter box. The kittens have their own litter box, separate from mama's, because they need a box that's shallow and doesn't have much litter in it. The breeder may make a litter box for the babies from a cut-down cardboard box that once held soda cans. The breeder throws away the whole box daily and replaces it with a clean one. When the kittens are little, the box should hold only plain, fine-grain clay litter.

The adorable little ones learn to climb over the whelping box and into the litter box. When they're little, it takes a couple of days for them to learn to use it.

Many queens teach their kittens to use a litter box, although it's extremely rare for any human to see them taking the kittens, one at a time, to the litter box, stimulating them to eliminate, and then showing them how to cover it up. More commonly, it's the kittens who watch their mother eliminating in her own litter box and climb up and tumble into their litter box to copy mama. Kittens are wonderful observational learners.

The breeder may also help things along. They might set up a smaller box next to the queen's litter box and put some of mama's litter into the small box so the babies get the smell and the idea. As soon as the kittens start to squat, the breeder might put the kittens in their little litter box.

It's important to start with a box that is low enough for the kittens to climb into—maybe two inches high—with just a small amount of litter.

As the kittens grow, the kitten litter box can be replaced with a box that has three-inch sides, then four-inch.

Kitten Containment

Most breeders have only one litter at a time, allowing more time and space for the kittens. The kittens stay in their kitten-proofed room with a barrier that enables them to see what's going on around the house but doesn't allow them to have run of the house quite yet.

Breeders have different methods of keeping the kittens in one kitten-proofed room. They may set up baby gates stacked two high across the doorway so the babies can see out. (Soon enough, a healthy, active kitten will learn how to climb up and over a single baby gate. That's why two are needed.) Other breeders will add a screen door to the kitten room. This provides the same effect but is a permanent change to the house. One breeder I know puts a tall baby gate in the hallway. The gate comes up to her waist and is angled in toward the kittens. Mama can jump over but the babies can't climb because gravity takes over.

When they're a little older, the kittens can be moved around the house using a portable pen. This way, they can get used to all the household activities—the sounds, sights, and smells of cooking; the television; vacuuming; even dogs running past. If the breeder has one or more dogs, the dogs can also watch the kittens, who are safely out of reach in their pen. A breeder who has both cats and dogs told me she will hold a kitten and let the dogs come and investigate while she carefully watches the interaction so the dogs don't injure the kittens. Different breeds of dogs have different levels of prey drive, so it's important to know your dogs and never take chances. This breeder's kittens are usually 12 to 14 weeks old before they can run with the dogs, but only when she is there to supervise. Having kittens who are raised with dogs is a definite plus if they're going to a household that has at least one resident dog. Both dogs and cats should learn to live together in peace and harmony. Many dogs and cats have become best friends in a multi-pet household.

Handling and Socializing

Kittens are often helped by the breeder to push their way out of their mother, so they are held from the moment they're born. They're also picked up and weighed daily, and their tummies are felt. Their gums are checked weekly. An experienced breeder can tell a lot about how the kitten is doing from that interaction. Plus, the kitten is getting used to human scent and touch.

The kittens are handled constantly. The ones who will be chosen for the show ring will have to get accustomed to handling by a cat show

Linda Aronson, DVM

Early handling is important for the well-socialized kitten.

judge. And the rest of the litter gains the same benefits from early handling, making them wonderful pets. One breeder points out that male kittens, especially, don't like to have their tummies touched, so they have to be acclimated early on. She kisses and nuzzles their little tummies so they are accustomed to loving, consistent touching. Some cats don't like having their paws touched, either, and this can make nail clipping a chore. Early playful touching of the paws and feet helps avoid this problem.

As the kittens are moved around the house, people come and go, handling them gently, kissing them, and letting them learn how wonderful it is to be with adoring humans. The breeder who doesn't have children will invite children over to interact with the kittens, when they're old enough for visitors. The breeder will carefully supervise, making the children sit down to play with the kittens using small, soft toys, and will only allow children to carry the kittens after they've learned the right way to do it.

The kittens are carried around by the breeder, who puts them in every position, including laying them on their backs and rubbing their little tummies. Kittens are groomed at an early age, too, even if they don't need it, just to get them used to these routines. They may be combed or brushed with a very soft-bristle brush. They're handled while the breeder trims toenails. Pedigreed cats destined for the show ring are given short pretend baths, and then each is wrapped in a towel so they get the feel of that. (Pet cats generally don't need a bath unless they get into something really nasty. But show cats are routinely bathed before a show. Pet cats who aren't accustomed to being bathed can find it stressful, so it's not something you'll do unless it's absolutely necessary. Kitties keep themselves meticulously clean.)

Responsible breeders get their kittens used to being in a carrier and even take their kittens on car rides in their carriers. Some breeders drive hours away to see a veterinarian who is experienced with young kittens. The kittens and their mother can ride in a large dog crate with a

Kittens need to stay with their mothers for at least twelve weeks. They learn valuable lessons from mom and their littermates.

litter box inside on such long trips. If the breeder must travel a distance—perhaps to a cat show—the kittens will go along so they get used to traveling. This is what it all means when a breeder tells you their kittens are raised "underfoot."

Kittens also get lots of toys, things to climb on, things to swat, tunnels to go through, and lots of other activities to exercise and help develop their bodies and minds. One breeder puts a Ping-Pong ball in the bathtub with a few kittens. New types of toys are added at each developmental stage of the kittens. Toys are also traded out and rotated back into the mix to increase their novelty. Of course, mama cat's tail is also a great source of amusement for kittens—a built-in toy.

It's interesting to watch the way the mother interacts with her kittens, teaching them things such as climbing stairs, what to be afraid of, what not to be afraid of, and how to interact with other cats and with people. She will teach her kittens how to hunt, too—even if that just means stalking and "killing" their toys. Often the queen will walk through the house holding a small toy and calling her kittens, then inviting the kittens to follow her. She'll put the toy in the bed, and the kittens will curl up with the toy and sleep. She's further solidifying their desire to cluster together and sleep cuddled near one another for warmth, companionship, and security. The queen will teach her babies to play, picking up a toy mouse, for example, and showing them how to stalk the mouse, perhaps peeking around at it or a larger toy from behind a chair and then pouncing on it. This is actually practice for hunting, as well.

Stray and Shelter Kittens

Stray and shelter kittens don't have the same wonderful start in life. Shelter volunteers do their best to handle the little ones so they are socialized to people, but there are so many kittens and only so many volunteers. They certainly do the best they can, but it's not the same as being raised by a responsible breeder.

Volunteers who take care of colonies of stray cats often pick up kittens when they are very young—perhaps younger than is ideal for them to leave their mother. The window of opportunity for socializing a kitten born in the wild is quite brief, and these caring volunteers must balance the kitten's need for mama against the chances of helping that stray kitten get adopted and become a good pet. These kittens tend to be little scaredy cats at first, but with love and patience they become sweeties and can really bond to their humans.

Kittens are dumped at shelters or in empty lots and feral cat colonies by irresponsible owners who don't spay or neuter their pets and allow them to roam. The end result of a roaming, unspayed cat is always an unwanted litter. The kittens aren't born into a nurturing environment and are dumped outside or sent to a shelter quite young. But don't let that put you off. Adopting a kitten from a shelter means you are saving a life. And with careful, loving nurturing, you can have a wonderful companion.

Socialization is especially important with shelter and stray cats. Be slow and patient in introducing your cat to unfamiliar people and experiences, and you can certainly help your new little family member become the cat of your dreams. We'll discuss the things you can do to enrich your kitten or cat's environment and create an even closer bond a little later in this book.

Vaccinations

Kittens get their first immunity from the colostrum (first milk) of their mother. How long this protection lasts varies from kitten to kitten; maternal antibodies disappear between 6 and 16 weeks of age. At this age, kittens will need protection of their own from dangerous diseases. This is where vaccines come in.

Vaccines all work by exposing the cat to a safe version of a disease. This exposure stimulates the cat's immune system, so if she is exposed to the disease again, she has already developed immunity. There are several types of vaccines available. Modified live virus vaccines contain a virus that is alive but that has been changed in some way so it doesn't cause the actual disease. Killed virus vaccines use a dead version of the virus; sometimes this is combined with an immunity stimulant called an adjuvant. Recombinant vaccines stimulate immunity using DNA taken from a single protein that is part of the disease agent.

Injectable vaccines with an adjuvant have been associated with inflammatory reactions at the injection site. The degree of inflammation varies among products. This inflammatory response may or may not be linked to a type of cancer in cats called vaccine-associated sarcoma. There is an association between vaccination—particularly for feline leukemia and rabies—and this type of sarcoma. But the potential role of vaccines with adjuvants in causing vaccine-associated sarcomas remains controversial, and an exact link between adjuvanted vaccines and vaccine-associated sarcoma has not been proven. It's also important to remember that vaccine-associated sarcoma is very rare and seems to be associated with a genetic predisposition.

There has been a great deal of controversy about what vaccinations cats need and how often they need them. There are many terrible diseases that once killed kittens in alarming numbers, and without vaccines kittens (and adults cats, too) would still be dying. But most veterinary groups now agree that older recommendations for vaccinations left our companion animals overvaccinated. So the American Association of Feline Practitioners and the Academy of Feline Medicine formed a committee bringing together some of the best veterinary minds in the country to study what we know about communicable diseases and vaccines. They came up with a set of recommendations for vaccination schedules that abandoned the former "one approach fits all cats" model. Instead, they divided the available vaccines into three categories:

1. Core: vaccines every cat should have

2. Noncore: vaccines only some cats need

3. Not generally recommended: vaccines that either have not been proven to be effective or that are for diseases that don't pose a serious threat to cats

Specifically which vaccines a cat needs depends on the cat's age and circumstances. The cat's owner and veterinarian need to review the recommendations and together come up with a plan that is right for each individual cat.

Keep in mind that if you keep your cat indoors, not only will she be healthier and live a longer life, but she will require fewer vaccines. Many infectious diseases are passed on by contact with infected cats, wild animals, parasites, or the droppings of wild animals. Lack of exposure means lack of risk.

In 2006, the vaccination recommendations for cats were revised to take into account new vaccine technologies. As of this writing, these are the current vaccination protocols issued by the American Association of Feline Practitioners.

Core Vaccines

Feline panleukopenia virus (FPV) is a highly contagious virus that attacks the white blood cells. It's a leading cause of death in kittens who have not been vaccinated. The vaccine is very effective and safe, so there is no need for any kittens to die from this disease.

FPV is usually administered as a combination vaccine along with **feline herpesvirus-1 and feline calicivirus (FHV-1/FCV).** These are the two main groups of viruses that cause upper respiratory infections in cats. Upper respiratory infections can be deadly in kittens. The FHV-1 and FCV vaccines are highly effective, but they won't prevent all cases of upper respiratory illness because the cat may be exposed to a specific virus strain that is not in the vaccine. However, if this happens, a vaccinated cat will usually have a milder case of the disease than an unvaccinated cat.

The combination vaccine comes in many forms. Injectable forms include a modified live vaccine and both killed adjuvanted and killed nonadjuvanted vaccines. There is also an intranasal modified live vaccine.

Kittens can be vaccinated with this as early as 6 weeks of age and then revaccinated every three to four weeks until the kitten is 16 weeks old. If an adolescent or young cat hasn't been vaccinated, the protocol is two doses, three to four weeks apart. For all cats, booster shots are given one year after the last dose of the initial series, and then no more frequently than every three years.

Killed vaccines are preferred for pregnant cats, and then only if vaccination is absolutely necessary. Killed panleukopenia vaccines should be used in kittens who are less than 4 weeks old. All kittens and cats should receive at least one injectable panleukopenia vaccination.

Rabies is a disease that is always fatal. It is transmitted through the bites of infected animals. The vaccine is required in every state and is highly effective. It comes in a recombinant form and a killed adjuvanted form.

Initially, the rabies vaccine can be given as a single dose to a kitten as early as 8 to 12 weeks of age, with a second vaccination a year later. The killed adjuvanted vaccine has been tested and shown to be effective for at least three years, but how often it must be administered varies from state to state.

Noncore Vaccines

Feline leukemia virus (FeLV) can cause a large number of diseases in cats, including cancer, and contributes to the severity of many other feline diseases. It is highly contagious, and kittens can acquire it before they are born or from an infected mother's milk. There is no effective treatment, although cats who test positive for the virus but are still healthy can live a long life if they have excellent care.

This vaccination is highly recommended for *all* kittens, but booster shots are recommended only for cats who are at risk. The vaccine comes in a killed adjuvanted injection or a recombinant transdermal patch. If the cat needs this vaccine, the first dose is given when the kitten is 8 to 12 weeks old, depending on the product, with the second dose given three to four weeks later. Adult cats who haven't previously been vaccinated will need two doses, three to four weeks apart. If necessary, a single dose is given a year later. However, this vaccine is given annually only to a cat who is considered to have a continuing risk of exposure to FeLV.

Only cats who have tested negative for FeLV should be vaccinated, so it's important that cats be tested before vaccinating them. They should also be tested if they have been exposed to FeLV since their last vaccination for it.

Feline immunodeficiency virus (FIV) attacks the cat's immune system. Cat bites are the main source of transmission. There is currently no effective treatment for the disease. The FIV vaccination will provide protection from some strains of FIV but not all of them. The vaccine is recommended only for cats who are at high risk of infection, such as cats who roam outdoors and fight and those who live with FIV-infected cats.

This is a killed adjuvanted vaccine. When it's indicated, three doses are required. The initial dose can be given to a kitten as young as 8 weeks old; two subsequent doses are given at an interval of two to three weeks. When it's necessary, a single dose is given a year after the initial series, and each year thereafter if the risk of exposure to FIV continues.

Vaccination interferes with the ability to diagnose an FIV infection, because cats who test positive for FIV may have FIV or may simply have been vaccinated. Cats should be tested for FIV before being vaccinated to be sure they are FIV-negative. Kittens may have FIV antibodies from their mother and therefore may test positive, but this immunity appears to wane by about 12 weeks of age.

Chlamydophila felis is a bacteria-like organism that causes conjunctivitis and a mild upper respiratory disease called feline pneumonitis. The vaccine should be used only as part of a control regime for cats living in a multicat environment in which some cats are infected with the disease. It comes as either a live or a killed adjuvanted injection. Kittens can be vaccinated as early as 9 weeks old, with a second injection three to four weeks later. Adult cats will need two doses, three to four weeks apart. An annual booster is advised only for cats who are at continued risk.

Bordetella bronchiseptica causes upper respiratory infections in cats. The illness is more severe in young cats and in cats living in poor housing. Vaccination may be considered before a cat enters a rescue shelter, a boarding facility, or a cattery where bordetellosis has been confirmed. This is a live nonadjuvanted vaccine. It can be administered in a single dose intranasally in kittens as young as 8 weeks old, and to adult cats. It's only administered where cats are determined to be at risk. An annual booster is administered to cats who continue to be at risk.

Not Generally Recommended Vaccines

Feline infectious peritonitis (FIP) is a fatal disease that develops in a very small percentage of cats who have been exposed to the coronavirus. The disease is not contagious. The coronavirus is an extremely common virus that does not cause serious illness in most cats. Most cats who are exposed encounter the virus before the age of 16 weeks, but the vaccine cannot be given before that time. And there have been some studies showing that only cats who have never been exposed to coronavirus at the time of vaccination are likely to develop some level of protection from the vaccine. Therefore, vaccination is not recommended for cats living within households in which FIP is known to exist or cats who are known to be positive for coronavirus antibodies.

The existing vaccine comes in a nonadjuvanted intranasal form. It's administered at 16 weeks of age, with a second dose three to four weeks later. The efficacy of the vaccine is controversial, and the duration of immunity is short. The manufacturer recommends an annual booster.

Feline giardia is caused by protozoa that's usually picked up from infected water. Most infections are extremely mild, although, as with all diseases, they affect young cats more seriously. The vaccine is in a killed, adjuvanted injectable form. There aren't enough studies available to show that the vaccine will prevent giardia in cats. It's also not known whether vaccination will help infected cats recover. The vaccine, if administered, can be given as early as 8 weeks of age. A second dose is given two to four weeks later. In adult cats, two doses are given two to four weeks apart. The manufacturer recommends an annual booster.

Meeting the Breeder and the Kittens

If you're thinking of getting a pedigreed kitten from a breeder, the breeder will want to talk with you on the phone first. If the breeder lives nearby, they will want you to visit, preferably with all the family, so the breeder can meet them all and see how your family members interact with one another and with the cats and kittens.

Breeders are friendly, not confrontational, but they will ask a lot of questions. Some breeders will ask potential kitten owners to fill out a questionnaire. The purpose is to get to know the person or family to make sure they are the right owner for one of the kittens. The breeder is responsible for each of the kittens they have brought into the world, and that responsibility extends to finding each of them the best, most loving, most responsible home possible.

While the breeder is checking you out, you should also check out the breeder. Ask to see the kittens' parents; the queen, at least, should be there, although the father cat may not be. Ask about the health and genetics tests that were done on the parents before breeding. Ask about socialization and the types of interactions the kittens have had.

The breeder's home should look clean and smell clean. Ask to see where the kittens are kept in the house. Is it clean, tidy, orderly? Do the kittens have enough toys, food, water, litter boxes?

Ask about the warranty the breeder has. What is the policy if your vet finds your new kitten is sick? What if a genetic illness shows up later?

Nancie S. Belser

This is a Scottish Fold Kitten. Mi-ki, or tricolored, cats have long been taken by Japanese sailors on their ships to bring them good luck.

The Best They Can

A lot of rescue groups and shelters release kittens at 6 weeks old or when they weigh at least two pounds, but neither the age nor the weight is ideal. The kittens are released so soon because there are so many in need of homes, and when one kitten Is adopted, that space in the shelter can be occupied by another kitten or cat in need of a home. Some rescue groups wait until the kittens have had two sets of vaccinations, while others will wait until the kittens are 3 or 4 months old. There is no one-size-fits-all.

Shelters and groups do the best they can to balance their resources with the needs of the cats they have. Sometimes releasing kittens at a young age will make room for them to take in more cats and kittens in need of care. Sometimes adopting feral kittens out at an early age (perhaps earlier than might be considered ideal to take them away from their mom) will help the kittens better adapt to human interaction.

It's important to remember that every group does what they can with what they have. The population of homeless cats in the United States has reached crisis proportions, and just about every group trying to save them lacks the resources (money, caregivers, space, permanent homes) to do things the "ideal" way.

If you've gotten your kitten at an early age, it will be up to you to do the socialization I've described. In any case, you should continue socialization throughout your kitty's life so she is as loving and adaptable to any situation as possible.

How much of the vet bills will the breeder be responsible for, and for how long? The warranty should be for at least a year. Some breeders will warranty genetic diseases for the life of the cat, but that's unusual. Be aware that if the breeder does not have a contract, you will have no legal recourse if the kitten is sick.

Does the breeder take cats back at any age if there's a problem? Sometimes a death in the family or loss of income can put owners into an untenable position. Will the breeder take the cat back? A responsible breeder will also take cats and kittens back if, for any reason, the owner can't keep them. (Of course, in those circumstances you can't expect to get a refund of your purchase price. You just want to know your cat will be safe and cared for.)

Also ask if the breeder will be available if you or your veterinarian have any questions.

A responsible cat breeder will keep kittens until they are about 4 months old. Sometimes they stay with the breeder for as long as 5 or 6 months, or even till 7 months old, depending on the kitten. Each kitten is an individual, and they have to be fully confident before they are sent off to begin their new life. The more time they spend with their mother and siblings, the better, since their littermates and mother teach them how to interact with other cats. The mother also teaches them play skills that hearken back to hunting skills.

The kittens who are meant to be pets may be spayed and neutered before leaving the breeder, often at 16 weeks or four pounds—whichever comes first. Early spay and neuter can be done when a kitten weighs two pounds, but that procedure is generally reserved for shelter pets. It's also preferable to have the kittens recover in the home they know, where they're comfortable. Cats do not respond well to stressful situations, so it's important to make this procedure as easy and comfortable as possible for them. That said, kittens recover quickly from spay and neuter procedures.

If, for whatever reason, your new kitten is not spayed or neutered, it will be your responsibility to get this done. It's really important to have the surgery before the cat is 6 months old because many cats become sexually mature as early as that! There are free and low-cost spay and neuter programs all over the country. Ask your veterinarian if they participate in one of these programs. You can also call your local animal shelter, humane society, or rescue group to find out about low-cost spay and neuter options in your area.

CHAPTER 2

READY, STEADY, GET YOUR CAT

Before you decide to bring a cat or kitten home, you need to do some serious thinking. Loving cats and wanting your own is one thing; being a good cat owner and providing a good home is another. Love is not enough when it comes to cats. You're also going to have to assess your life and your lifestyle to decide if a cat is right for you—and if so, what kind of cat. Do you really want a kitten, or would an adult be a better match for you, your home, your lifestyle? Are you prepared for the activity level of some breeds? The activity level of a kitten? Do you have the time and patience to groom a longhaired cat every single day? Are you willing to scoop a litter box twice a day, every day?

One thing to consider, no matter where you get your kitty, is to get two cats at the same time, especially if you are away at work for long hours and kitty will be home alone. Most (although not all) cats love the company of other cats. If you have an older cat in residence, it is easier to bring in a kitten than to try to introduce another adult cat. It can be done, but it will require a lot of time and patience, not to mention understanding.

Are You Ready for a Cat?

Do you have time for a cat? Seriously. There's a perception that cats don't require any care other than to be fed and have the litter box scooped. That's such an old wives' tale! (And who are those "old wives" anyway?)

Cats are loving pets who require a lot more than just food, water, and a litter box. If you're at work all day, your cat is going to be lonely. Yes, he may be sleeping all day, but he also may be bored and getting into mischief, amusing himself in ways you are unlikely to find very funny. Kittens are especially active, so you will need to keep this in mind. If you opt for a particularly active breed or an active kitten, your smartest move may be to get two at the same time so they'll keep each other company.

You simply cannot go off and forget that you own a cat. Granted, you don't have to walk them several times a day the way you would a dog. They take themselves to the litter box and can get plenty of physical exercise indoors with some thoughtful environmental enrichment provided by you. But make no mistake: You do have to interact with your cat when you're at home—a lot. Otherwise, what's the point of getting a cat? Your cat will eagerly seek your attention. Are you willing to provide it?

One of the things that makes cats appealing to people who live in a cold climate is that you don't have to take a cat outside for walks. But your feline will require a clean litter box. Will you scoop the litter box, or boxes, at least twice a day? Faithfully change out the litter and clean the box every time it smells?

Your cat will need indoor exercise, too. Are you willing to spend time playing with your cat every single day? And will you set up areas for your cat to climb and perch and scratch?

Are you thinking of getting a cat for your children? If so, there are some very serious points to consider. First, how old are your children? Do their friends run in and out of your house? Are you willing to properly supervise the children and the cat or kitten? Have you taught your children to be gentle with animals? A kitten or cat isn't a stuffed animal. That said, some children are wonderful with pets and can develop an amazing relationship with them. A pet will also teach them about kindness, caring, and responsibility.

Getting a pet "for the children" only goes so far, though. As a rule, children quickly get bored, as they do with a new toy. A kitten or cat is a living, breathing, sentient being who will become a member of your family. You can begin to teach responsibility that is age-appropriate, but you, the adult, will be responsible for the cat's well-being. You cannot leave it to your children. Small children can "help" feed the kitten or cat and help with the water dish. This doesn't mean that they carry or fill bowls before they're old enough to have the manual dexterity these tasks require, but that they come with you when you perform these tasks.

Home Alone?

There are people who go away overnight and think nothing of leaving their cat home alone with food, water, a litter box, and maybe a few toys left on the floor. They believe cats can fend for themselves. While it's true that a cat will eat when he's hungry, drink when he's thirsty, use the litter box when necessary, and sleep, that's not all a cat does. Your cat will get bored and lonely for companionship. If you have two cats, they will occupy themselves and be companions, but they will still crave affection and attention from you. They love their owners and thrive on human interaction.

Bad things may happen when you are away. What if your house catches fire or there is a severe storm or other natural disaster? Many pets have been lost while the owner was away.

At the very least, you should arrange for someone to visit your cats no less than once a day while you're gone—even if it's just for the weekend. Cats get stressed when they're left alone. Have a pet sitter or a friend or relative come in to check on your cat and play with him, scoop the litter box, and spend some time with him every day. Even if kitty doesn't come out from a hiding spot while that person is in the house, he'll still know that he's not alone.

More than likely he will be happy to appear, particularly for someone he's met before—especially if that person is willing to play an interactive game and give kitty a kiss and a treat.

It's often possible to exchange cat sitting with a friend who also has a cat. It's a nice trade-off with someone you feel you can trust with your cat and someone your cat knows, as well. There are cats-only boarding facilities, but your cat will be much happier in his own home.

The children can begin to take on more responsibility as they grow older. Part of that responsibility is playing with the cat, but appropriate play is something that needs to be done by all members of the family.

The adults will be responsible for buying food and equipment, for taking the cat to the veterinarian at least once a year (more if there is a health problem), and for the cat's general health care. These are things children simply can't do—although they can accompany you as you go about these tasks, and it will provide an invaluable learning experience.

While you don't have to bathe a cat, you will have to set aside time for grooming. This includes brushing and combing, nail trimming, wiping ears (and learning to clean them if your cat is one who produces earwax like a cottage industry), brushing teeth, and other grooming help.

Another thing to consider is how much time you have to devote to your cat or kitten just to be together. All pets require time and love. Of course, what you pour into them is returned to you multiplied too many times to count.

If, after carefully considering all of this, you are prepared to add a cat and all the joy and love he brings to your family, here's the next step.

Kitten or Adult Cat?

Most people want a kitten. But this is not always the best choice for their lifestyle. Let's talk about the options.

Kittens are cute, silly, and will leave you laughing. Well, laughing when you're not weeping over the shredded drapes or watching your little kitty seem to fly through the air and land on you or chase your ankles when you walk into a room. Kittens fly and pounce because it's fun. It's a game for them, but it can be a nuisance for anyone who doesn't realize that this is normal behavior in kittens. You can teach a kitten alternate behaviors (we'll be discussing how to do that, and more, later in this book), but you can't make him calm down. Kittens have *a lot* of energy.

Kittens are curious little creatures, and that curiosity can get them into a world of trouble, especially when they're also cute and small. Curiosity is a trait cats don't outgrow, but they usually do become more mellow and sensible with time and training.

Another thing to consider is that kittens don't stay small very long. They're so adorable when they're tiny, but they grow so fast that it seems as if you can see changes overnight! That tiny little fluff ball who fit into the palm of your hand the day you brought him home will rapidly become the size of a grown cat with the mischief making of a four-legged juvenile delinquent. Kittens' personalities often change, too, as they grow and become more confident.

With adult cats, what you see is pretty much what you get. Of course, they will change some as they become comfortable in your home and their shyness subsides. But, by and large, an adult cat's personality is what you see when you meet and interact with him before you bring him home.

Adult cats can be an absolute delight, and since a healthy cat will live a long life, you'll have plenty of time to enjoy a wonderfully bonded relationship for many years to come. You'll also be giving a cat a new chance at life. There are many reasons why an adult cat may need a new home: Perhaps his previous owners couldn't keep him; perhaps he would do better in a home as an only cat.

Particularly wonderful is the trend of older people adopting older pets. Senior cats often can't find a new home, and senior people benefit

Thirty-two muscles control a cat's outer ear, or pinna, so he can rotate his ears independently. This is a Russian Blue.

from the companionship of a pet. This is definitely a win-win. Research has shown that seniors with pets are more active and feel less lonely and isolated. Senior cats are more mellow and less active, which is safer for a senior. An active young cat can get under the bars of a walker or the wheels of a wheelchair, or may be frightened of a cane. Also, an older person with an unsteady gait can all too easily trip or fall over a kitten or young cat who hasn't learned to get out of the way. The last thing an older person needs is a fall.

As humans get older, one of the issues that must be faced is arranging, in advance, for someone to take their four-legged companions if they become incapacitated or die. That becomes more of an issue with a senior who has a kitten or a younger cat.

An older cat has mellowed out from that active kitten stage and yet is still wonderfully playful. You can have many rich, fulfilling years together. And age won't stop some of the more active ones from flying onto your shoulder from on top of the refrigerator or swinging from the

Ready, Steady, Get Your Cat   25

dining room chandelier. You are not losing anything by getting an older cat, but you and the cat have everything to gain.

If you are still deciding between a kitten and a cat, think about how much patience you have and what your schedule is like. Do you have any dogs, other cats, or at least one human at home to entertain a lively, curious kitten while you're at work? And don't forget those sleepless nights you'll have with a kitten who is running around with the nighttime crazies.

An older kitty would be grateful to spend the day napping, waiting for you to come home from work. These cats just want to be loved, cared for, protected from the elements, and secure in their later years. They have so much love to give.

If you *must* have a kitten, get two of them for the sake of the cat. They might trash your home as they explore and learn, but they will be much more behaviorally healthy than an underexercised only kitten would become as an adult.

For optimum human sanity and humane care, think about adopting a mother and her kitten from a shelter. Cats live in female-centered groups, so mom and her kitten will already be comfortable with the social structure. You'll give the kitten the best behavioral start possible and you'll save the life of an adult cat.

Pedigreed or Moggie?

There are so many cats from which to choose. Do you want a pedigreed cat whose lineage is known? A pedigreed cat has been bred to conform to the standard for his breed—a written guideline for what cats of that breed should be like. You will know what to expect in the way of size, appearance, activity level, and, to some extent, personality.

In chapter 10 I'll talk about some of the cat breeds and their characteristics, but suffice it to say for now that a Persian won't have the activity level of an Abyssinian or a Bengal, who are far more athletic.

Some people are vastly amused by a cat who is always active, always busy and interacting with them, while others prefer a cat who lies around the house or lies on their lap. Of course, an active cat will still be affectionate, but he will be more interested in playing and interacting with you than he is in settling down for a long cuddle. If you don't have the time for a very active feline, one of the more active breeds will find ways to keep himself amused that might not seem as amusing to you.

A moggie, or mixed-breed cat, can be the best of all worlds. However, you may not be able to predict what he will be like as an adult and what his activity level might be. That said, someone who is good at reading cat body language and has been around the kitten or cat for a while should be able to make some predictions. And you're going to

Ramona Marek

African wildcats, the ancestors of our domestic cats, are among the oldest mammals still on earth today. Their fossils have been found dating back 38 million years.

have some input, too, in how your cat's behavior develops. That's another topic I'll be discussing later in this book.

Long Coat or Short?

Another consideration is whether you want a longhaired cat or a shorthaired one. You may like the look of a long, luxurious coat, but it requires a lot of care. All cats need some grooming, but a longhaired cat, such as a Himalayan or a Birman or a longhaired moggie, is going to require careful, consistent grooming daily.

Virtually all cats shed, but a longhaired cat's fur will also mat if you're not careful. A mat is a clump of tangled hair that can also contain other tangled-up dirt and debris. Mats keep gathering hair and getting closer and closer to the skin, until eventually they pinch and cause the cat pain. When you try to untangle a mat, that just hurts more; most likely you'll have to cut it out—with special care not to cut the cat's skin! That won't be nice for the cat or for you.

Shorthaired cats need less grooming, of course, but that doesn't mean you never need to brush them. Weekly brushing is about right for the shorthair. You will have to decide what maintenance you are able or willing to do. It is only common sense not to get a longhaired cat if you don't want to groom your cat every day.

If you don't want hair on your clothing and furniture, a cat may not be right for you at all. There are hairless cats, but make no mistake: They require enough special care to make up for the combing and brushing time. Hairless animals have skin-care requirements that will keep you busy.

Where Will You Get Your Cat?

Now that you've decided you have the time to share with a feline companion, and you've decided whether a kitten or an adult cat will share your life, it's time to figure out where you will go to find that new family

Allurophilia is the love of cats.

member. You have several options, depending on the type of cat you want.

One caveat: Beware of people giving away free kittens at a fair, roadside, or parking lot. Those kittens are no less deserving of a home, but they are unlikely to have been seen by a veterinarian and may have all sorts of health problems that will run up your veterinary bill in short order. Just be ready for that if you want to take a "free" kitten home with you.

The same goes for the stray you pick up. I am by no means discouraging you from taking in a stray, but please be aware that you will have all the usual veterinary costs, and probably some additional ones to treat parasites (inside and out) and illnesses that cats pick up when nobody cares for them. At the very least, a stray cat will likely also have fleas and/or ticks that will need treating, as will your house. This isn't meant to frighten you away from adopting such a cat or kitten but to prepare you for what will come as part of the package. And no matter where you get your cat, you're going to have veterinary expenses. That's part of responsible pet ownership.

Shelter

Shelters can be a wonderful source for a new feline companion. Shelter cats come from a variety of places and land in a shelter through no fault of their own. They can come from the street as strays or may have wandered away from home and have no microchip or tag to identify them. Others are dropped at the shelter because an irresponsible pet owner didn't have their cat spayed or neutered and then ended up with kittens they didn't want.

Some cats lose their homes because the owner truly can no longer afford to keep them; others because their owner has died and the family or friends won't give a home to the well-loved pet who was such a deep source of joy and comfort. Now the poor cat has lost not only his beloved owner but a home as well.

It's important to remember that cats in shelters—even the best of shelters—are frightened. It's a noisy environment, where they're in a cage and hearing all sorts of scary sounds. So the personality you see at the shelter may not be the true personality of the cat. For example, a cat who is quiet in a shelter may be withdrawn out of fear, and may end up being quite gregarious once he settles into your home.

Getting a cat out of the shelter and into a foster or a permanent home is the best possible solution, but there are not enough homes for every cat who needs one. A cat in foster care often settles in and reveals more of his true personality.

Animal Shelters and City Politics

You may have heard about kill and no-kill shelters; it sounds like the kill shelters are awful places. But actually, most municipal shelters are required to accept every animal brought in. These kinds of shelters receive some sort of public funding and are not allowed to turn animals away. So they have no choice but to hold an animal for a maximum number of days until they're either claimed by their owner or adopted. If neither happens, the animal is killed to make room for more animals. Because so many more cats than dogs are surrendered to shelters, the number of days a cat is held might be very short—sometimes less than a week.

No-kill shelters keep the animals until they are adopted, but of course, that means they do not have the space to accept every cat brought to them. Usually, they are not publicly funded.

When an animal shelter is under the direct control of the municipality it serves, the funding is controlled by the city and, often, the director is a city appointee. It's important to remember these things, because there are instances when the staff and volunteers at a shelter would like to do better by the animals but do not have the funding or the leadership to make that happen.

Here's one example of what can be accomplished when the shelter director really cares and understands the issues: The Albuquerque, New Mexico, city shelters had a dreadful reputation until Jeanine Patterson became the city's Director of Animal Services. Patterson, a registered nurse who brought not only her love of animals but her professional expertise with her, as well as management skills, brought in a shelter medicine specialist from the University of California–Davis School of Veterinary Medicine to assess the shelters and make recommendations about bringing them up to optimum standards. The recommendations were followed, and the incidence of illness among shelter animals dropped dramatically—and the number of adoptions went up.

However, when the mayor of Albuquerque changed, so did the Director of Animal Services. Only time will tell if the new director will maintain the standards set for veterinary care and behavioral enrichment—or if the city has the will to fund such initiatives.

Shelters vary in the quality of their facilities and attention to such things as sanitary conditions, environmental enrichment, and how much hands-on time the cats receive from the volunteers and staff. There may or may not be one or more veterinarians on staff. When shelters are not well run, the conditions may be unsanitary and the animals may get little or no attention and enrichment. When they are well run, the animals are clean and healthy, and the shelter staff will be able to tell you something about the personality of each one.

When you go into a shelter, you have to be prepared for the tug on your heartstrings as you walk from cage to cage, looking at all the cats and kittens who need a loving home and want to love you in return. Some of them will reach an insistent paw out of their cage to get your attention. It's not unusual to go into a shelter with one type of cat in mind and leave with a cat who doesn't look in the least bit like what you'd envisioned but who has captured your heart. When you meet your cat, you know he's "the one." Maybe it is the look in his eyes, or the way he reaches out for you, or the expression as he sits, winsomely, in his cage waiting for "his" human to come along.

Many shelters have a room into which you can take your potential new family member and get acquainted. You can get a better idea of what his personality is like out of the cage and in a quiet room, where you can get acquainted and see how he interacts with you and anyone you may have brought with you. You'll want to know if he's happy, healthy, curious about you and the world around him. If he's an adult, you'll want to know about his background. Why did he lose his home? Does he like children? If you have one or more dogs, you'll want to know if he likes dogs. Does he like other cats or is he better off as an only cat? Is he active? Is he a lap cat? These questions will help you determine if he's right for your home and your lifestyle. Shelter workers should be able to fill in some, if not all, of the blanks.

Some shelters have foster programs in which the kittens and cats are placed in homes to be kept as loved family members, nurtured and cared for, as well as socialized, and then released to a properly screened home. Often these are kittens who have been dumped at the shelter and need the type of nurturing and health care they can only receive in a private home.

Before you can adopt a cat or kitten, you will be screened by the shelter volunteers to ensure that the kitten or cat is going to a good, responsible home. No one wants to place a cat, only to have him brought back to the shelter—or worse. Change is hard for cats, and returning to the shelter would surely place the cat in a very confusing situation.

Rescue Group

Breed rescue organizations are groups of volunteers who rescue cats of one or two breeds. There are also groups that rescue cats of all types—often from shelters when the cats are scheduled to be killed. Rescue groups might be organized with a small shelter and a list of foster

The top two rows of a cat's whiskers can move independently of the lower two rows.

families. Or there might be a rescue point person who hears about cats in need and calls upon a network of foster families. Breed rescue groups are often set up this way. Often, the group is actually a network of breeders, and they rescue cats of the breed they're involved in. When the rescue point person doesn't have room for more cats, they will contact someone who is involved in the breed, who may be able to help. Whatever way the rescue group is set up, they're all volunteers, helping cats because they love them and want to save as many as possible and place them in loving homes.

If you're looking for a pedigreed cat, breed rescue may be right for you. It's hard to believe that after someone has paid for a pedigreed cat they would give him up, but pedigreed cats lose their homes for as many reasons as any other cat: the owner has died and no one wants the cat, a child in the family has become allergic, the family is moving to a place that won't allow pets, or somehow the cat just doesn't fit into their lives anymore. (Why anyone would choose to move to a place that doesn't accept pets and therefore give up a member of their family is incomprehensible to those of us who truly accept the responsibility of a lifetime commitment and who genuinely appreciate the human-animal bond. But that's another book.)

Sadly, another group of pet owners has been forced to give up their pets because of the economy. Fortunately, there are groups springing up to help them with everything from pet food to discounted veterinary care in an effort to keep these pets in their homes. Still, many pets slip through the cracks and are relinquished. It's hard on everyone, pets and owners, when this happens. Stepping in and adopting one of these needy pets can give a cat a new lease on life. The rewards are great for both the cats and the cat adopters.

With any rescue group, expect to pay an adoption fee. Even when they are run by volunteers, there are still expenses, including veterinary care, spaying and neutering, food, litter, towels, beds, laundry that must be done, and administrative costs.

You can also expect a thorough screening to be sure that yours is a good home. The people in rescue groups and in shelters are no less concerned about the homes in which they are placing cats and kittens than is the breeder of pedigreed cats.

Friends and Relatives

A great many people get their cat from a friend or relative. That doesn't mean you shouldn't ask questions before bringing kitty home. Your friend will certainly know if the kitten has been vaccinated and has had a veterinary examination to rule out any health problems. Ask for a copy of veterinary records. This way, your veterinarian will know just what your kitty needs—and doesn't need.

Ask about socialization, too. Has the cat been handled? If you're adopting a kitten, be sure they're not sending the kitten home too soon in their haste to place the kittens. Ask them to keep the kitten with his mom for at least ten weeks, and promise you will take him then.

Volunteer!

Volunteers are invaluable to any shelter or rescue group. If you're not quite ready to bring home a cat of your own, you might think about volunteering at a local shelter or humane society, or fostering a cat. There's always a shortage of volunteers and foster families for needy animals.

Breeder

If you have decided to buy a kitten from a breeder, there is something to consider first: Sometimes breeders have retired show cats that they are willing to place in a pet home. Yes, you will pay for the cat, but you will get a cat who has been thoroughly socialized, is accustomed to being handled by total strangers (the judges at cat shows), is used to traveling to show venues, and, for the most part, is pretty much imperturbable. Retired show cats make great pets for older people as well as for singles and childless couples. If the cat likes children (and the breeder will know), he can fit well into a family with gentle children. The cat will be spayed or neutered and in good health before leaving for your home.

Breeders sometimes give up a show cat because the cat has been retired from their breeding program or they have decided not to breed that particular cat. While that cat is very much loved, there is only so much attention and time to go around. Reputable breeders will keep retired cats, but sometimes they can see that a cat would flourish in another home with more attention. And so, despite their own sadness at parting with a beloved cat, they will try to find an exceptional home where the cat will get far more individual attention and will enhance someone else's life. That is a truly unselfish attitude. Placing the cat's needs ahead of one's own love for the cat is an act of selflessness and generosity.

When you buy a pedigreed cat or kitten from a reputable breeder, there are certain things that are assured. You know what the cat will look like, you'll know his breed characteristics, and you'll have a good idea of his temperament because the breed standard outlines it. The queen and the male will have had proper veterinary care, including tests for genetic diseases. (You may not realize it, but cats can have hip dysplasia, luxating patellas, hypertrophic cardiomyopathy, and other inheritable diseases. Cats with these problems are not bred by ethical breeders.) As a potential owner, you have the right to ask to see the health clearances for any cat's parents, and the breeder should certainly show them to you. If you meet a breeder who has not had these tests done or who can't show you the results, find another breeder from whom to buy your cat.

Seeing the queen will give you an idea of what the kittens might be like as adults—although, like children, they will each have their own personalities. Physical breed characteristics, however, should be uniform.

Another thing you should expect, want, and need if you're buying a pedigreed cat is a written contract—one that details responsibilities for both breeder and owner. If you're spending money on a cat or kitten,

The nose print of a cat is ridged in a pattern that's unique, just like the fingerprint of a human. This is an Abyssinian.

make sure you know what you're willing to pay and what the breeder is willing to do or pay for with regard to that cat. Is the breeder willing to stand behind the health and temperament of the cat? For how long and to what extent? Remember, this is a very different situation from when you are adopting a cat from a rescue group or a shelter—in that case all future bills are your responsibility. But you are *not* rescuing a cat or kitten from a breeder. If there are problems later, you will need to have a legal document in hand. Many responsible breeders' kittens come with a lifetime guarantee, including paid bills for genetic illnesses. If there are veterinary bills later due to some inherited physical defect and you don't have a contract, don't complain when you're not reimbursed.

A responsible breeder will never walk away from the cats they've bred. The contract will often say that at any time, if you can't keep the cat, you must return him to the breeder.

You don't want to get your pedigreed cat from someone who just breeds cats to make money. A responsible breeder breeds cats who meet the breed standard and because they love and want to improve the breed. They often lose money on a litter. It's a hobby they love because they love their breed and their cats.

As I mentioned in chapter 1, the kittens are kept by the breeder for a minimum of twelve weeks. This is the time period that is setting the foundation for their lives. Everything is done to ensure that nothing is scary for them and that they are bonding with their mother, building confidence, and having positive experiences. The kittens have every opportunity to develop confidence. These developmental stages are critical and help set the stage for the kind of pet you want in your home. That's why it's so important to get your pedigreed cat from a responsible, knowledgeable hobby breeder.

With all that care and love poured into every kitten, expect to be rigorously screened by the breeder. After an initial contact by telephone and possibly e-mail, you will want to visit the breeder's home—and most breeders want you to do that. If the breeder doesn't know you, how can they entrust that little life to you? And if you don't meet the breeder in person, see the queen, and meet the kittens, how can you know what you're really getting?

The breeder will want to see you interact with the kittens and will also want to screen you as a potential owner, just as you are screening the breeder. You have to be comfortable with each other.

You should do your due diligence in discovering as much as possible about the breed before you begin to look for a breeder. Each breed has their own characteristics, and you want to be sure those characteristics will match your lifestyle. But this is also a good time to talk to the breeder about the breed and what you will need to know, including grooming, exercise, and diet requirements.

Look for a kitten who is confident, not shy, especially if you have an active household. The older a kitten is, the more likely he will be to come up to you or play with a toy. The breeder will have a better idea of the kittens' individual personalities and likely adult size. So talk over your choice with the breeder and let them guide you.

CHAPTER 3

Gearing Up for Kitty

I n the winter of 2010, archaeologists unearthed a 2,000-year-old temple in Alexandria, Egypt, that was dedicated to a cat goddess. It was the very first trace of the royal quarters of the Ptolemaic Dynasty to be discovered, and it provides confirmation that the early Egyptians did, indeed, worship cats. The temple is 200 feet high and 50 feet wide—certainly impressive.

It's not necessary for you to build a temple to your new kitty, but be warned, you may find yourself worshipping at her little paws. Cats, with their endless charm, seem to have that effect on their people. You do, however, have to provide a safe home and environmental enrichment. And, please trust me on this: The right home environment will help prevent behavior problems later on.

There are definitely some basics you will need for your new cat, and you should get them *before* you bring home your newest family member. You'll also need to prepare your home so it's safe and comfortable for kitty's homecoming.

Kittyproofing Your Home

Cats and kittens are innately curious. The old saying "Curiosity killed the cat" can be sadly true, depending on where that curiosity leads your kitty. If cats are curious, kittens are doubly so, and they appear to be fearless. Depending on your kitten's activity level, you could easily find her swinging from the dining room chandelier, climbing the drapes, or perched atop the refrigerator, all within a short span of time. A cabinet

Cats, like this Abyssinian, can jump five times their height.

door is open? Don't be surprised if you see a sleepy kitty napping on a plate or curled up in a bowl.

Anything left out on counters is fair game for a curious cat. Burners on the countertop range or the stove can be downright dangerous. Be sure to buy covers for them. Sooner or later your kitty will decide to explore that surface, and you don't want any accidents.

Be sure to pick up paper clips and pins that have dropped on the floor, any tiny toys your children might leave around, your own small knickknacks, and anything small other than the cat's toys (it is not unheard of for a cat to swallow a shiny piece of jewelry). Once a cat begins to swallow something, she can't stop. This is because kitty's tongue, which is so good at giving you sandpaper kisses, has tiny hooks called papillae that help her clean her fur, hunt, and eat. However, the catch is that those little papillae all point toward the back of her throat, making it just about impossible for kitty to spit out things like string and yarn.

The more string a cat swallows, the more dangerous it becomes to the cat, and that can lead to surgery or possibly to death, depending on what has been swallowed and whether it does any internal damage.

Holiday Hazards

Tinsel on Christmas trees presents a serious hazard because it can cut the cat on the way through her intestinal tract. Don't use it. And keep breakable ornaments off the bottom of your tree—go for large wooden or cardboard items on the bottom branches.

Candles are another kitty hazard. Light them in the room only when you are there all the time to supervise. Bowls of potpourri are toxic for cats, so find some other way to give your home a holiday scent. Aerosol sprays can also be hazardous to kitty's health, as can scented oils. An air purifier would be safer, although it would also be more expensive.

And at Easter time, skip the lilies; they are so toxic to cats that even one bite can kill.

Long, stringy things of any type may also be swallowed and cause an obstruction. These include yarn, ribbon, thread, and string. It can also be dangerous if you catch your cat swallowing string and you try to pull it back out. Instead, rush your cat to the veterinarian immediately.

If kitty is adept at opening cabinets, you're going to need childproof locks for cabinets and drawers. A curious kitty might decide to stick her paw in an electric socket, so it's wise to buy socket covers as you would for a toddler. Tape wires to walls, because if kitty chews on an electrical wire she can be electrocuted—or, at the very least, badly burned.

Many cats enjoy deliberately knocking things off bureaus or other pieces of furniture just for the fun of it. If those things are breakable, you may be dealing with shards of glass or china, which will be dangerous to everyone in the house, including the cat.

That fascination extends to the bathroom. If you keep various items on the back of the toilet, don't leave the seat up, because some cats really enjoy knocking each item into the toilet and watching for the splash. Keeping the lid down is always a good idea anyway in case your kitty decides to leap up on the toilet back and misses, landing in the water. She probably won't enjoy the impromptu bath very much. And skip drop-in toilet cleaners of all types, because they are toxic.

Computers and printers are another source of entertainment for kitties—not just because they're there but because *you* are so often there. You can get a system to put on the keyboard that shuts the computer off when kitty walks on the keys, or you can keep the keyboard covered when not in use. It would be interesting to know how many pounds of cat hair are shed into keyboards worldwide! And watching the paper come out of the printer is a great source of entertainment. But the paper feeder can catch little paws, so be careful.

Shredders can also provide a danger unless they have an automatic switch-off mode to prevent accidents. On the plus side, especially if you have a home office and spend a lot of time there, you can get a cat bed that will attach to the side of your desk. Or you may just want to put an extra cat bed in the room. And at least you'll have company while you're working.

The Litter Box

Obviously, you need to bring the litter box home *before* you get your cat. And if you have more than one cat, you'll need more than one box. The basic rule is one box per cat, plus one for the house. While you can probably get away with one box if you have only one cat, the optimum is to have two boxes in different places in your home. And if your house has more than one floor, there should be a clean box on each level.

You might consider asking what sort of litter box your kitten or cat has been using before she comes home with you. Generally speaking, a cat will do well with a large, open, uncovered litter box. If you have only one cat, you can buy a covered box as one of the two options in your home, and see what your cat likes best. Cats prefer privacy when they eliminate (so do we, which is why bathrooms have a door), so you can put up a screen in front of the uncovered litter box if you have placed one in an open area, such as your family room.

There are several options when selecting a litter box. You will also need a scoop for all boxes, even the electronic or automatic boxes, since they require an occasional scooping if litter gets stuck on the sides or the bottom of the box. The scoop choices are plastic or aluminum, deep or shallow. Which one you buy is purely a matter of personal preference.

Uncovered Box

This is the plain box you can buy at any pet supply store. It's not very large but is sufficient for most cats. It's very easy to scoop and clean.

Covered Box

The oblong covered boxes seem to be getting harder to find, while the round ones are becoming more popular. The problem is that the round ones are kind of cramped, and cats don't like that in their bathroom any more than we do.

Where's the Bathroom?

There's nothing worse than arriving somewhere and not being able to find the bathroom, so be sure you show your cat where all the boxes have been placed. This is like someone giving you directions to the restroom in a restaurant or a store. You know there's one somewhere, but someone has to tell you how to find it.

When you first bring the cat home, place the carrier near a litter box. Then, when you take her out of the carrier, show her the litter box by putting her down next to it or even right in it. Every cat who has used a litter box will know exactly what it is and will be happy to know where to find the facilities. It's okay if she immediately jumps out.

You will likely be confining kitty to one room until she's comfortable with the house or if you have another cat in residence. While she's waiting to be able to explore more of her new home, she should have a litter box in her room, as well as a scratching post, food, water, and toys. Be sure you show her the box before letting her explore the rest of the room. And please don't put the food and water dishes near the litter box, because nobody like to go to the bathroom where they eat.

Electronic or Automatic Box

These are the boxes that scoop themselves. They are activated a couple of minutes after the cat leaves the box. These, too, come in covered and uncovered versions, round or oblong, depending on the manufacturer.

These boxes are made for people who don't particularly like scooping a box. When the box is activated, it rakes through the clumping litter and drops the waste into a bag set into a bottom shelf under the box, then combs the litter so it is once again fresh. You replace the bag when it's full, and how often that happens depends on how many cats you have. All you handle is the bag when you put it into the pan or shelf at the bottom of the box and when you remove and dispose of it. Some models have a tub instead of a bag.

This can be an excellent option for pregnant women who don't have someone else to scoop the litter box, as well as for some multicat households. But not all cats will accept an automatic box (they don't like the idea of moving parts in their bathroom) and some cats find them to be too small, while other cats actually prefer them and enjoy watching them move.

Do-It-Yourself Plastic Box

If you have a large cat, like a Maine Coon Cat or a Norwegian Forest Cat (or just a really big cat!), your best bet may be a plastic storage box, like the kind you buy to store sweaters. Take off the top, and if the sides are very high, cut down one side so the cat has easy access. For an older cat, be sure the opening is low so there's no problem getting into and out of the box.

Disposable Box

These cardboard litter boxes are perfect for travel. You can buy them in multipacks at pet supply stores and supermarkets. They last about a week, or less, depending on the number of cats using them. These boxes also need to be scooped daily and at the end of their use put into a plastic trash bag and thrown away.

The Litter

There are clay litters, scented litters, unscented litters, litters made from natural sources, and even litters made from newsprint. The choice of litter you use is personal—for your cat. If kitty doesn't like the litter you pick, she'll soon be thinking outside the box.

The wisest thing is to ask what kind of litter kitty was using before she came into your home, and have the litter boxes set up with that kind of litter ready for kitty.

Let's talk about litter for a few minutes so you'll have a better understanding of the various types of litter and their different qualities. There is nothing quite like an educated consumer. The more you know, the better it is for you and your kitty.

Before the invention of litter, people who kept their cats mainly indoors put ashes into a box for their cat. When cat litter was invented by Ed Lowe in 1947, the whole idea of cat ownership changed. Suddenly it was cleaner and easier to keep a cat.

The first litter was made of absorbent clay, and for years that's all that was available. Then along came clumping litter. And in recent years a bewildering array of choices has become available.

Nonclumping litter is still quite common, but it isn't as easy to keep the litter box as clean as you can with a clumping litter. With some types, though, kitty tracks less on her paws when she leaves the box. Also, some nonclumping litters produce less dust than some of the clumping litters. If the dust is inhaled over a long period, it can cause upper respiratory infections and trigger long-term health problems. If you suspect that your cat is having respiratory problems, see your veterinarian immediately—and while you're there, discuss litter. Changing to a litter that doesn't create much dust is a wise course of action. The litter will have to be changed gradually so the cat becomes accustomed to it.

But nonclumping litter does have its negative aspects. While excrement can be scooped daily, the urine is absorbed and stays in the box until the entire box is emptied out and thoroughly cleaned. With a nonclumping litter, that should happen once a week. With a clumping litter, it can be less often—depending on the type of litter you use.

Absorbent silica crystal litter is designed to make litter boxes as odor-free as possible. It was among the first of the alternative litters and was designed for that purpose. The catch here is that many kitties don't like the texture of the little round silica crystal pellets. Those cats may find the silica litter that comes in irregular crystal shapes more acceptable—or not, because some cats may not like the feel of the crystals under their feet, either. The silica absorbs urine effectively, but you really should stir it around to be sure all the urine is being absorbed. You'll have to dump the litter, clean the box, and put in new silical litter at least every thirty days.

Clumping litter is advantageous in that the urine forms clumps in the litter that are easily scooped using a slotted litter scoop. This makes the box cleaner overall. But when it first came out, there was a problem: Some cats, and especially kittens, licked their paws after being in the box, swallowed the clumping litter, and developed an obstruction in the intestinal tract. Many types of modern clumping litter don't present this problem and are safe for all but the youngest kittens. Still, it's better to be safe than sorry. Don't use clumping litter for kittens younger than 8 weeks of age.

As you scoop clumping litter, there will be less of it in the box. You can add some fresh litter, but be aware that you should still empty the entire box and thoroughly wash it at least once a month if you have one cat, or more often in a multicat household. Some of the clumping litters contain baking soda to help with any odor in the box.

While some clumping litter does produce dust, and the cat will usually track some litter out of the box, you can put a mat in front of the box so the litter drops off kitty's paws and onto the mat. There are several types of mats made for this purpose. You'll have to find one that your kitty doesn't mind stepping onto when exiting the litter box.

Flushable clumping litter is a great option for those who don't want waste matter sitting in the trash. It flushes right down the toilet. At least one brand is safe for septic systems, so be sure to read the labels. If your kitty likes the flushable brands of litter, it's a very reasonable solution to the kitty waste question. (When you empty the entire box, you'll still have to throw that litter in the trash, though; it's too much for your toilet to handle.) One such litter is made from corn and is a good option since it's natural and has much less dust than clay types. But some cats are allergic to corn and others don't like the texture—although it works just fine for many cats and their owners.

Paper litter and other assorted natural litters made from pine or other substances are often flushable in small amounts. They tend not to be clumping, although there are exceptions. Many of these litters are bio-degradable. Again, whether or not you can use any of these litters will depend on your cat: Some cats won't like a particular scent; others won't like the texture. You have to go with what your cat wants. This is the time when you want to remember that kitty knows best!

There are so many options that it can be confusing. In general, though, most cats prefer an unscented litter with a fine grain and a softer texture. And they tend to prefer clumping litter because the box is cleaner and doesn't smell like urine.

Still, at least in the beginning, it's wise to use whatever litter your cat has been accustomed to using. There will be enough changes in her life without upsetting her in this very important area. If you want her to think inside the box, then give her every chance to do so. If you want to switch your new kitty to another type of litter, do it slowly. Add small amounts of the new litter to the old brand in the box. Gradually add more of the new and less of the old until you've completely made the switch. Be aware that if you're switching to a clumping litter, it won't clump if it's mixed with a nonclumping variety.

And let me repeat that you will need to scoop the box twice a day, more if you have a multicat household. Cats appreciate clean facilities just as much as we do. No cat wants to eliminate in the kitty version of a grungy gas station restroom!

Just one more thing: There is a litter made to attract cats who don't use the box as they should. It's more expensive but certainly a worth-while investment—along with a behavior modification program—to encourage kitty to use the box again. It's called Dr. Elsey's Cat Attract.

For disposing of kitty waste, there are also waste disposal systems that you can buy, some more inexpensive than others. The less expen-sive ones will sit right next to the litter box and hold an ongoing supply of bags that are kept in such a manner that no odor escapes.

The Scratching Post

Every cat needs at least one tall, sturdy scratching post. It's an essential for your cat. Scratching is a natural behavior for cats, and you can't teach a cat not to scratch. However, you can teach a cat where to scratch and where not to (more on that in chapter 5). And it's up to you to supply the proper place to scratch.

Scratching serves several purposes. Cats remove the dead outer layer of each claw while scratching, which allows the nail underneath to grow and remain healthy. Cats also leave a scent mark and a visual mark when they scratch. Even though your kitty is indoors and may be an only cat, she still needs to designate her scratching post as her property and the room it's in as her territory to let everyone know that she is there. Think of it as a kitty calling card. Cats also need to stretch out their entire body length, and the scratching post is one way in which they do it. They anchor their front claws up above them and pull down to stretch their entire spine. The post often represents a tree, which is tall, solid, and allows for such action.

The scratching post must have a heavy, solid base—it can't tip or jiggle because it's too light or flimsy or is hanging from a doorknob. There are a lot of inexpensive vertical scratching posts on the market, but they are likely to tip over, which will probably frighten your cat and may discourage kitty from using the post again.

The scratching post should be a minimum of 32 inches high. And I do mean a minimum. Again, think of it in terms of a tree. Thirty-two inches is fine for a kitten if it's a very solid scratching post, but a kitten will outgrow it rather quickly. So invest in the tallest, most solid post you can afford right from the start, rather than having to replace it with a taller post before too long. Frankly, that would be penny-wise and pound-foolish.

Scratching posts may have sisal wrapped firmly around wood. Some are left natural and have bark or rough wood on the outside. Some have carpet material wrapped around the post, but if your house is carpeted, how is kitty supposed to know the difference between her post and your expensive rugs? You really can't tell her that scratching one rug is okay and scratching another rug isn't.

Some people make their own scratchers out of a log, or will do something even more elaborate by combining sisal wrapped carefully around the log with exposed areas of wood so their kitty has a choice of scratching surfaces.

Place the scratching post next to a sofa or chair in a part of the house where you and kitty like to hang out. If she's already scratching your furniture, place the post right next to the piece of furniture she likes to stretch out on and scratch. This will encourage her to scratch on an acceptable piece of furniture—her scratching post—and not on your sofa or chair.

Some cats also like to scratch horizontally. If your cat does, you'll know because she will scratch rugs and mats. Horizontal scratching pads are usually made of corrugated cardboard, and most cats love them. They come with a small packet of catnip to encourage use. Some cats prefer both a vertical and a horizontal scratching post. The cardboard ones are so reasonably priced that there's no reason not to buy one or two and put them in different rooms.

Other scratchers are built on a slant. Some are made of cardboard and others are made by the companies that make scratching posts and cat trees and are sturdy enough to serve as a small ramp near a chair, sofa, or bed.

The Cat Tree

Cats see rooms in a different way than we do. Where we will walk into a room and think the sofa looks nice when it's juxtaposed near that armchair, providing a nice conversation area, a cat will walk into the same room and view the sofa, the chair, and any other raised surface as various levels available for her to go up. So we see the floor and she sees the first level. We sit on the sofa or the chair, but she sees it as one level up. And then she might move to a shelf or the mantelpiece over the fireplace because it's higher. Some cats like to go really high up and seem to be extensions of the Flying Wallenda family, while others are more conservative. And if you have a multicat household, the one who always goes to the highest level is the one who probably has higher status in the family.

Having a cat tree in your home is the best way to give your cat two things she craves: a sturdy scratching post and an elevated spot from which to survey her territory. A cat tree isn't just a tall scratching post, although it does incorporate one into the design. It has cat beds on several levels. Some have a curved platform on one or two levels and a barrel-shaped bed on another. Cats love little hidey-hole places where they can rest undisturbed, and they feel safer and more comfortable in a closed-in place, and sometimes kitty just wants a safe window on household activities, so try to choose a tree with a variety of platforms. Often, the scratching posts are covered in sisal and the beds are covered in carpet.

Cats both like and need an escape route—someplace comfortable and close at hand (or paw) where they can climb and get away from it all. Unless you want your cat to use your dining room table, breakfront, and other fine furniture, you have to give her a cat tree. In fact, you should have one even if you have other places for your cat to perch.

A cat tree is safe, not slippery like furniture, so your cat won't slide all over it. This is the best of all worlds from a cat's point of view—a place

A cat rarely meows at another cat. This sound is typically reserved for humans.

of her own, a room with a view, as it were. It also is a scratching post where she can stretch out to her full length (which is very important) without worry of it tipping over. The cat tree is where she can safely go if you have a family dog or children who are pestering her. Or just because . . .

Buy the sturdiest cat tree you can afford, and the tallest. Like the scratching post, it needs a very solid base so it won't tip over, and as much height as your pocketbook and house can handle. This is a piece of furniture for kitty and for your home. Some companies make them in quite elaborate designs and colors, and they will work in with your décor, much like an objet d'art. Think of this as an investment that should last for many, many years. And it will be used daily.

The Window Perch

All cats need environmental enrichment. While a sliding glass door can provide a wonderful version of kitty TV, with all of the birds and squirrels presenting the entertainment, a window perch offers the cat version of a luxury recliner from which to watch. It's usually a hammock that serves as a perch so kitty has a choice of watching the world go by or napping happily in the sun as it streams through the window. It's also elevated, so it allows your kitty to get away from a pesky kitten or puppy.

Food and Water Dishes

It's a good idea to try to get the same kind of food and water dishes your cat was using at her previous home, so she's comfortable with them—at least at first. That said, there are some wonderful choices that you might enjoy seeing as much as kitty will enjoy using.

You will need anywhere from one to three dishes for food and one to two for water (aside from folding travel bowls, which you may want if you travel with your cat). Why so many food dishes? It's simple: one for dry food, one for wet food, and a third in case your cat has some regular dry food diet and a "side order" of hairball formula or other special food. Some cats don't mind having the two types of dry food mixed together, while others prefer to have them separated. Think of the little kid who doesn't want her peas next to her mashed potatoes.

Plastic dishes can cause skin problems, so you want to avoid those. There are cute crockery dishes and aluminum ones as well. Do not buy the food and water bowls that are made as one piece with two sections. Cats don't like their food near their water. Cats need separate dishes, cleaned daily.

Cat dishes need to be wide and shallow. A cat's whiskers are very sensitive and cannot be crammed into a deep bowl. It's more natural and comfortable for a cat to eat and drink from flat, wide dishes. Keep the word *dish* in mind, not *bowl* when shopping for kitty.

Water should be fresh, not stale and flat. If you can splurge, a water fountain is a wonderful addition to kitty's life. The water is filtered and aerated, and cats find it fascinating to watch. The water fountain usually encourages cats to drink more water, which is far healthier for the cat because it helps to prevent urinary tract and kidney problems.

There are long-term feeders that you fill with food in one compartment and water in another, but I think the convenience is far outweighed by lack of freshness. Food will be sitting in that container for a good long while before being released into the dish, and so will the water.

Dish placement is very important. Cats certainly don't want their water or food near their litter box. That's just common sense; you wouldn't want to dine in the bathroom either. The cat is more likely to stop using her litter box than to stop eating, so just separate the two. As for the water dishes, you should put out at least two, each in a different part of the house. Be sure to wash all the food and water dishes every day.

Toys

Your kitty will need an assortment of toys. This is not a waste of money or an indulgence; it is an investment in your cat's overall health. Toys provide mental as well as physical stimulation, which means that they also provide much-needed environmental enrichment.

Cat toys are so cleverly designed that they are nearly always irresistible to cat owners. Cats, however, will soon make their preferences clear. Give some thought to what cats do: hunt. Simulated hunting is a big part of their play, so many of their toys will be designed to tap into their hunting instinct. They also like to carry around small, soft toys, and they enjoy batting things that move (there's that hunting instinct again).

Remember when shopping for toys that it is up to you to assess the safety of the toy. Beware of sharp objects, parts that kitty might pull off and swallow, and any interactive toys with strips of Mylar—Mylar strands can easily give kitty the equivalent of a paper cut on her lips or tongue.

Soft stuffed toys come in a variety of sizes and shapes. While shape, size, and fabric texture can be meaningful to your cat, chances are she won't care very much if the toy looks like a former president, a dog, a fish, or a veterinarian. You are really buying those to attract *your* eye. Think more about size and shape.

Some toys come stuffed with catnip, but the quality of the catnip varies from toy to toy. We'll be discussing catnip in a moment, but for now it's important to know that depending on the manufacturer, the toy may contain low-quality catnip, high-quality catnip, or no catnip to speak of at all, even though the package says it's a catnip toy. Some toys come with a replaceable catnip packet, or a pocket to hold catnip, so you can always put fresh catnip inside the toy for maximum enjoyment.

Balls are another kitty favorite. Not only do some cats like to play fetch, but they love to play their own version of hockey—kicking the ball with their back feet, running and pouncing on it, and then kicking it again. Many kitties seem to think that you can never have enough balls. For self-amusing fun or interactive play, balls are inexpensive and fun. Balls come in several choices. Crinkle balls (a safer way to enjoy Mylar) make a noise when touched, somewhat akin to the sound of a rustling paper bag. Sparkle balls are very sparkly to attract the cat. (One cat owner I know insists that her cat is going to take over the world with sparkle balls. Obviously, those are her cat's favorites.) There are hard balls to kick around, soft balls that can also be carried like a soft toy as well as kicked, rubber balls that bounce, and plastic balls that have a bell inside for cats who like the sound. Those break rather easily if you accidentally step on one.

There are seemingly countless styles of mouse toys. Some are small and hard, some small and soft. Some are filled with catnip while others are made of a crinkly material. Some are made of fabric or fur, while others are made of colorful rope. There is seemingly no end to the types of mouse toys you can buy.

The trackball is a round toy that comes in two sizes and is made of plastic. It's shaped like a doughnut. There is a deep groove around the edge of the toy with a ball inside that can be batted but cannot be removed. Kitty hits the ball and watches it spin around the track. Some also have a scratching surface in the center. This toy is a little more expensive but is well worth it if your kitty enjoys it. Some cats love this toy and others are completely uninterested. You won't know unless you either try it or have been told that this was a favorite before kitty arrived in your home.

There are tunnels and sacks and crinkly sounding toys that also provide mental and physical stimulation. There are treat toys for cats, too. They will release a treat or a piece of dry food when manipulated by the cat. This is a great idea, because it makes the cat hunt for her food and use her mind to figure out how to get the toy to release the morsels.

There are plastic toys that pop back into position if pushed over and others that bear a strong resemblance to baby toys, such as a roller with a bell inside. There's a good reason for this: Some of these toys have been designed by the same creative people who have designed baby toys. Why? Most likely it's to catch the eye of owners who love to baby their pets. But also, what's safe for a baby is often safe for a cat as well—sometimes. Some flame-retardant toys are dangerous to animals, since they contain a chemical inside that if ingested can kill the pet. They weren't meant to be chewed open by pets and have their chemicals ingested.

Interactive toys—the ones you play with together—are important, not just to create a wonderful playtime and bonding experience for you both, but for the cat's emotional and physical health. Your cat needs to exercise as well as use her mind. These toys must be put away between play periods because they come attached to a stick or string, and your cat can get into serious trouble playing alone with one of these toys. She can get tangled in the string or wire and injure herself, or chew it off and swallow it and it can create an intestinal obstruction. A bonus to putting the toy away is that when you take it out, kitty knows it's time for special fun with you.

Fishing pole type toys have string tied to a stick, with something on the end of the string—often feathers to make it seem as if kitty is chasing a bird. You can swing the toy around so it looks as if the bird is flying and kitty can jump to catch it, or you can drag it across the floor so kitty can chase it. Some of these toys sound like a bird as it flies through the air.

Wand toys come with a piece of fur or feathers on the end or a long piece of fabric. They are similar to fishing pole toys in that you need to put them away between play sessions. A shorter stick with the fur or tassel-type end allows kitty to bat at it and play pounce and jump games. The longer stick with the very long fabric at the end is great for dragging along after you so kitty can chase it. There is also a wire toy with cardboard pieces at the end that bounce around. Cats seem to love it.

Laser toys are somewhat controversial. There are those who say they are perfectly safe and there are others who feel they are potentially dangerous. The laser can damage the cat's eye if it is shined directly into the eyes. As someone who has had two laser surgeries, I am hesitant to use a laser toy for fear of accidentally causing eye damage to my cat. Cats move so fast that it's easy for their eye to suddenly be in line with the laser beam. If you do want to use a laser toy, animal behaviorist Karen Pryor has long recommended starting the laser game as if the light is coming from inside your shoe and ending the game with the light seeming to go back into your shoe so the cat isn't going crazy trying to find it. Kitty knows that the game has a beginning and an end, and then the laser toy is put away.

Catnip

I'm sure you've heard of the herb catnip, which is a member of the mint family. But did you know that not every cat likes it? The feline reaction to catnip is genetic, and not every cat is born with the catnip gene. Young kittens don't react to it, but if they're going to react it will be when they're a little older. When cats are affected by it, it works like a stimulant, causing the cat to act rather silly and happy. You can buy catnip toys or bags of fresh or dried catnip. There are also mats for kitty to lie on that have an opening into which you can place some catnip. It's also possible to grow your own fresh catnip on your windowsill or in your garden. Catnip starter plants are for sale in many pet supply stores.

Give your cat a catnip toy every few days or once a week, and then put it away when she's finished playing so it becomes a special treat. That includes both fresh and dried loose catnip, and catnip toys. The immediate effect is seen in a minute or two, and it probably takes an hour or two for the cat to return to a normal state—although she will appear so much sooner.

Toys that are filled with catnip will stay fresher if you put them in a plastic bag in the freezer. Also, squeezing the toy will release some of the scent, which likely releases a chemical that reacts in the cat's brain. The scent is also released when kitty plays with the toy, kicking and biting it and even rolling on the toy.

You can also sprinkle catnip at the base of kitty's scratching post to encourage her to use it. It won't hurt if she eats a bit. Catnip is also used as an enticement for cardboard scratching pads to attract a kitty's attention. There is also a catnip spray that you can use on the scratching post to encourage your cat to check it out.

If your cat becomes overly aroused, remove the toy and replace it with something else. In the future, keep play sessions with catnip toys shorter so kitty won't reach that overaroused stage. One cat I know would play so actively with a catnip toy and become so aroused that she would end the play session by urinating in the bathtub. Don't let your kitty reach that state of arousal. All good things in moderation.

While catnip definitely has an effect on those cats who respond to it, it is not a drug. You don't have to be afraid of giving it to your cat. There's no addiction involved. It does alter her mood, but it's not dangerous like a drug would be. It is simply another thing to stimulate her. Just don't overuse it, and it will always be something special.

Grooming Tools

While cats are famous for how well they groom themselves, you will also need to groom your cat every day to help her remove dead hair and prevent some of those notorious hairballs that you may find around your house from time to time. Even shorthaired cats shed, so brushing daily certainly won't hurt and will help to remove dead hair from kitty's coat. You can use a chamois cloth to wipe down a hairless cat each day.

There are few things less enticing than hearing your cat hack up a hairball while you're eating. And hair in the intestinal tract isn't good for kitty. Here's how hairballs happen.

If your kitty licks you, you will notice that a cat's tongue feels rough, a little like sandpaper. That's because there are little hooks (the papillae that I mentioned earlier) on the tongue that help remove hair. Where is that hair going? Well, since cats can't stop swallowing once they start, that hair goes into the intestinal tract. And from there, it's either passed in the feces or gathers in the stomach until the cat throws it up. And then you usually find it by stepping on something squishy. That's the "yuck factor"—a good reason to groom your cat regularly!

You'll need a comb and, depending on the type of coat your cat has, a brush. If you have a shorthaired cat, you may want to use a rubber brush with little nubs on it to loosen dead hair, which can then be combed out more easily. Longhaired cats will benefit from a good brushing with a slicker brush.

Let's talk a bit about combs and brushes. There are so many types, and deciding which one you need can be pretty confusing for most of us. What you will need depends on your kitty's hair and its condition. If

Cats spend about a third of their waking hours grooming.

you have a pedigreed cat, you can ask the person from whom you got the cat what works best on that particular coat.

Combs come with teeth spaced close together (fine), wide apart (coarse), or in between. A fine comb is for cats with smooth or fine coats. A medium comb is suitable for most cats. And a coarse comb is for coarse-coated cats with short hair. You may also want a flea comb if your cat is exposed to fleas and you need to go through her coat, literally, with a fine-tooth comb!

Some people also get a shedding blade to remove dead and semi-dead hair. This is a loop of metal with teeth that rake through the coat. A dematting comb helps remove dead hair and comb out most tangled hair. There is also a product called a Furminator to remove loose or dead hair. These types of products cut down on shedding, and, as I said before, combing and brushing kitty's hair cuts down on hairballs.

Zoom Groom is a product I use and my cat loves. I don't have anything to do with the company, but I can say from experience that this was a good (and relatively inexpensive) investment. A Zoom Groom removes dead or semidead hair, even from my double-coated cat, without pulling or any chance of accidental cuts to the skin. It's made of rubber and also provides a nice kitty massage. Once the hair has been loosened, I simply go over the coat with a comb and collect the hair.

A slicker brush has lots of fine metal bristles that are set at an angle. It's good for longhaired cats and can also remove mats after they have been loosened with a mat splitter. Find a slicker brush with extrafine bristles if you have a kitten, an older cat, or a cat with fine, short hair.

A bristle brush helps you keep your cat's coat in good condition when used regularly. It is especially good at distributing natural oils from the skin throughout the coat.

If you comb or brush your cat regularly to remove dead hair and gently ease out any tangles, you won't need any of the products made for removing mats because your cat won't have mats. If you do find one, you should be able to work out most mats that haven't progressed with a comb. Be gentle, because snarls and mats hurt!

You will also need a set of clippers to clip claws. It's not tough to do if you start your cat out right with nail clipping. (More on that in chapter 7.)

You also need a toothbrush and kitty toothpaste. It's important to brush your cat's teeth because debris and germs leaching down from the teeth and gums get into the cat's bloodstream and can cause a plethora of health problems that may shorten your kitty's life. It's easiest to start brushing teeth when your cat is a kitten, but some adult cats can be tolerant.

By the way, any time there's a strong odor coming from your cat's mouth, it's time for a veterinary visit. Your cat's teeth will likely need a professional cleaning. Cats are very good at hiding pain, and a toothache isn't something you'll know about, although bad breath is one sign; not eating well can be another. We'll talk more about that later in this book.

Cats do a good job of bathing themselves, but if you need to give your kitty a bath, you'll need a shampoo made only for cats. If the label doesn't say that it's made for cats, don't buy it. The pH that is ideal for a cat's skin is not the same as it is for people. *Do not* buy any shampoo that contains tea tree oil. While it's okay for dogs, tea tree oil is deadly for cats. Exposure is lethal. Do not ever bathe your cat with a shampoo that contains it, and don't let anyone else do it, either. If you take your cat to a professional groomer, insist that they know not to use any product with tea tree oil on your cat. Don't rely on the fact that a product is labeled for use on cats; read the ingredients and be sure!

The Cat Bed

When it comes to cat beds, the choices are almost endless. They come in an assortment of styles and colors and sizes to go with any décor. You can find pillows of all sizes and shapes covered with any type of fabric. Some create a nest when the cat lies in it. Some are shaped like sofas; others like beds, tents, and royal crowns; and still others like sacks lined with faux sheepskin to keep kitty warm.

That said, you will probably find kitty dozing on your bed or a sofa or chair, or napping in the sunlight as it streams in through the window. If you are going to buy a cat bed, make sure it's set in a place where you've seen your kitty napping.

Cats love warm places. They also like dark small places in which to snuggle down for a nap. So you might also put a cardboard box with a towel inside in each of several rooms so kitty can jump in and nap or play. Cats don't care if it's expensive as long as it's comfortable.

When kitty becomes a senior, you might want to buy a cat bed (or make one) that is filled with foam in an egg crate pattern to ease any pressure points on arthritic joints.

The Carrier

A carrier is important not just for bringing your kitty home but for taking her places such as to the veterinarian's office and on trips. You will also need a carrier if you and your cat must leave home in a hurry for

Domestic cats spend about 70 percent of their day sleeping.

any reason. Whatever the reason, kitty will have to be contained in a comfy carrier when she goes out, and you want it to be well constructed and safe.

Many people just use the cardboard carrier in which they've brought kitty home from the shelter. But these carriers do not stand up to use over time. It's best to buy your cat a sturdy carrier that will last her a lifetime. The better the carrier you invest in, the longer it will last. A cheap one will have to be replaced sooner, which means you will have to pay twice for the same item.

The carrier you buy should be sturdy, and it shouldn't tip over or have canvas sides that sag inward. Check to see that the zipper that closes it can't be easily opened with a paw. Cats are very clever about opening zippers and squirming out of small places. Check to see that the stitching is uniform and won't separate. The material from which it's made should be safe and strong; check that first, and then you can think about the color and/or design that suits your taste. The carrier should also have good ventilation. Hard plastic carriers are mainly used for shipping animals and must be airline approved. They're a bit more awkward to carry. Many rescue groups use them as well. But for your purposes, a good, canvas carrier with sides that don't sag will suit you and your kitty quite well.

Creating a First Aid Kit

Everyone should have a first aid kit for their cat or kitten. In case there's an emergency, everything you need will be in one place.

You have two choices here. You can buy a ready-made first aid kit, or you can make one yourself. If you decide to make one yourself, you can go to the fishing gear section of your local store and buy a small tackle box. These boxes have slots for fishing tackle, which you can put to good use for separating first aid supplies so you can easily see and grab them.

It's a good idea to prepare two identical boxes: one for the house and one for the car. Most of the items will be similar to those in a first aid kit for people, but you must be very careful never to give your cat any human medicine without consulting your veterinarian. Many of the over-the-counter medications we take are just not safe for cats—most notably, acetaminophen.

Inside your cat's first aid kit you will need sterile gauze and adhesive tape or, preferably, vet wrap to use as a bandage. (Vet wrap is a bandage that sticks to itself and doesn't require any tape or pins. In fact some hospitals now use it instead of bandages after a blood test. It's very handy stuff to have around, since it's so easy to apply.) You'll also need tweezers, scissors, petroleum jelly, hydrogen peroxide, nail clippers, a muzzle (a pet in pain may bite), cotton balls, a tongue depressor or something similar to use for a splint, a flashlight, sterile saline solution, a chemical ice pack, an oral syringe, antiseptic wipes, an antibiotic ointment, eye wash, burn and insect relief lotions or creams, and a thermometer. Ear cleaning solution can also come in handy, as can latex gloves for you. You'll want to have towels handy to wrap up kitty, and you'll need the cat carrier for transport, so keep everything together in the same closet.

Keep your veterinarian's phone number and address, along with directions, in the first aid kit, in case a pet sitter is with your kitty. Include an emergency after-hours veterinary phone number, poison control phone number, and a copy of your cat's medical records, including proof of rabies vaccination. If your cat is on medication, write that down on a piece of paper in the first aid kit.

If you're traveling, before you leave home get the name of a good veterinarian in the area to which you're traveling. Ask your vet to make a referral.

These Maine Coon Cats are in a great carrier: It's strong and lightweight and ribbed across the top, so the fabric doesn't collapse in on the cat.

While it's true that cats prefer to be in their home, there are also cats who enjoy the adventure of traveling with their people. If you're one of those people who will take kitty along on vacations or other trips, you will want to buy a carrier that will fit underneath an airplane seat without collapsing on kitty. Yes, such carriers do exist. There is at least one company that makes a carrier that is so lightweight that all you feel is the weight of the cat!

A small, hard plastic carrier will also do for trips to the veterinarian and should fit under an airplane seat—despite the fact that there seems to be less room on planes than ever before. But know that even with a nice soft crate pad or towel, it still won't be as comfy as some other carriers that are soft-sided and weigh less. The soft-sided carrier will often have a shoulder strap to allow for more comfortable traveling if, as usually happens to me, your plane leaves from the very last gate. The carrier should be a pleasant place for kitty. Kitty should feel safe in the carrier and away from the noise and hubbub of the airport terminal.

Always have a cat carrier easily accessible and teach your cat that it's a fun place to be before she needs to go in for an emergency. Get kitty accustomed to the carrier by having a comfy mat inside (some carriers come with a nice one), a toy or two, and a treat. Leave the door or flap open and, especially if you plan to fly with kitty, keep it near your feet. Don't forget that this will be her main view during a flight! Let her wander in and out and nap in it. Occasionally close it and then open it while she's inside. She'll gradually become acclimated to it and will view her carrier as a safe haven. You can experiment with taking her out for short periods—trips to nowhere. And you can take her for car rides in the carrier.

You might also think about buying a harness and leash for your kitty for trips to the veterinarian or elsewhere. When you go through airport security, you have to hold your cat while the carrier goes through the X-ray machine. You may think kitty is calm and will be fine in your arms, but it only takes one loud sound or sudden movement to startle a cat enough to escape, even from the safety of your embrace. You need to know that kitty is safe outside your home, and a harness and leash will provide that.

Do *not* use a collar to walk your cat. Cat collars are made to break open if the collar gets caught on something so the cat won't choke to death. They're fine as a place to hang kitty's ID tags, but for walks nothing less than a harness will do.

This is all the basic equipment that kitty will need. So plan on a shopping spree before bringing your cat home.

CHAPTER 4

HOME AT LAST!

N ow that you've chosen your cat—or, more likely, your new feline friend has chosen you—and you have all of the accoutrements you'll need (at least in the beginning), it's time to bring kitty home.

Before you go to pick up your cat, set aside a room for kitty's homecoming. Whether kitten or adult, your cat will need a period of adjustment when going from his previous home to his new one. He'll feel more secure in a smaller space, rather than being given the run of the house right when he first arrives.

The room should contain a litter box, a scratching post, a couple of toys (you can bring an interactive toy in with you each time you go into the room to play with kitty, then take it out with you), a water dish, and a food dish. Fill the water dish when you get home, so the water is nice and fresh.

If the person with whom kitty has been living up to this point hasn't given you a bottle of the water kitty drinks and a small bag of food, you'll want to know in advance what food to buy. And tap water changes from place to place, so if kitty is coming from a different city, start him off with bottled water. You don't want him to get sick, and local bacteria he's not used to may upset his tummy. The change of home will be enough of an adjustment for kitty without adding to it a bout of diarrhea. You want to keep everything as positive as possible.

When you first bring kitty into the house, make sure he knows exactly where to find his litter box. Show him the litter box by gently putting him down in it, so there's no question of where the facilities are located when nature calls. You've already asked what type of litter and box he prefers, so I know you've got that all set up before you bring kitty home.

Add the Mat, Skip the Liner

You may want to add a mat where kitty enters and exits the litter box, because litter can stick between the pads on the cat's feet and be tracked out of the box. And that can be a bit messy. If the litter falls on a mat, you only have to shake the mat over a wastebasket or into a trash bag. Be sure to sweep or vacuum up any litter that's not caught in the mat.

When you're setting up the litter box, skip the litter box liner. Liners are often a waste of money because many cats will avoid a lined box. They don't like the feel of the liner under the litter or are startled by the way it can crinkle under their paws. A liner can also come away from the sides of the box and cause the kind of mess you're trying to prevent.

Be certain to scoop his litter box as soon as you see that he's used it. Once he gets used to using the box, it should be scooped twice a day. No one wants to use a dirty restroom. Cats are quite fastidious, so if you don't want litter box problems, remember to be diligent about scooping and cleaning the litter boxes from Day One.

Of course, it's not enough just to scoop. You must wash the box regularly with soap and water. Be sure to thoroughly rinse it, too. (See page 88 in chapter 5 for more on litter box hygiene.)

Make your cat feel welcome but not overwhelmed. Don't get him overexcited that first day, because going to a new home is excitement enough. Sit in the room with kitty. Let him explore on his own. Offer him something to eat. Let him investigate his new toys, his new bed, and his scratching post. Let him check out all of your stuff, too. Bring a book in with you; if he doesn't want to interact with you, you'll be a quiet presence in the room, and he will gradually approach you—all in his own time, of course. Family members should visit him quietly in the room. Everyone should remember that the cat will need some naptime.

Let the cat come to you and see how much affection he'll accept. He may very well surprise you by being a happy little camper who is eager for attention and affection right from the start. If he's hiding under the bed or under a piece of furniture, just sit there calmly. He may, or may not, come out. It may take a bit of time. You may not see the cat at all for a few days, but you'll see the telltale signs in the litter box and food and water dishes that he has been taking care of business when you're out of the room. Just give him some time to adjust.

A cat's collarbone, or clavicle, doesn't connect with other bones; it's buried in the muscles of the shoulder area. This unique anatomy is what allows a cat to squeeze through spaces no wider than her own head.

If the hiding goes on for more than a few days, you can tempt him out by using a toy on a stick. For this I especially like the Quickdraw McPaw, a tube with a control at one end and a toy at the other that slips in and out of the tube. Slip the toy part under the bed and use it to interest kitty. Start to slowly bring it out from under the bed, playing with it all the while. Kitty will follow. You can try any toy on a stick if that one isn't available. You can also try putting your hand down with your forefinger pointed out and let him come and sniff it. Again, this is all in his own time. Just let him sniff at first; don't reach for him. The key is to give kitty time, space, and as much affection and attention as *he* wants.

Newest Cat in the Family

If you already have one or more cats in residence and are bringing home a newbie to add to the family, you will have to proceed slowly and carefully to ensure that all cats are properly introduced. There's a myth that you can just bring a new cat home, turn him loose, and all will be well. Are you ever in for a surprise! This is akin to your spouse bringing home a new roommate one day and expecting you all to get along.

There's another myth that says if the cats don't get along, you can just let them "fight it out." That doesn't work in our human culture, and

Picking Up a Cat

Knowing how to properly pick up your cat is important. Queens hold their kittens by the scruff of the neck, but that's not the best way for us to do it. Kittens grow quickly, and when the cat begins to weigh more, scruffing can be darn uncomfortable.

The best way to pick up a cat is to put one hand under his chest between his front legs and use the other to support his hindquarters. This avoids putting stress on any part of the body. There shouldn't be any dangly parts hanging down to make your cat uncomfortable. You need to support him the way you would support a human baby, so he's comfortable and safe.

Once you've got him up, place his tummy against your chest, high enough so that he can put his front paws over your shoulder if he wants to. Hold him close to your body for maximum security and comfort. Don't hold him too tight but not so loose that he doesn't feel secure.

And remember that, mostly, cats don't really like being picked up. Kitty will often simply choose to sit near you or climb on top of you, perhaps for cuddles, perhaps for a nap. Many cats are fairly selective about human companionship; you've been chosen.

it doesn't work among cats, either. Cats have different personality types, just as people do. They need to get to know each other.

You're much more likely to have cats who like each other if you take the time to do a proper introduction. Here's how you go about introducing the newest kitty to the rest of your feline family—whether you have one resident cat or more.

Set up new kitty's room for comfort, as I've already described. You may also want to leave a radio on a low volume to a calming music station—although some cats prefer quiet. If you've brought him home in a regular carrier, not a cardboard one, you can also put that in the room, but leave it open. He will probably want a little hidey-hole of his own. Cats enjoy small, enclosed spaces.

Spend time in the room playing with the newcomer. Be sure to spend time playing and interacting with your resident cat(s) too, who will be curious about the newcomer and will certainly be concerned about losing your attention.

The newcomer should be completely isolated, not just for behavioral reasons but in case he is harboring something infectious. After several days, when you know your new kitty isn't carrying anything contagious, put towels on the floor in the areas where the resident cats and the new cat

The tabby pattern is the basic coat pattern that underlies all of the variations we see.

lie. If you already have cats, you know that when you put down a towel, a cat will lie on it. As each cat lies on their towel, it will pick up the kitty's scent. Then exchange the towels so they each smell the other's scent.

This is just a scent exchange. The optimum is not seeing each other for the first week. Cats aren't fond of change, so your resident cat will need time to adjust—as will the newcomer. You can also give each cat a treat on the opposite sides of the door.

Rubbing your cats with each other's scent is another way to exchange scents. Simply run the same towel along each cat's flank to accomplish this.

After a week or more of exchanging scents, you can exchange places. Allow the resident cat to spend time alone in the new kitty's room, and allow the new kitty time out in at least one other room of the house. It doesn't have to be for a very long time—just an hour or two. Then put the new kitty back in his room while you let the resident cat out. They will now have had the experience of smelling each other's scent in the house.

Remember the old story of the tortoise and the hare? Slow and steady wins the race. Now you can start feeding the cats on opposite sides of the door. Food is a great icebreaker for cats as well as for people. If the newcomer's room has a screen door, allow them to see each other without contact. Yes, you can expect hissing. Ignore it. It's normal behavior under the circumstances.

In another week, with new kitty in his carrier, bring your resident cat into the room for their first introduction. There will be more hissing, and you may see some posturing. If this portion of the introduction leads to anything that looks like aggression, don't move to the next step; just do this same sort of intro for another few days with newbie kitty in his carrier. He'll feel (and be!) safe in there. Don't leave the cats alone together. Stay in the room so each cat has the security of knowing that you're there.

When things have settled down and they are peaceful together, you can open the carrier and allow the new kitty to walk into the household. Supervise this introduction carefully. It is best done at mealtime so they're distracted by food and are busy dining in harmony.

When you finally allow the new cat out into other rooms in the house, be sure to supervise all interactions and play games that include all the cats. A wand toy will help get the games started. You want all interactions to be positive so you're not setting up the equivalent of a sibling rivalry. When they're playing side by side, there will be a better chance they'll all accept each other. Be sure that your resident cat knows that fun things happen when the new cat is present.

To make the cats smell alike, you can put a dab of vanilla extract on each cat's rear end. Some cats can be agitated by this, although others are just pleased that they share the same scent.

If there are any problems, put the new cat back in his room and slow down the introduction to the rest of the house. Always be there to supervise when the cats interact. And when you leave the house during the next few weeks, be sure that kitty is safely in his room if no one is there to supervise. Do not leave them out together with someone who is not capable of supervising. Better safe than sorry. Eventually, the cats will either make friends or at least learn to tolerate each other.

It can take anywhere from a couple of days to a couple of months to properly introduce them. Meanwhile, they can play under the door, touching paws.

If there are problems, such as fighting or excessive hissing and spitting or growling, separate the cats and start the process over, going much more slowly this time. If there's only one place where they have problems interacting, I recommend a Feliway plug-in. Feliway is a pheromone-based diffuser that's plugged into an outlet in the wall and releases a comforting (to cats) scent into the area. It also comes in a spray and a wipe cloth, but the diffuser seems to work best in homes, since it automatically releases the calming scent (which, by the way, we humans cannot smell). The natural feline pheromones help ease the stress. (The spray can be used inside a carrier before you take your cat on a trip or to the veterinarian. You can also use the Feliway wipes for this purpose.) The bottom line with pheromone products is that some experts feel they don't work, while others claim they do. The only way to find out is to try them with your cats.

Once your cats bond to each other, or at least learn to live harmoniously, you're likely to find them grooming each other. This is called allogrooming and is perfectly normal cat behavior. Watching cats groom each other is very sweet.

If you also have a dog as well as cats, always introduce your cats first before you introduce the resident dog.

Sharing the House with Dogs

Before you even think about adding a cat to your canine household, there are some things to consider for the cat's safety and your peace of mind. Has your dog met cats before? Does your dog interact well with them? Does your dog have a high prey drive? Nature trumps nurture in most cases, and if your dog is the type who sees something small that moves and instinctively wants to chase and kill it, you may not be able to have a cat. Not every kitty is confident enough to swat the dog and stand his ground. And not every dog will back off from a confident cat.

If you have the sort of dog who is not likely to live peacefully with cats, you are going to have constant warfare, and no one will be relaxed, happy, or comfortable in your house again if you bring home a kitty. It's not fair to the dog or the cat. And you won't enjoy the situation either.

If you decide it's safe to bring kitty home to a house with one or more dogs, you still need to separate the newcomer in his own room where you will spend time with him. Your resident dog (or dogs) will smell the cat and be curious.

Take your time. Your dog will meet kitty under the door, the way I just described in the section on introducing cats. You can also do the towel exchange that I described. When you finally bring the cat out to meet the dog, be sure you are holding kitty and that the first meetings are brief, with the dog and cat having a chance to sniff each other while kitty is being held up off the floor.

Give the dog a treat for good behavior and be sure to give kitty one, too. Good things should happen for each of them when the other is present. Put kitty back in his safe room. Continue this daily, slowly increasing their interaction time. When they are both calm in each other's presence, kitty can be on the floor.

Always try to relax when introducing a cat to either dogs or other cats, because you don't want your pets picking up on your anxiety.

Suck on a breath mint if you have to. That will also help mask any fear odor that has been triggered, so the animals don't pick up on it. Dogs and cats are masterful at reading our body language. Please remember that!

Even if the dog likes cats and they become buddies, you will still need places where kitty can go up high to escape and feel safe. Cats see rooms as vertical spaces, so you want to give kitty the space she needs with a cat tree and other safe, cat-permitted elevated surfaces throughout the house.

Indoors Is Best

In the United States, it's not considered responsible to let your cat roam freely outdoors. When you get a cat from a shelter, a rescue group, or a breeder, they'll ask you to promise that you keep the cat indoors only. In the United Kingdom and some other countries, however, the shelters will often insist that the cat be allowed outdoors. Which is correct? Let's look at the issues.

The reason the people in the United Kingdom and elsewhere allow their cats outdoors is that they know cats need environmental enrichment. However, we are perfectly capable of providing that environmental enrichment indoors, and your cat will be much safer as well.

Outdoor cats are in danger from other animals, including other cats with whom they might fight and get bitten. Abscesses from bite wounds are common in cats allowed outdoors. They are also in danger from birds of prey, dogs, raccoons, coyotes, and other wild animals. They are exposed to the diseases of wild animals. They are exposed to internal and external parasites and all the diseases they carry as well. Outdoor cats require more vaccinations to protect them from more illnesses.

Cars are also a huge danger. Even an adult cat cannot read a street sign. Letting your cat out to roam is like turning your toddler loose in the streets.

There are dangers from the toxic fertilizers and weed killers people put on their grass, and from antifreeze spilled on the driveway or in the garage. All of these substances are lethal to cats. Your neighbor might have put out a mouse trap or rat poison as well, and that, too, is lethal to cats.

There are also people who will not appreciate your cat roaming around in their yard and using their garden as a litter box. And there are children and adults who dislike cats and will not think twice about injuring or poisoning your cat.

Outdoor cats have a much shorter life span than those who are kept indoors. Indoor-only cats live an average of ten to fourteen years, while

The Declawing Issue

Sometimes declawing is regarded as not okay for an outdoor cat (who needs his claws for defense and escape), but fine for an indoor cat. But (and I can't say this emphatically enough) even if your cat is indoors only, *do not declaw your cat*. Not even if the cat has been scratching the furniture or clawing the drapes. Getting a good scratching post and teaching your cat to use it is the easiest way to resolve the problem. Having different types of scratchers around is ideal.

Too many people don't understand declawing and ask their veterinarian to perform this surgery without actually knowing what it involves. Declawing is not a radical manicure. It is not just the removal of the claws; it's the removal of the last toe bone. In fact, it is the equivalent of cutting off your finger at the first joint. It's painful and it's disfiguring.

Cats need their claws for protection—especially if they're allowed to go outdoors. But even indoor cats use their claws for balance and to grasp toys and other items. *All cats need their claws.*

There have been some studies showing that declawing results in behavior problems, including litter box issues. There have been studies showing it doesn't result in behavior problems. Frankly, no large, definitive studies have been done on the long-term effects of declawing. But what we do know is that cats need their claws and removing them is cruel.

Cats absolutely do need to scratch, but there are ways to protect your furniture. Really, it's quite simple to keep the nails trimmed and to make sure that kitty uses the scratchers you buy for him. I'll talk about this later in chapter 5 when I discuss behavior problems.

Love your cat enough to let him keep his claws.

---

indoor-outdoor cats live approximately four years, on average. And indoor cats, when provided with proper environmental enrichment, are very happy and well adjusted.

Some cat owners want to give their cats a safe outdoor experience. You can take your cat for a walk using a harness or vest. Or you can build an enclosure where kitty can play outdoors in a safe place. Some of these enclosures will fit on a small apartment patio for urban cats. Discuss additional vaccinations with your veterinarian if you choose to do this.

Far less fun for most owners is when they allow their cat to go outdoors and kitty brings in a dead animal as a love offering. You can't train a cat not to hunt—that's just what cats do. On the other hand, if

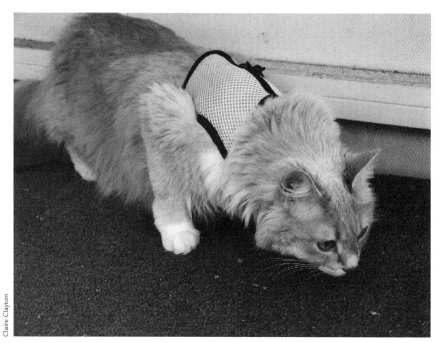

A stylish walking jacket is a safe way for your cat to enjoy the outdoors.

you live near woods and a mouse has gotten into your house—rather foolish of the rodent when you have a live-in predator—kitty will, indeed, be exercising his hunting skills and dispatching the mouse post-haste. The same will happen if a bird or a moth accidentally flies in. If your kitty is a good hunter, it won't take him long to capture his prey.

Environmental Enrichment

Environmental enrichment starts with kitty furniture, as I've discussed in chapter 3. Kitty should have the full assortment of soft toys, different types of balls, and other small toys to play with. Assorted toys should be switched around every few days, so there is always something novel to play with. He will also enjoy a plain paper bag from the supermarket or a crinkle bag made of cloth. There are also tunnels he can hide in and run through.

Kitty will also need to play with you. Toys are fine, but cats need human interaction, too. Cats who have regular play periods at least twice a day with their people are better adjusted and don't develop behavior problems. Interactive games provide them with a much-needed outlet for their prey drive, as well as companionship with you.

I know I've already said this, but it's worth mentioning again: Cats are *not* loners. Your cat craves your companionship and love. He wants and needs interaction with you. You will both enjoy it. Not only will you have a well-adjusted cat, but there is nothing—absolutely nothing—that can replace the human-animal bond. Those play sessions will make your bond grow stronger.

If you have more than one cat, and your cats play together, that's wonderful. But it's still no substitute for playtime with you. It's vital for cats to have interactive games with humans. We are part of their clowder, and they need interaction with us. Did you notice how happy kitty is to see you come home?

Some cats love to play fetch, whether with a ball, a mousey toy, or a crumpled-up piece of paper. Some are so enthusiastic at the game that when you want to stop, kitty may keep pestering you for just one more throw.

Interactive pole toys (like the ones I described in chapter 3) are a necessity of life with a cat. How your cat plays with these toys will depend on your cat's personal preference for hunting. You'll have to experiment to discover if your cat prefers toys that move and wiggle across the floor like a mouse or a snake, or fly through the air like a bird. (Remember that you want to avoid buying toys with Mylar strips because those can cause the equivalent of a paper cut on your cat's mouth.)

Sally Bahner

The average lifespan for an indoor cat is fifteen years, while the average lifespan for an outdoor cat is only three to five years.

Be sure to put the interactive toys away between play sessions. Each time you take an interactive toy out will signal to your cat that something special is going to happen, and you'll see the happy reaction it elicits. Your cat will know that you're about to have fun together. Cats are extremely intelligent, and once they learn that something good happens when you go to that special place where you keep the interactive toys, they will always remember. Show a cat something once, or do something once, and your cat has learned it.

A more controversial interactive toy is a laser light. There is a debate about whether the laser light can permanently damage a cat's eyes. A flashlight with a narrow beam will do just as well. You will need to remember to start the light-chasing game with the light appearing to come out of a specific place, and have it return to that place when the game is over. Otherwise, your cat will go crazy trying to find the light after the game ends, and that's just not fair.

Whatever toy you're playing with, allow the cat to catch it frequently so he doesn't feel frustrated. You can tell him what a good hunter he is! If your cat isn't playing yet but is watching the moving toy, then he's engaged in the action. He doesn't have to pounce to be part of the action.

Of course, you can't play with your cat all the time. But you can make the house interesting for kitty. You can put his food, or treats, inside a treat ball or hide small amounts of food around the house so he

Kari Winters

A cat's ears can pivot 180 degrees. This is an Oriental Shorthair.

has to hunt for it while you're out. (Eating more slowly will help some cats who are such gluttons that they eat and purge.) Rotate kitty's toys so the old ones appear to be new. If you haven't seen something for a while and suddenly discover it again, aren't you happy to see it?

Consider putting a bird feeder outside a window where kitty can watch the birds come and go, rather like Cat TV. You'll hear the different sounds he makes as he shifts into prey mode. It makes life even more interesting and serves as one more form of environmental enrichment—as do squirrels scampering up a tree and stealing the bird seed.

Another form of environmental enrichment is one that we'll discuss in detail in chapter 11: cat training. Yes, you've read that correctly.

According to the American Pet Products Association's most recent survey, there are 38.2 million cat-owning households in the United States. The majority of owners value the companionship a cat brings them. What you put into your relationship with your cat is what you'll get out of that relationship. It has every opportunity to be wonderfully beneficial for all of you.

CHAPTER 5

Understanding Cat Behavior

I t's commonly thought that cats were first domesticated about 8,000 years ago, so these beautiful creatures have been enhancing human life for a very long time. But housecats are probably the most misunderstood of the domesticated animals. *Felis catus,* domestic cats, have their own characteristics and behaviors that are unique to their species.

I know cats sometimes do things we don't like. With kittens there is often a concern about rough play or fearfulness. With adult cats the problems are usually aggression to other cats, fear of humans, and not using the litter box or scratching something that people consider inappropriate. For adults, these problems may overlap.

I will talk about behavior problems in this chapter. But first, let's go over the behavior basics. When we understand our cats' behavior and why they do the things they do, we can see that it all makes sense to them. And then we can learn how to change their behavior in ways they will understand and appreciate.

Four Myths about Cats

It's really amazing that so many myths have sprung up around cats, because they're such wonderful creatures. It's a pretty safe bet that the old belief that they were a witch's familiar has finally been put to rest.

Cats and people have identical regions in the brain that are responsible for emotions.

So has the idea that a black cat crossing your path is bad luck, which is just plain silly. Black cats are wonderful pets. Then there's the old adage that cats don't remember anything. Nonsense! They remember their names, people they've known, and much more. They are every bit as intelligent as other pets, and in some cases, more so.

So many old wives' tales have been taken as gospel for so long that just the fact that you are sitting here reading this book puts you head and shoulders above most cat owners. Let me take a moment to thank you for being ready and willing to learn more about cats so you can have the best possible relationship with your cat.

I want to start by dispelling four big myths about cats. Knowing that none of these things are true will go a long way in developing a great relationship with your cat.

Cats Are Low-Maintenance and Don't Want or Need Much Attention

In reality, cats are very social beings. They are solitary hunters, but when they're not hunting (and let's face it, today's kitty is often using her hunting instincts just to play), sleeping, eating, or taking care of litter box business, they want companionship. Specifically, your companionship. That's why you so often find kitty playing with the newspaper when you're reading it, lying across a book you're enjoying, or walking across your computer keyboard. Even sleeping cats tend to sleep in the room you're in.

Your cat wants your attention, interaction, and, yes, love. Cats don't particularly like being left alone with food, water, and a litter box while you leave the house. Kitty would rather be with you.

A Cat Is Like a Little Dog

You'd be surprised at how many people expect Fluffy to act like Rover, and then they're disappointed when things don't go as planned.

Cats are a different species. They want interaction but don't want you chasing after them. In fact, that's why they usually go to the one guest in your home who dislikes cats—they consider it polite behavior to be ignored so they can make the first approach. Unlike most dogs, who will go up to your guests and pretty much insist upon being petted and admired, kitty would rather take her time.

Once engaged, however, many cats will follow you around from room to room or will bring a toy for you to throw in a game of fetch—well, that is a bit like dogs. But you don't have to take kitty out for a walk in a blizzard or rainstorm, because she's happy to stay indoors with a clean litter box. She is definitely not a dog.

A Cat Is Like a Furry Child

While it's wonderful to love a cat as a member of your family, if you expect the cat to be a baby, you run the risk of interpreting the cat's behavior as if she were a human. This can lead to thinking the cat is being spiteful or "knows better" when she does something you don't like.

In reality, your cat is an animal and thinks like an animal. She is not doing anything to spite you. She has reasons for her behavior, but you'll have to look for them by understanding how animals see their environment. For example, if your kitty has always used her litter box but suddenly is not, think first about health problems and take her to the veterinarian. Once those are ruled out, you might consider what has changed in the household. Have you added a new family member, lost a member of the household? Can she see a neighbor's cat outside? Urinating around the house is one way cats cope with stress. This has nothing to do with spite but everything to do with how kitty perceives her world.

Many breeds, including this Maine Coon Cat, have a double coat consisting of a downy undercoat and a longer, harder outercoat.

Cats Can't Be Trained

This one is one of those myths that really puzzles me because we all see trained cats performing on television and in the movies. They're not just really good actors in a cat suit with a Screen Actors Guild card. They're trained to do whatever is required of them, whether it's opening a cabinet, sitting on cue, or staying in a certain pose. Cats who perform will jump through hoops, walk a tightrope, play a children's piano, or—like the cat who has become the rage of YouTube—learn to play a real piano through observational learning. The term *copycat* takes on real meaning when you see something like that.

Feline Body Language

Cats can read your body language, but can you read theirs? The answer is yes *if* you learn the basics and spend some time studying your kitty and others. This is a language that's not difficult to learn. I'll give you the basics, and then by carefully observing your cat you can learn the variations that make up her own unique "dialect."

Cats seem to have a million ways to communicate with you if you pay attention to their vocalizations and body language. Your cat will also tune in to you and the way you respond to her individual sounds and postures. Each cat has her own idiosyncrasies, and you'll come to know what your cat wants by paying attention to her. For example, when my cat wants to be petted, she does the usual arching of her back and will often also sit near me, reach over with one paw, and pull my hand over to her while looking meaningfully into my eyes. I know what she wants, just as if she had spoken English and told me!

The position of a cat's ears and tail will tell you a lot, as will body posture, fur, eyes, and even whiskers. But looking at the cat's entire body will give you a better idea of what's going on than just picking out one body part. Sometimes there's more than meets the eye at first glance.

For an excellent illustration of feline body language, point your Internet browser to www.messybeast.com/cat_talk2.htm.

Ear Grammar

Your cat's ears can move independently of each other—a wonderful advantage while hunting or if there is a need to hear something in the house. Kitty's ears are also really interesting when it comes to signaling her feelings. Ears that are upright and point forward indicate your cat is relaxed and alert. It's also possible that this can be an aggressive

Sally Bahner

Cats, like this Russian Blue, have exceptional peripheral vision and can see 120 degrees around them.

positioning of the ears, but you can tell the difference between aggression and alertness by looking at the rest of the body.

If her ears are sideways, she's alert to sounds but isn't sure about what she's hearing. Ears back and flat against her head indicate submission but, again, she may become aggressive. Don't push your luck. If she's feeling very defensive, you can count on her ears being back and flat against her head. Her body will also be signaling defensive aggression, and the best thing you can do is stay away from her.

Tail Talk

Kitty's tail is another barometer of her mood. When her tail is upright, she's indicating that she's content or happy. If, however, you see her tail upright with hairs bristling, she's feeling defensive. If her tail, held high, is curled down at the end, then she's not really sure about whoever is approaching her. If she's holding her tail halfway up, it's an indicator of a friendly cat who is not sure about the pet or person who is in her line of sight.

An upright tail that is flicking is telling you that kitty sees or hears you but has more important things on her mind at the moment. It's sort of like waving hi to someone when you're in the middle of a discussion with someone else. Frankly, a squirrel or bird outside is more interesting at the moment. Be flattered that kitty is acknowledging your presence when she has something that has so piqued her interest.

Here's an example of a dialect in feline body language: When a cat swishes her tail back and forth, that's a warning sign that kitty isn't happy. And if kitty isn't happy at that moment, then no one will be happy, so leave her alone. However, there are some cats who have a "happy tail." In other words, they wag it rather like a dog when they're happy. It's up to you to know your cat and learn to discern between the warning and the welcome. The rest of her body, including her eyes, will point you in the right direction.

Sometimes a Look Is Just a Look, but Sometimes It's Not

The eyes are best read together with body signals to come to a conclusion about your cat's mood. When your cat looks at you and slowly blinks her eyes, it's known as kitty kisses; it means she trusts you. If her pupils are dilated, she may be signaling aggression, excitement, pain, or fear. That's why you have to take the entire body into consideration. If her eyes look like narrow slits she may be self-assured or just plain angry. Or sleepy.

A cat who stares at another cat is being confrontational. The standoff is broken by blinking. Whoever blinks or looks away first has capitulated.

Body Posture

You'll see body posture clues in the other parts of this section, and it's important to factor them into any translation of your cat's body language.

Arching her back with her hair raised is a warning to stay away, because she's really aroused. On the other hand, if she rubs against you with her back arched and her hair flat, she's asking to be petted.

Some cats like to have their tummy rubbed. But most cats have a low tolerance for this, and some of them seem to sucker people into petting their stomach so they can grab the person's hand and bite it. Gentle bites that don't break the skin are known as love bites. The worst thing you can do is pull your hand away, because kitty will only clamp down. Just freeze. She will eventually release your hand—and it really won't take that long.

Aroused Cat

It's fascinating to watch a cat as she contemplates a squirrel or bird outside the window. Cats are natural predators, and there is an intensity about a cat who is paying attention to prey or possible prey. You'll see that body language when the ears are moved forward to hear better and the body also leans forward. Your kitty's lip will curl a bit and her mouth will open. She'll crouch and then you'll see her ears move back.

If her head is low and she looks intent, then she moves forward with her head shifting from side to side, she is looking at her prey.

Tasting the Air

Cats sometimes exhibit an unusual reaction to smell called the flehmen response. You see it when a cat grimaces in response to an odor. The cat is actually using her tongue to sweep the scent molecules into a special organ in the roof of her mouth called the vomeronasal organ. This is a way your cat tastes as well as smells the scent.

If you've used a scented grooming spray or shampoo, chances are that you will see this response from your cat. You will also notice it when she's smelling something on the floor or anywhere else that has captured her attention. She may also use it when she's stalking prey. And in intact cats, it's part of mating behavior; they're checking out the pheromones in the air.

Defensive Cat

If your cat's head is held to the side and she's crouching, she is defensive. If her ears are up and pointed back, she is troubled and may become defensively aggressive. Hissing and growling are also defensive language. They're a way a cat says, "Stop, I've had enough." You may also see a ripple of her back that indicates defensive aggression.

Signs of Love

When your cat follows you, licks you, and head butts, she's showing how much she loves you. So is rubbing her cheek on you or something you own. That cheek rubbing is called allomarking. Your cat has scent

Nancie S. Belser

Domestic cats are the only cat species that can hold their tail vertically while walking.

glands in her cheeks, and by rubbing them against everything from furniture to your leg or your shoes, she is marking those items (and people) as hers. It's definitely a compliment!

Another way of showing love is head butting. This is when your cat puts her head down and uses her forehead to gently butt you. Head butting is a wonderful greeting that tells you she's so very happy to see you. Cats will also greet each other this way.

Your cat may also play with you by using her back feet against your arm. Cats play with one another using their back feet, and she's showing you that you're everything to her, including her playmate.

Some owners are confused when their cat kneads them or, as it's sometimes called, "makes biscuits." This kneading behavior is comforting to the cat because it is what kitty did to help her mother let down her milk. When kitty does this to you, she is comfortable with you and is comforting herself by showing a kittenish behavior that she used with her mother. As long as her nails are trimmed, there is no reason why you both shouldn't enjoy it.

Some cats will show one or two of these behaviors with you, and some will show all of them. Relax and enjoy these expressions of love and comfort.

How Cats Vocalize

Cats vocalize for a variety of reasons. You will likely pay a lot more attention if you live with a particularly quiet cat, because it's unusual to hear from her. But all cats use vocalization to make their needs known, whether it's through purring, meowing, or chattering. Some can't wait to talk to you when you come home. And they're just as happy to hear about your day as to tell you about theirs.

Did you know that there are at least nineteen different types of meows? They each have a different pitch, volume, tone, rhythm, and situation in which the cat uses them. Cats can yowl, squawk, scream, and more. One study found there are about thirty different sounds a cat can make.

Interestingly enough, cats communicate their desires to us in ways that we may not have considered. Recent research has shown that a cat will purr at a low level that connects with a part of the human brain that prompts nurturing; it's a subtle "feed me" signal. Purring can also be used for reassurance, to request close contact with you, or to show contentment.

And while we're talking about purring, research has shown that cats purr at a frequency that facilitates healing in cats, and in people as well. Ask anyone who has a cat and gets migraines if the cat's purring during an attack doesn't help make them feel better. In fact, I'm living proof of this. It's very calming to get my breathing in sync with my cat's purring. And I begin to feel better. No, it's not a cure—you can't take two purring cats and call me in the morning. But that purring definitely makes a difference.

Litter Box Issues

Litter box problems by far are the most common complaint people have about their cats. Eliminating outside the box can be a behavior problem, but it can also be a physical problem. Sometimes, it's a combination of both. Often, there are a lot of different issues, so it isn't really possible to pinpoint a single cause.

There can be almost as many reasons for house soiling as there are cats who do it. Perhaps something happened to frighten kitty when she was in the box. If another cat didn't startle her, then someone may have dropped something that made a loud noise, and she now associates that with eliminating in the box. Think back and try to remember if anything unusual happened around the time she stopped using her litter box. Often, you're not aware of what happened—it may even have been a loud noise outside when you were out of the house.

There may have been an upset in her routine or there may have been some sort of household stress that she has picked up on. These, too, can cause litter box issues.

Medical Issues

If your cat typically is good about using the litter box and suddenly is not, the first thing on your agenda should be a trip to the veterinarian to have kitty checked out. The culprit could be anything from kidney disease to hyperthyroidism to diabetes. It could be stones or crystals in the urinary tract or a complex and poorly understood syndrome called feline lower urinary tract disease (FLUTD). (I'll talk about all of these in chapter 8.)

Let me burst another myth here: Urinary tract infections are quite rare in young and middle-aged cats. But just because the cat doesn't appear to have an infection doesn't mean there isn't a medical problem. Stones may be the culprit. But some cats who appear on X-rays to be negative for any kind of urinary tract or kidney stones may still have a sort of mineral sediment in the bladder. New research by Dr. Jody P. Lulich, the head of the Minnesota Urolith Center at the University of Minnesota College of Veterinary Medicine, has found using ultrasound that these cats have struvite crystals that are irritating the bladder.

When the cats were fed a special struvite-reduction diet, the litter box issues often resolved after a few weeks.

Pain is often overlooked as a factor in litter box avoidance. Arthritis or other illnesses may also cause pain as the cat gets in and out of the litter box. Cats, especially those who eat an all dry or primarily dry diet and male cats who were castrated before puberty, are prone to urinary tract blockages. Older females are prone to urinary tract infections, which can burn and sting. These cats squeeze and struggle to get out the urine. If the cat is in the litter box when this happens, the box can be associated with the pain; wishing to avoid the pain, they go elsewhere.

Because cats are descended from desert animals, they tend to drink little water, and this is a problem if a cat is eating only a dry diet. The lack of water can cause constipation, which leads to pain in the litter box when the cat defecates and may have the same result as when a cat has pain on urination. Encourage the cat to drink more. Many cats love a water fountain and will readily drink water from it. Feed canned or wet food, add broth or water to soak the dry food—whatever it takes.

If you notice your cat straining in the litter box or if she's defecating on the floor, see your veterinarian. If the issue is medical, only veterinary treatment can clear it up. However, even after the cat is treated, you may have a residual problem of kitty not using the box because she was in pain when she was in it before.

If you have several cats, it may be a mystery which one is not using the litter box. But there is a way in which you can discover the culprit. Ask your veterinarian to give you some fluorescein dye. Add it to the food of just one cat. That cat's urine will glow green. Try this test with each cat, one at a time, until you find the culprit.

If a cat is marking with feces, grind up a little bit of crayon and add a different color to each cat's food. Write down which cat got which color. You will see the bits of crayon in the cat's feces the next day.

Marking Territory

When searching for the cause of a litter box problem, the most basic distinction is between marking and just urinating and defecating outside the box. Cats are most likely to mark if they live in a multicat household, if they can see other cats or other furry animals through the windows, and if they are male—although females may also mark.

Feces are rarely used in marking, although it isn't unheard of, and cats will mark territory with feces in the great outdoors. You may notice that some cats cover their poop and others leave it uncovered. When it's uncovered, it's a statement that Big Bad Kitty was here.

When urine marking, cats tend to back up to a vertical surface and spray urine at it. The male cat's penis faces the rear, so this is pretty easy for him to do. If your cat is spraying, you will see urine on the vertical surface as well as on the floor just below the marked spot. (If you can't see the urine, a black light can help you locate it.) If the cat is just urinating outside the box, you are more likely to find larger puddles on the floor.

Intact males who have reached sexual maturity and females in heat will mark territory. Having your pet spayed or neutered before sexual maturity is the best thing you can do to prevent this. If you wait until after sexual maturity, the spraying will likely have become a fixed behavior, and it will be more difficult to resolve the issue. Male cats who are not neutered *will* mark. There's no avoiding it. Neutering usually helps. (Spaying female markers is less likely to help with that problem, but it's still an excellent idea to spay females.)

Cats who live in a multicat household are more likely to mark because each wants to stake out their territory. (It's *my* house, and this mark says so! No, it's *my* house!) If stray cats are coming around, your cat will also feel the need to mark. Usually, kitty will mark around windows and doors to try to tell those outside cats to stay away from her territory.

When you ask a cat to stop marking, you are asking your cat to stop doing something that comes naturally. This is always difficult to accomplish.

If she is spraying because she sees intruders outside the window, blocking off the view is helpful. If the problem is a multicat household, you may need to partition off the house to keep the cats separated so the two who are instigating marking behavior don't see each other and so have no need to make a territorial exclamation point.

If these measures (and some I will discuss under "House Soiling") fail to clear up the problem, then drugs may be helpful. The two most commonly used are buspirone and fluoxetine. Sometimes, using drugs while making environmental changes speeds up the relearning process. Once the behavior has been extinguished, the cat can be weaned off the drugs.

Cat-appeasing pheromones like Feliway may also reduce marking. If you're using the spray, make sure it has dried before the cat returns to the area, though. If it is still damp, it may actually increase marking behavior.

House Soiling

House soiling means urinating, not spraying around the house. There can be almost as many reasons for house soiling as there are cats who do it. For example, both spraying and urinating may be ways of marking territory or expressing anxiety. Usually, though, a cat who is dissatisfied with the litter box sticks to urinating. Almost always, the reason goes back to something about the litter box that the cat doesn't like. And if your cat doesn't like the box, she will go outside of it.

Certainly, some cats have distinct preferences when it comes to the type of litter or box they want to use, and if you don't respect these, the cat will let you know of her displeasure. Clumping and unscented litter get high marks from most cats, but each kind of litter has its adherents, so you may need to experiment. If you've recently changed the brand or type of litter, your cat may be expressing her displeasure at the new litter.

Some cats like the privacy of a closed box, while others like to keep an eye out for incoming attacks by other cats or the family dog and want the full visibility of an open box. Open boxes are crucial in multi-cat households, because kitty needs a fast escape route if another cat decides to use the same box at the same time. If it's uncovered, she can just jump out of the other side of the box. If it's covered, she'll be cornered and have nowhere to go. And then she's unlikely to put herself in that situation again.

Speaking of being bothered in the box, if you have a dog and she's hanging around while kitty's in the bathroom, you need to know that cat litter is bad for dogs. That, however, doesn't prevent most dogs from craving the feces left by the cat, as if it were some sort of delicacy. Cat food and feces have a higher protein and fat content than dog food, which means that dogs find it yummy. But having a dog waiting by the box can be a deal breaker for the cat. Keep the dog away. Gates, a bolt or chain that limits how far the door will open so a cat can get into the room with the box but the dog can't, or even a small cat door entrance in the bottom of an appliance box might help. And if the dog has scarfed the "appetizers" in the box, you probably won't want to kiss her on the lips.

The litter box must be easily accessible when the cat needs to use it. If your house has three stories and your cat spends most of her time on the top floor, having the litter box on the first floor or in the basement isn't going to help the cat use the box. Personally, I keep an open one in the bathroom and a covered one in the den. That's for my one cat. Since I have a one-story home, that's plenty. If you have a two- or three-story home, or a home with a basement, you'll need one box on each level.

And, as I said before, multiple cats mean multiple boxes. Not all cats like to share boxes, so the rule is one more box than you have cats. Or, put another way, one box for each cat and one for the house. Do not line up the litter boxes side by side. Spread them out around the house. Some cats are bullies and will guard the box so the other cats can't use it. Other cats will lie in wait for the cat to finish using the box and then pounce on that cat. But even bullies can't guard more than one box at a time.

The location of the litter box is very important. Choose a quiet place for the box. If it's a busier place like a den, you can either opt for a covered box or a screen in front of the box at that location.

Litter Box Hygiene

It's no secret that cats object to a dirty litter box. If you do not keep the box clean, the cat won't use it. Your cat doesn't want to go in a dirty litter box any more than you want to make a rest stop at a filthy gas station. The cat will simply find a place she likes better—and that won't be a place that you prefer.

Scoop out excrement and all clumps from every litter box twice a day. If you use a clumping litter, you need to dump the litter and wash the box every few weeks. If you use nonclumping litter, you'll have to do that weekly. Clean one box at a time so kitty has one available while the other is being washed.

When you wash the box, don't use harsh chemicals, because the lingering scent can cause a cat to avoid the litter box. Wash the box in hot water and dishwashing detergent. Use a bit of bleach in the rinse water to kill the germs, and then be sure to thoroughly rinse it again so none of the bleach remains.

Rinse thoroughly, and when you think you've rinsed it enough, rinse one more time. Then let the box air dry. When you're done, the litter box should smell like nothing at all. When the box is completely dry, you can pour in fresh litter.

All cats object to a dirty box, and cleaning out excrement daily and dumping the litter, washing the box, and putting in clean litter once a week may help with some litter box problems.

If the cat is only soiling around the litter box, it's possible the box itself is too small. A lot of cats prefer large plastic under-the-bed storage boxes instead of a standard litter box. And if your cat tends to urinate horizontally, a high-sided storage box with one side cut down for easy entry will keep everything in the box.

The Aftermath

When you have figured out your kitty's particular aversion to the litter box, you must clean all areas outside the box(es). Be sure to clean scrupulously with enzymatic cleansers, which break down the biological molecules in urine rather than just mask the smell for you. Vinegar will not remove all traces of urine, nor will any household cleaner. You need an enzymatic cleaner made just for cleaning urine. An area may smell clean to us, but not to the cat with her superior sense of smell.

If your cat has only one other area that she uses outside the litter box, put a box there. If that spot is in the middle of the dining room or living room, start there and gradually move it to a place you can both live with.

Cats tend to prefer absorbent substrates, because they stop urine from splashing back on them. This is why beds, carpets, and piles of clothes may be favored if the litter box is not. Some cats get hooked on these new substrates, and you may have to put a disposable baby diaper or a wee-wee pad for puppies in the litter box at first to get the cat back in the box. Gradually add regular cat litter after you have resolved the original problem.

There are special litters with additives that attract cats. One of them is Dr. Elsey's Cat Attract. (I don't endorse products—I'm just giving you an example of a product that I've seen work.) Once the cat is using the box successfully and regularly, you can slowly transition to another litter.

Litter Box Retraining

If you've encountered litter box problems, even after you resolve the problem you may find that you need to retrain kitty to use the box. Here's how to do it.

1. Never ever yell at or punish your cat. All that will do is make her afraid, and that will only make the problem much, much worse.

2. Put a brand-new litter box in a nice, quiet spot so kitty can have her privacy. The box needs to be easily accessible, both in where it's located and in kitty's ability to get in and out. Be sure the box is not near her food or water.

3. Look carefully to be sure the place where you put the box hasn't been previously marked by a cat. If it has, use something that removes the urine odor, not something that just masks the smell for you. Kitty can still smell it!

4. Put about two or three inches of litter in the box. She's not building sandcastles, so more than that isn't necessary.

5. Keep an eye on the box and praise kitty lavishly when she uses it.

Destructive Scratching

As I said in chapter 3, cats need to scratch. But that doesn't mean you have to let kitty use a chair as a scratching post or rip out your upholstery. The first step is to get a good scratching post, as I described in chapter 3. Put it next to the favored scratching spot, where kitty has already left her scent and visual markers. Now, cover up the favored

Impulse Control Aggression

There are cats who exhibit a form of impulse control aggression. This used to be called the "leave me alone bite," but that label implies that the cat is just fed up with the human and is biting to chase the human away. That's not what cats with impulse control aggression do. These cats feel the need to control their environment and the humans in it—their movement, activities, access to the cat—because otherwise they are so anxious that they cannot function.

Obviously, this is based in a neurological problem. The cats are in a constant state of arousal and cannot turn it off. They constantly need to know whether you represent a risk, but the line between okay and pathological arousal is very thin for them. They never feel safe, and they cannot process the calming signals they get from you.

The pathology, unfortunately, means that even if they can control what's happening around them, at some point they become so aroused and distressed that they bite and may hurt someone if that person walks in front of them or touches them. Many of these cats actually seek attention and then bite when the attention becomes too much for them.

Fortunately, this is not a common problem in cats. But you need to recognize it when you see it. And you must work with a veterinary behaviorist. Treatment involves both drugs and behavior modification. Cats often respond to a class of drugs called selective serotonin reuptake inhibitors (SSRIs), or to fluoxetine (Prozac), which makes them less impulsive and gives them more mental space to think through their real risks. Then, you must learn to watch the cat's physical signals and to work with the cat so that she gets no attention unless she is calm (and then reward her for being calm). With a careful treatment plan, the cat improves dramatically.

Part of the improvement is because the cat's neurochemistry is better balanced by the medication, and part of the improvement is because the people have basically choreographed a very clear set of rules and expectations for interaction. If these rules are consistent, humane, and absolutely unmistakable, they provide a very predictable social environment in which the cat can learn that she can take her cues from what is happening around her and need not be perennially aroused.

scratching spot, perhaps with an old shower curtain or a plastic tablecloth, so it's smooth and no longer fun to scratch. If your cat is scratching chair or table legs, you can put socks over each leg of the chair. Some cats are discouraged by double-sided tape applied to furniture, although others actually enjoy the feel of it.

Kitty will gain no satisfaction from scratching in an inappropriate place, and this will stop that behavior. Meanwhile, be sure to praise her every time she uses her new scratching post. Eventually, you can remove the protective cover from your furniture.

Make sure to keep your cat's claws well trimmed. If your cat really fusses about clipping, you can use a nail grinder—something many cat and dog owners prefer. As with clipping, be careful not to hit the quick, or blood vessel, inside the nail.

If these measures aren't helping, ask your veterinarian or a local groomer about nail caps. These are plastic caps that glue on right over the nail. Each cap goes over each claw, rather like wearing false nails. Usually you don't need more than one set. However, you don't want to end the scratching entirely, since it's a normal and healthy cat behavior. Be sure kitty has an alternate place to scratch and finds satisfaction there when the caps are removed.

And please, please, do not declaw your cat. You can work through the problem without cutting her toes off.

Fear

Fear often has a genetic component. To some extent, which kitten in a litter will be bold and outgoing and which will be nervous and shy or timid depends on who the father is.

Adult cats may become fearful if they are undersocialized or traumatized. If the fear in the adult cat is because of the lack of opportunity to interact with humans or because of mistreatment or neglect, but the cat is predisposed to interact, you can work with her. With patience and time, the cat may well come out of her shell.

Some strategies you can try for dealing with a fearful cat include using an interactive toy to entice her to engage in short play sessions and tossing an occasional treat her way when you're in the same room.

The best-kept secret in helping fearful cats is that they are perfect for and do superbly well with clicker training. I'll talk a lot more about what this is and how you do it in chapter 11. For now, I'll just say that training builds a cat's confidence and also teaches her that you are the person who gives out goodies.

Rough Play

The responsibility for being bitten or scratched during play with kittens and cats almost always falls on the humans. Never encourage rough play by swatting the cat with your hands or using hands, feet, or other body parts as toys.

Instead, watch how cats play with other cats and encourage the chase, pounce, and bite behaviors you see by using toys that keep your hands well away from the cat. Interaction should be fun, aerobic, intellectual, challenging, and safe for everyone. If that's not the case, you're playing too roughly with your cat, and your cat is responding the only way she knows how.

While we're talking about bites, you should also watch for the "I've had enough" bite when you're petting your kitty. Cats love petting but eventually get to a point where they want you to stop. They give you signals to stop, but if you don't notice and heed those signals and keep petting beyond a cat's level of tolerance, you'll get bitten. It will be a mild bite but will state unequivocally, "I told you to stop and I meant it!"

Ankle Attacks

Kittens are especially fond of running out from a hiding place and jumping at or biting your ankle. Adult cats sometimes do this, too. It's a fun game for kitty but a really obnoxious behavior. The cat can hurt someone when she is older and bigger and could cause an older person to fall.

Never encourage kitty to bite by responding to an ankle attack with a game. This is another time when clicker training comes in handy. You can teach kitty to go to her mat or some other appropriate place instead of attacking your ankle. There is a wonderful award-winning video about this on YouTube at www.youtube.com/watch?v=jrGj246t57Y. It was made by Jacqueline Mason Munera, a Certified Cat Behavior Consultant.

Intercat Aggression

Aggression between cats is not uncommon and tends to appear as they move through social maturity, between 2 and 4 years of age. It may appear in cats who have previously gotten along or between newly introduced cats who have mismatched styles of behavior.

Cats who are uncertain, retiring, or a bit shy may not be good with really pushy, young, bold cats. And no one does really well with a bully. That's why combining households of cats or introducing a new adult cat into the household can be so challenging.

The first sign of aggression between cats in a household may be a litter box problem. Fearful or retiring cats may not want to share a box with a cat who intimidates them. Bold cats might start urine or fecal marking.

It's also important to note that aggression between cats is often more subtle, though—at least at first. If one cat walks into a room, surveys it, stares at the cat on the sofa, and the cat on the sofa leaves, there was a "fight" as cats understand it, and the staring cat won.

If you have cats who are entering into or are in the social maturation period, it is wise to monitor them for changes in behavior associated with overt (hissing) and covert (leaving the room, staring, covering another cat's urine) aggression. If the problem is not addressed, the cats will not grow out of it. As it grows worse, one cat may stalk another—without anything we humans would recognize as provocation—and become wholly focused on driving that cat out of the house.

If you have a real cat fight on your hands, you will have to separate the cats. You want to put the more agitated, aggressive cat in a dark room. And both cats need to calm down.

Unfortunately, when they're in this mode, the cats are so aroused that people attempting to separate them can be mauled. When stalking or fighting cats need to be separated, you can throw a blanket over the cat that you want to pick up—or even over both. Tuck the blanket under one cat, scoop her up, and deposit her in a separate room behind a closed door. If you can't quickly grab a blanket, either wear heavy gloves or use a broom or a big piece of cardboard to "herd" one cat into another room. The room needs to have food, water, a litter box, a scratching post or a horizontal cardboard scratcher, and perhaps a toy so kitty will have the necessities while in the room. You can expect it to take anywhere from several hours to a full day for kitty to calm down. Leave both cats alone until you are certain they can be calm.

Once aggression reaches this stage, it is hard to treat. In fact, veterinary behaviorist Dr. Karen Overall warns people that these cats may forever have to live separated in the same house.

The earlier you intervene in an intercat aggression problem, the better chance you have of solving it. After that, you have to realize that all you will get are negotiated settlements. You won't end up with a peaceable kingdom. But everyone can be more or less happy and live in a humane world, although there may be some restrictions.

One problem is that many people don't recognize and understand that very elegant language that is "cat." One way to overcome this is to take videos of your cats interacting with each other, with any other pets, and with the humans in the household. Once a month is not too often.

Get in the habit of making a fifteen- to twenty-minute survey video in a few specific circumstances, such as when the cats are passing each other in the house and when they eat, and also video how each interacts with toys when the other is present and where they tend to rest.

Seeing where the cats settle in the same room will tell you something about their hierarchy. The cat who has chosen the highest point in the room is the one with the superior social position.

These videos are best shared with a behaviorist to see what is going on between the cats. If you look for and record interactions once you first notice problems, you can begin to try to resolve them, preferably with professional help.

If you can get the cats to calmly interact and realize that good things (games, treats, attention) happen when they're in the same room at the same time, you will be going a long way toward resolving any intercat issues. But remember that not all of these issues can be resolved.

Discussing the management of cats under these circumstances, veterinary behaviorist Dr. Debra F. Horwitz has suggested setting up several feeding areas, places to rest, and litter boxes. She also suggested the owner put a quick-release collar with a bell on it on the aggressor cat so the other cat(s) can hear that one approach soon enough to avoid a confrontation.

The Importance of Interactive Play

It's impossible to say enough about the importance of playing interactively and vigorously with your cat at least two or three times a day. A bored cat is an unhappy cat, and an unhappy cat may express her unhappiness in ways that won't please you.

The result of a bored cat is almost always a behavior problem. That can include inappropriate elimination, dragging clothing around, or chewing or sucking on fabric. Some cats who are feeling very insecure will urinate on the bed for the feeling of comfort of surrounding herself with her own smell. If kitty isn't happy, no one will be happy.

This can easily be avoided by giving the cat what she really wants— interaction with you and a chance to exercise her prey instinct. Get out a wand toy and see how excited your kitty becomes! Play with her using whatever motion makes the toy move in a way that engages her. Let her catch the prey often so she has that satisfaction and doesn't become frustrated. Tell her what a good hunter she is!

A cat who is happy, satisfied, and has exercised is far more likely to be mentally, as well as physically, healthier. And it's fun for you, too. The close bond you form will be enriching for each of you. Other family members can take turns doing this so kitty interacts with everyone.

You also stave off boredom by providing your cat with plenty of environmental enrichment, as described in chapter 4. Having a kitty companion will also help keep both cats occupied. But remember that interactive playtime is crucial to your cat's well-being, even in a

On the Move

People sometimes want to move to a new home. Cats, not so much. Whether you're moving to another city, across town, or across the country, you'll have to make some special plans for kitty.

Move your cat last, and have as much as possible already set up in your new home, so kitty won't have to listen to a lot of people banging around, moving furniture, and so on.

Before you move, arrange your packing so you can put the litter box, scratching post, cat tree, food, and bottled water in a special room in your new home. This way, kitty can have a place to call home without being overwhelmed by all of the new space at once. It's going to be confusing enough to have her familiar home emptied of belongings and then arrive in a new space. Let her settle into the new space a little at a time, starting as you did when you first got her, with one room that's set aside for her and where you spend time in with her. Gauge her reaction, and when she seems to have settled down you can allow her out to explore the rest of her new home and begin to rub up against her special places. It's her way of marking the new place as home.

multicat household. If you have opted to allow your cat outdoors, even with all the dangers that presents, she will still need interactive playtime with you when she comes into the house. There's no getting around that—cats want and need to play with us.

Do you often hear kitty thundering through the house in the middle of the night, playing some wonderfully self-amusing game? Cats are, for the most part, nocturnal. Of course, you may not be nearly as amused if you have to get up early for work the next morning. Cats can sleep thirteen to sixteen hours a day, depending on their age and activity level. Some sleep even more. Some of that time is spent in light cat naps. You want kitty to sleep at night rather than racing through the house in joyful, noisy abandon. Scheduling one of your daily playtimes with kitty before bedtime may tire her out sufficiently to stay quiet through the night. And don't forget at least one more interactive play session during the day.

The Baby Myth

Since I started this chapter talking about cat myths, I'm going to end it the same way. There are a lot of myths about cats and babies, and some of them continue to be passed along by medical professionals.

Cats and kids can grow up to be fabulous friends—as this pair did.

They lead to women giving up their cats, and that's not fair to the women or the cats.

One absolutely infuriating myth is that cats steal a baby's breath. How strange! Cats do no such thing. In fact, they are often lovely companions for babies if the parents are wise enough to supervise interactions.

For some families, their rule is that a cat should not sleep in a crib with a baby. But that's easy to prevent with a crib cover. Some people have no problem allowing their cat to sleep, supervised, at the foot of the baby's crib. And for infants, a cat's purring is probably quite calming, just as it is for adults.

Sadly, some medical doctors are still espousing the old belief that pregnant women should get rid of their cat because of toxoplasmosis. This parasite can cause serious birth defects in the first trimester of pregnancy. Cats are the only animals who pass on the infectious stage of this parasite through their feces. This sounds scary, but the danger cats pose is minimal. That's because the main sources of toxoplasmosis infections in humans—by a wide margin—are handling raw meat and digging in infected soil. Cats get the parasite the same way humans do, which means if you have an indoor cat who eats only cat food, she's not likely to ever be infected.

Even if a cat does get toxoplasmosis, she's only capable of passing it on for seven to ten days *of her entire life*, when she has an acute infection. On top of all that, it takes anywhere from one to five days for her feces to become infectious; in other words, the litter box would have to sit unscooped for one to five days before the infection could be passed on. So scooping the box twice a day is an effective prevention.

But even if you didn't scoop so often, to get the infection you'd have to touch the cat's feces and then touch an opening in your body without first washing your hands.

All you need to do to be safe is wear rubber gloves when scooping or cleaning the box. Or just have someone else take over all the litter box chores while you're pregnant. A self-cleaning litter box is another possible solution, since it places the waste in a bag that can then be removed and put out with the trash. A little common sense is all that's needed.

CHAPTER 6

FEEDING A CARNIVORE

There are so many thoughts about pet diets today that it can be quite confusing. Let's start with one irrefutable fact: Cats are obligate carnivores. This means that they *must* eat meat. Sure, they can have vegetables, and some enjoy a bite of fruit, but your cat gets his primary nutrition from animal sources. A cat absolutely cannot be a vegetarian. Even if you're a vegetarian, you need to feed your cat a diet that's designed for the unique needs of the feline body.

In truth, the perfect diet for a cat is a mouse. Nature designed cats to catch mice and then eat them. Mice contain all the vitamins, minerals, and other nutrients required by a cat, in exactly the right proportions. But these days, most of us don't feed mice to our cats. So what's the next best thing?

There are commercial diets, home-cooked diets, and raw diets (which may be prepared at home or purchased fresh or frozen). Which food is best is currently the subject of a good bit of controversy. Where does that leave you and your cat? Well, it leaves you with choices.

At first, it's always best to keep your kitty on the diet he was on before he came home with you. A food change can sometimes upset kitty's tummy, especially with all the other upheaval going on as he settles into his new home and routine. But if it's not the diet you want to feed him, you can gradually make a transition after a few weeks to the diet you have chosen for your cat.

Commercial Diets

Pet food companies have been doing research for decades to scientifically develop diets that mimic the mouse and meet the nutritional requirements of cats. Commercial pet foods can sometimes be the target of strong criticism from raw diet proponents, but the simple truth is that the major pet food manufacturers can afford to hire excellent veterinary nutritionists and monitor the diets as they are fed to colonies of test cats. (If this sounds like cats in the lab of evil scientists, think again. I got to tour one of the test cat facilities at a major manufacturer, and the cats were kept in a large, sunny room filled with toys. It looked like a preschool. They had plenty of people to interact with, as well—perhaps spending more time with their people than many cats spend with their working owners.)

If you decide on a commercial diet for your cat, be sure to choose one from a reputable company. It should say on the label that the food meets AAFCO standards for a complete and balanced diet. (AAFCO is the Association of American Feed Control Officials, a regulatory body that helps develop and enforce regulations for safe and healthy animal foods. The Food and Drug Administration also shares responsibility for pet food safety and appropriateness, and it also regulates pet food labeling.)

However, that's just a start, because AAFCO requirements are the minimum for feline nutrition. You want your cat to have the optimum. Generally, with cat food you get what you pay for, because the higher the price, the higher the protein content—and the greater the amount of protein that comes from meat. When you feed a better food, you will soon see the end results in kitty. His coat will be glossy, his eyes bright. His coat will *not* be greasy or oily. You'll see less poop in his litter box, too, because better foods are more highly digestible. Digestibility is a measure of how efficiently the nutrients in a food are absorbed and metabolized. It's important because if you can't easily digest your food, it won't do you much good.

Commercial cat food comes dry and in cans. The dry food is crunchy and may help keep kitty's teeth clean. Dry foods are usually higher in carbohydrates, which cats don't really need. So you must be aware of protein and carbohydrate levels in dry food to ensure that you are feeding the correct levels for your kitty. You do that by reading the label on the food packaging—I'll explain how in just a bit.

Many veterinarians are encouraging their clients to feed their cat canned food because it contains fewer carbohydrates and has a high water content. It's important that your cat drink water for the sake of his general health—and especially kidney and urinary tract health—and canned food ensures water intake. However, most cats do fine with dry food and will drink more water to compensate. You'll want to be sure kitty has clean, fresh water available at all times.

Senior cats are more at risk of becoming dehydrated, and of developing kidney disease, so feeding more canned food may be the best option for them. But a cat who has been eating crunchies all his life may not want to switch. So, to keep their options open and give the cat the best of both worlds, many cat owners opt to feed both canned and dry. It's important to talk with your veterinarian about which might be the best choice for your particular cat.

Some cats may develop an allergy or intolerance to one or more ingredients in their pet food. This could be seen as scratching around the ears and face, or licking the tummy or legs or in between toes. Symptoms of an allergy are not always external. Kitty could begin vomiting or have diarrhea. (Note that diarrhea can also occur if you change kitty's food too quickly.)

Diagnosing a food intolerance can be tough. It's important to work with your veterinarian to figure out exactly what the cat is allergic to. This is usually done by feeding the cat a diet with very limited ingredients (called an elimination diet) to determine the culprit in kitty's food dish.

Reading Pet Food Labels

It's important to learn the basics of how to read pet food labels. Let's start with the ingredients. The ingredients in the food are listed in descending order, so the ingredient there's the most of is listed first. You'll want to see a protein source listed first, and then listed again several times more in the first few ingredients. If you see grain products listed several times in the first few ingredients, that means there could be more grain than meat in the food—even if meat is listed first.

You'll see a section called Guaranteed Analysis that will tell you how much protein, fat, fiber, moisture, ash, magnesium, and taurine is in the food. Protein is very important, because as obligate carnivores, cats metabolize protein for energy. The source of protein (fish, chicken, beef, turkey, and so on) isn't relevant unless your cat has an allergy or intolerance to a specific protein.

Cats require only two fatty acids, linoleic and arachidonic. Fats are burned for energy and help keep kitty's skin and coat glossy and healthy. Cats don't have cholesterol problems the way humans do. However, too much fat ends up being stored, and the last thing you want is a fat cat.

Fiber actually helps with digestibility by slowing down the transit of food through the intestines. If the food moves through kitty's system too fast, it can't be absorbed.

The magnesium levels are important for urinary tract health, which is why they are listed separately. The other minerals in cat food are listed on the label collectively as ash. Yes, that sounds like something you wouldn't want in cat food, but it's simply the minerals.

Taurine is an amino acid. Cats have a particular need for it in their diet; without sufficient taurine, they will go blind and also develop a potentially fatal heart disease. Because of this, all commercial cat foods are now supplemented with taurine (although commercial dog foods are not—a good reason cats can't eat dog food).

There will also be feeding instructions that tell you how much of the food to feed your cat. It's important to remember that this is only a suggestion based on the average cat with an average energy level. You will have to adjust the food portions depending on your individual cat's weight and the energy he expends. His body type or breed and his age will also factor into how much food he needs.

Homemade Diets

A cooked diet consists of food that you have cooked at home. A cat cannot live by meat alone, so you will have to add vitamins and minerals in just the right amounts to make a balanced meal for your cat. It's not as easy as preparing meals for yourself, so you'll have to do some research. For example, the types of meat we buy in the supermarket—even chicken and turkey—don't have the meat-to-bone ratio a cat needs.

Gary Rohde

Cats and dogs have very different nutritional needs; cats cannot survive on dog food.

Most people who cook for their cats end up adding vitamin and mineral supplements that are specially formulated for felines.

A raw food diet has even more to think about. Not only will you have to create a complete and balanced feline diet, but you will be dealing with raw meat and all its inherent risks. Salmonella and trichinosis are present in many types of raw foods. All food-preparation surfaces and tools must be scrupulously cleaned, both before and after preparing a raw diet. And if you are immune-compromised, you shouldn't be handling raw foods.

For those who feel qualified, who can find a source of good, clean, high-grade meat, who are adept at handling it, and have a good recipe for a complete and balanced feline diet, this is certainly an option. If you are feeding a high-quality commercial or a well-balanced cooked diet, there is no particular nutritional advantage to feeding raw food to your cat. There is, however, a risk of your cat getting either a mild or a deadly gastrointestinal disease.

If you really don't like commercial cat foods, the best recommendation is to cook all meat surfaces. Pathogens multiply on the surface of the meat, but they will be mixed throughout the meat during the grinding process. Another consideration is that after the cat eats a raw diet and licks himself, any pathogens can be transferred to you or other family members when you pet him, or if he decides you need grooming, too. That's just one more thought.

I'd like to say a word here about board-certified veterinary nutritionists. There are many specialists in veterinary medicine—recognized experts who have taken additional training. If your cat has nutritional needs that aren't being met, or if you want to formulate an optimum homemade diet, you may be referred to a veterinary nutritionist. These are the people who know about feline nutrition. It may be tempting to take the nutrition advice of a friend or neighbor who has cats, but only a board-certified veterinary nutritionist has all the science at their fingertips to help you formulate the best diet for your cat.

There is nothing at all wrong about feeding your cat a homemade diet, as long as you do it right. But do remember that proponents of homemade diets sometimes make claims about these diets that have not been backed up by scientific studies. They may also believe so strongly in the benefits of these diets that they suggest even top-quality commercial diets are harmful to cats. I can't stress too strongly that no one should be made to feel bad about what they are feeding their cat. The end result is what counts, and if your cat is happy and healthy and your veterinarian approves of the diet, you have found what is right for you and your cat.

Hairball Diets

If your cat has hair (as opposed to a hairless cat or a Rex breed, which is nearly hairless), you may need to feed your cat a specific hairball formula, either as his regular food or as a side dish to help him eliminate hairballs in a way other than upchucking them. There are also pastes your cat can eat to help prevent hairballs from forming and clogging up his intestinal tract.

It's important to take hairballs seriously, because if they aren't ejected from one end or the other, they can cause a blockage—and that will require surgery. However, the best remedy is prevention. Brush your cat regularly and hairballs will not be a problem.

Dining In

In general, cats eat to satisfy their energy needs. Many cats are excellent free feeders—they just eat when they're hungry. Cats normally eat several small meals over the course of the day, so that's actually the more natural way to feed—as long as the cat won't overeat. But some cats are foodies who are making up for a period in life when food was scarce. Cats may also overeat out of boredom.

If your cat is good about only eating what he needs, you can leave food down and he will naturally graze on it throughout the day and night. Cats who can't be trusted not to overeat should be fed two or more measured meals a day at specific times, to keep them at their optimum weight. It's also important to remember that spaying or neutering a cat will decrease their energy needs. Energy needs of cats drop by about 25 percent after they are altered. It's important to work with your veterinarian to select a diet geared to your specific cat's needs, and don't forget that exercise will also play a part in that selection process!

If you have several cats and only one or two need to lose weight, you can put a weight-control formula out for all the cats to nibble on all day, and then supplement the skinny cat with a nutrient-dense food once or twice a day. Or put the skinny cat's food in a box with a small entrance, so the fat cat can't get inside to the food.

This is also a place for some environmental enrichment. You can use food balls (toys with holes cut in them that dispense pieces of dry food), so the cat must play with the ball and get some mental and physical activity while he eats. You can also use a clean, dry, empty yogurt container or a water bottle with holes in it. Fill it with dry food, and the cat

Sue Janson

This Maine Coon kitten needs to get about 30 percent of her energy from protein.

will have to manipulate it to get the food out. These kinds of containers can be better for cats who like to play with their back feet while holding on with their front feet.

Life Stage Feeding

Cats require different foods at different stages of their life. Just like all creatures, including us, they change as they grow. And so do their food requirements.

The first meal a kitten has is from his mother. The colostrum in her milk passes along protection in the form of her antibodies against illnesses for which she has been vaccinated. The kittens knead the mother, causing the milk to move to the nipples, where they can suck and be nourished.

Kittens need extra protein, fat, vitamins, and minerals for optimum nutrition during this stage of rapid growth and development. Since kittens are so active, they require more energy, hence the need for extra protein. Their bones and supporting tissue and muscle are also growing rapidly, and that means they need the extra nutritional support they get from a kitten formula food.

During the middle years of his life, your cat will eat a basic maintenance diet. Senior diets are reserved for elderly cats who are no longer as active as they once were.

Avoiding the Fussy Feline Foodie

Cats are notoriously fussy about their food. They often get so accustomed to one food that they won't touch anything else. You might think that's good, but it's a double-edged sword. If your cat gets sick and requires a veterinary diet, he's not going to eat it, and that's going to cause problems.

To keep your cat from becoming a fussy eater, frequently offer him a side dish of another food or another flavor. You can give him a variety of foods, as well—just be sure the protein amount is in the same range and that you're not overfeeding him.

Some cats like to take food straight from your plate. This is more a case of manners than anything else. If the food itself won't hurt the cat, that's fine. But you may want to place his share in his dish rather than allowing him to eat from your plate—unless all of your guests are like-minded people who will enjoy sharing with a feline dinner companion.

Our seniors are such treasures, no matter if we've had them from kittenhood or brought them home as adults. By the time a cat is a senior, your close relationship is such a comfort to both of you. You'll need to think about things that will make your older kitty more comfortable, and one of them is diet.

If your cat was finicky before, he may well become even more so, and his favorite food suddenly may not interest him. Your cat may not drink enough water, which is vital, so you'll have to be sure he does. This may be the time to switch to a canned-food diet, because canned food has a high water content. You might put a bit of tuna juice or low-salt chicken broth into the cat's water or on the food to encourage kitty to drink.

Like people, older cats can get fatter because they are less active. However, in senior cats (those age 12 and over) energy requirements go up and lean body mass goes down, so they need to take in more food to maintain their body weight. One in three senior cats has a reduced ability to digest fat, and one in five has a reduced ability to digest protein. They are not absorbing the nutrition as well as they did when they were younger and can become malnourished even though they are eating as much as they always did.

As in people, renal disease, diabetes, and cancer are more likely to develop in cats later in life. That's why if your cat has an unexplained weight loss, he needs to be seen by the veterinarian right away. Studies have shown that cats lose weight two to two-and-a-half years before a terminal event. Keeping weight on your senior cat can help him live a healthier life. This doesn't mean a fat cat, but a normal weight for the cat's size.

Most senior cat foods are formulated for middle-aged cats, not the true geriatric cat. What can you do? If you can't find a nutrient-dense food for seniors, buy a kitten food instead, because kittens also need food that is dense in nutrients.

At every age, your cat should *always* have fresh water available at all times, in a clean bowl or a water fountain. You wouldn't want to drink stale standing water, and neither does your kitty. Nor would you want to drink from a dirty glass. Please remember this when it comes to caring for kitty.

Cats love water fountains. They filter the water and aerate it. Watching the water running down into the bowl is also quite fascinating, which makes it all the more interesting to drink. And some cats like to drink right out of the faucet in your sink. If you have no problem with this, you can buy a special spigot that the cat can touch to turn the water on, and it will turn off when the cat walks away. That is better for the environment than letting water drip for kitty all day and night.

Veterinary Diets

There may come a time in your cat's life when he will need a special diet to help him cope with a medical problem. Special veterinary diets are available from several pet food manufacturers. They are created with the specific health problem in mind to support your kitty for optimum nutrition and not make his health problem worse.

Sometimes a special diet is needed only for a limited time. Sometimes it's for the rest of the cat's life. The circumstances vary depending on the individual problem.

The best food in the world, however, won't do your cat any good if he turns up his nose at it and walks away from the dish. You can try microwaving the food for a few seconds to release the aroma (warm— *not* hot enough to burn your cat's tongue and mouth). Or you can change to another company's diet made for the same health problem. Never feel that you have only one choice; you have multiple choices for your cat. Ask your veterinarian for a list of suggested alternatives if the first diet is completely rejected. Surely something will tempt that picky palate!

And remember to keep presenting the new diet to your cat every day, even if he walks away at first. Your persistence and patience will really pay off.

Enticing Your Cat to Try a New Food

There are times when getting your cat to eat a new food is of the utmost importance. If your cat has a health problem that requires a special veterinary diet, for example, or if the food you've been feeding suddenly turns up on a recall list, you will have to get kitty to eat something else as soon as possible without upsetting his system.

You always have to change food slowly, so that kitty's digestive system isn't disrupted. Patience is important. But here's the tricky part: Cats are notoriously picky about food. Once they fall in love with something, it's hard to convince them that something else is better—or even just as good as their favorite food. They're like little kids who get hooked on eating hamburgers or hot dogs or pizza.

Tempting the palate of a cat is pretty much like tempting the palate of a small child. This is why you need to introduce your cat to a variety of tastes early on. If you haven't done that—well, here's where it pays to have a trick or two up your sleeve. I can't give you help with your fussy small child, but I can help with your fussy kitty.

Cats love anything smelly. To get the most odor out of a canned veterinary diet, put it in the microwave and nuke it for a few seconds. Be sure it's not too hot, because you don't want kitty to burn his mouth. You just want to bring out the smell. It only needs to be a tad warmer than room temperature. (This also works for older cats whose sense of smell isn't what it used to be.) You can also try putting a little bit of warm chicken broth onto dry food to entice kitty. Opt for the low-sodium chicken broth, because commercial soups tend to have a very high salt content.

Obesity

Sadly, obesity is as much of a problem for our pets as it is for us. The expression *fat cat* may be funny, but the reality is no laughing matter. Being overweight is just as bad for our pets as it is for us. It can lead to

Weather-Related Dining

You may find your cat eating less on hot days or eating more in the evening when it's cooler. Or he may eat more during the cold winter months. A cat will feel like eating more or less depending on the weather. They are like us in this respect. Their metabolism will respond to climate change. Make sure your cat is maintaining his proper weight throughout the year.

A cat has five more vertebrae in her spinal column than her human does, making this longhaired Scottish Fold very flexible indeed.

all sorts of health problems, including cardiac problems, diabetes, and arthritis. In other words, you will just be shortening your kitty's life if he's not in shape.

We tend to share food, including snacks, with our cats. And there are so many special snacks made for cats that it's hard to resist. What to do? I'm not suggesting you deny your cat treats, but dole them out judiciously. Be sure you are not giving so many that they are no longer special and your cat is no longer his best weight. Treats and special extras must be balanced with a cat's overall diet to make sure you're not adding more calories than kitty can manage without a weight gain.

Diet and exercise go paw in paw for cats, so avoiding obesity is not just about what they eat, but also about how much they play. Cats are natural hunters, so one way you can feed your cat and make sure he's getting exercise is to put his food in little dishes hidden all over the house so he has to "hunt" for it, or use a treat ball that will release tiny pieces of dry food.

Treats can be placed on levels of his cat tree so he has to climb in order to get them. They can also be used solely as training rewards (we'll discuss training later on in this book).

The Perils of Rapid Weight Loss

If your kitty is starting to look a bit overweight, nip it in the bud before he becomes obese. But crash or fad diets are not a good idea for cats.

A Cat's Ideal Weight

If your cat is eating properly he will be at his ideal weight. Here's how you can tell: When you look at him from above, you should see his waist behind his ribs. When you touch his flanks, you should be able to feel his ribs with a slight covering of fat. And he should not have too much abdominal fat. Looking at your cat this way will help you determine if kitty is too thin or too fat.

Veterinarians have developed some general terms to help assess a cat's body condition. They are:

Emaciated: The ribs are visible on a shorthaired cat, you can't feel any body fat, and his tummy is tucked up. You can easily feel his bones.

Very Thin: This is between Emaciated and Thin.

Thin: You can feel his ribs; there is minimal body fat and his bones are obvious.

Underweight: This is between Thin and Ideal Weight.

Ideal Weight: You see an indentation behind the ribs, a kind of "waist." When you touch the ribs there is a slight covering of fat, and there is a minimal abdominal fat pad.

Overweight: This is between Ideal Weight and Heavy.

Heavy: You can't easily feel the cat's ribs, and he has moderate body fat covering them. His tummy is rounded and he has moderate abdominal fat.

Obese: This is between Heavy and Grossly Obese.

Grossly Obese: You can't feel this cat's ribs because they have such heavy fat covering them. He has heavy fat deposits over his lumbar area as well as his face and ribs. He has no waist, his tummy is distended, and he has extensive abdominal fat deposits.

Just as you would check with your doctor before embarking on a weight reduction program, you should check with your veterinarian before embarking on a reduction diet and exercise program for your cat. Your veterinarian will have to do a full work-up, including complete blood and thyroid panels.

There is one very important thing to consider when putting an obese cat on a diet: You *must* do it slowly. Rapid weight loss in cats can result in death.

Felines have a unique, and dangerous, metabolic response to rapid weight loss: They develop hepatic lipidosis, or fatty liver disease, which is an accumulation of fat in the liver tissue. It develops when an overweight cat stops eating. The cat's body starts releasing fat cells to be processed for energy. But cats aren't really good at processing fat, so it ends up being stored in the liver. If this condition isn't treated, the liver will fail and kitty will die.

If your cat loses weight rapidly, stops eating for any reason, or begins to salivate a lot, *run,* do not walk, to your veterinarian. Anorexia and weight loss can be indicative of other diseases, too, such as pancreatic disease or liver cancer. Whatever the case, it needs immediate veterinary attention.

Your best bet for safe weight loss is to put your cat on a high-protein diet and carefully measure how much he gets each day. Carnitine, an amino acid, is the key here, and meat protein, not vegetables or carbohydrates, provides carnitine. Carnitine helps the body metabolize fatty acids and burn them for energy. Some weight-loss diets contain L-carnitine, and there are also supplements made for pets. But talk to your veterinarian about whether this is a wise choice for your cat and if so, how much to give your specific cat.

You should take your cat back to the veterinarian every few weeks for weight checks and to monitor how he's doing on his new diet and exercise regime.

If your cat develops anorexia and constipation, you will need to help nature along. One of the most popular and easy ways to do that is to give kitty a bit of canned pumpkin. Not the pie filling—plain canned pumpkin. It is high in fiber and filled with vitamins. Offer kitty a taste of it, and if he likes it, you can give him as much as two teaspoons of pumpkin per day.

Sometimes, when a cat stops eating, you can tempt his palate with baby food. Just be sure that the one you choose doesn't have onion in it; read the label *very* carefully.

Diane Smith, RVT

Helmi Flick

Craig Zeichner

Ramona Marek

Tetsu Yamazaki

Alan Robinson

Diane Smith, RVT

Lisa Allison Clay

Robin Burkett

Teresa Keiger

Ramona Marek

Alan Robinson

Tetsu Yamazaki

Lisa-Marie Padilla

Lisa Allison Clay

Robin Burkett

Helmi Flick

Linda Aronson, DVM

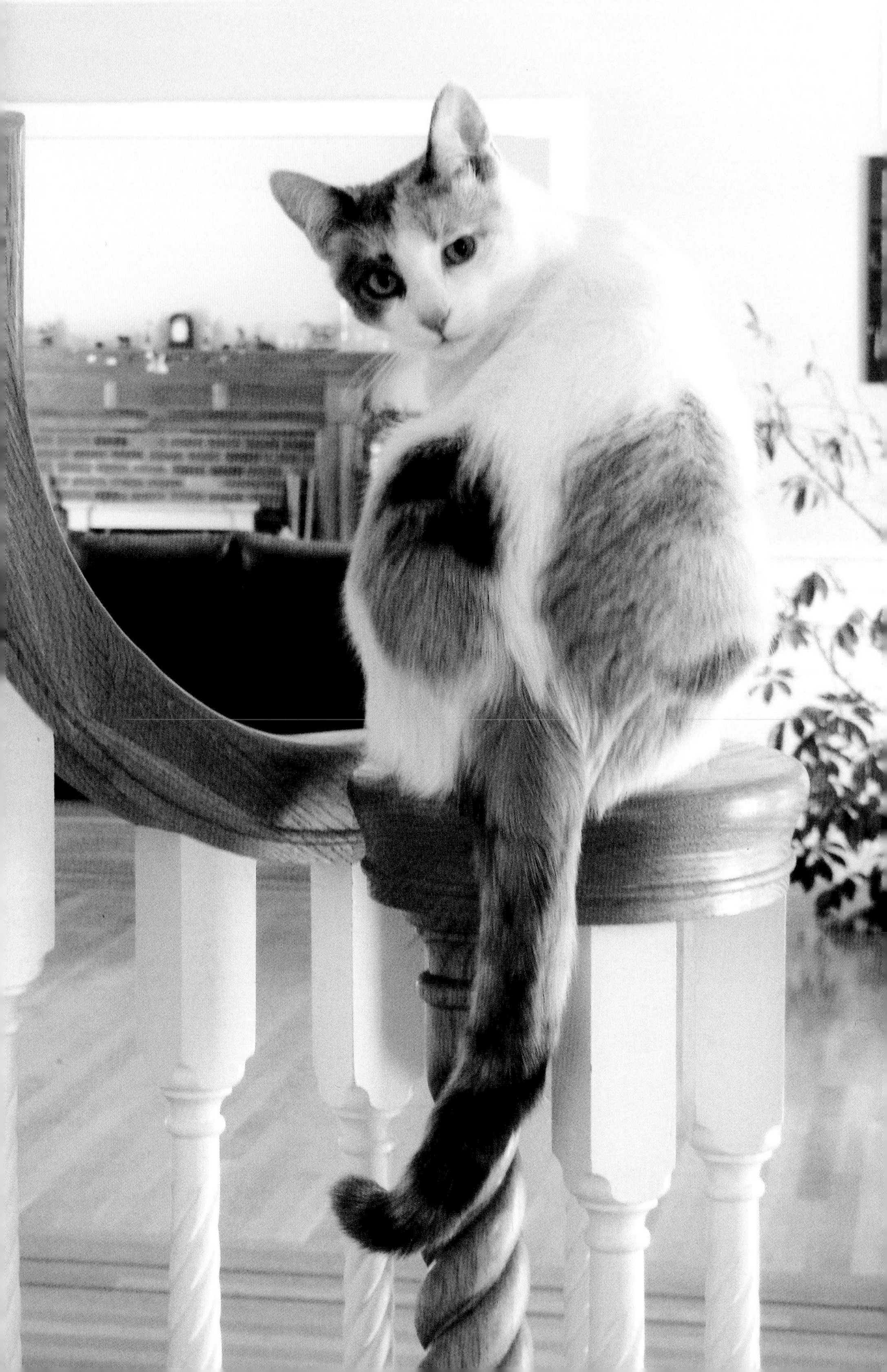

ROUTINE HEALTH CARE

Part of what you sign up for when you get a cat is being responsible for your kitty's health. There are many things you can and should do yourself to keep your cat healthy. These include giving kitty a great diet (which I talked about in chapter 6), keeping her well groomed, and noticing when she isn't feeling well.

Among the most important things you'll do for your cat is find a great veterinarian and take her there for regular visits—even when she's feeling fine. You and your veterinarian will work together in a special partnership to ensure kitty's health and wellness.

Cats are the most popular pet in America, but studies show they go to the veterinarian about half as often as dogs do. One study found that about a third of pet cats are never taken to the vet. I know you want what's best for your cat, and that includes regular checkups called wellness visits. And there's good reason to do that twice a year. Cats age faster than people, and depending on your cat's age, one cat year can be from four to fourteen years, relative to a year in our life. Besides, your cat then gets accustomed to being in the carrier and visiting the veterinarian when she's not sick—which can actually be pleasant. Plus, there's a lot to learn from your veterinarian, and you can follow your cat's weight and other health parameters more closely.

Your Cat's Veterinarian

Before you get your kitten or cat, you'll need to find a good veterinarian—one who knows cats and likes them. If you've had a veterinarian you liked in the past and they are still in practice, your problem is

Call your veterinarian sooner rather than later if you suspect kitty isn't feeling well.

solved. If you don't have one, you'll need to do a little investigating. Spend the time *before* your cat comes home.

There are several ways of finding a good veterinarian, and you may want to use any or all of them. The person from whom you get your cat may suggest the veterinarian they use, in which case that doctor has probably already examined your cat. If you got your cat from a shelter or a rescue group, they may be able to recommend a doctor in your area. You might also ask friends or relatives who have cats for a recommendation of someone they trust.

You can also call a local veterinary referral hospital, if you live near one. (These are hospitals that see cats who need a specialist or in an emergency.) Ask them who in your area sends cases that are worked up well. They may, or may not, feel comfortable telling you.

There are veterinarians who focus specifically on feline medicine, and some may be board certified as feline practitioners. Some have cat-only practices, while others have a general small animal practice. You may be able to find a feline practitioner, someone who specializes in cats. You can find the American Association of Feline Practitioners online at www.catvets.com. Their web site has resources for cat owners and a section where you can look for feline practitioners in your area.

Some cats don't like to travel because no one taught them that it can be fun, so you might want to consider a mobile veterinarian—someone who brings their van to your home to examine and treat your cat. This is fine for most things, but if you need a specialist for any reason, you will still have to take your cat to a referral hospital.

Once you've chosen two or three practices (if you're lucky and there are that many in your area), make an appointment to meet with each veterinarian and tour the hospital. Tell them why you are making the appointment. You may have to pay for this visit and should certainly expect to, since you will be taking some of the veterinarian's valuable time. Go prepared with a list of questions. Here are some very basic ones.

- How far in advance do you schedule appointments?
- What hours are you open?
- Are you open or closed on weekends?
- Is the hospital closed during lunch hour?
- Do you see emergencies after hours or do you refer out?
- Do you refer to specialists?
- What are your prices for typical services?
- Do you have a payment plan or work with a credit company?
- Do you take credit cards or checks as well as cash?
- What percentage of your clientele has cats?

Try to get there for your appointment a few minutes early. When you arrive, note how you are greeted. Let your nose do some work. Are there normal odors? A pet may have had an accident on the floor before you walked in, but the clinic should be clean and shouldn't smell foul. The clinic should be well lit, but not so bright that you feel like you're in an interrogation room. In fact, there is a new trend toward soft lighting to help keep cats from becoming aroused. Is there a separate waiting area or room for cats to make them feel more comfortable, rather than having to cope with the stress of hanging out with dogs? Watch how regular clients interact with the office staff. Does everyone seem friendly? Comfortable?

Take note of the way the hospital looks during your tour. It should be clean and well organized, with a place for everything and everything in its place. The staff in back should be pleasant as well. Try to watch them handling an animal and see what they do when they think no one is looking. Many veterinarians practice cat-friendly handling, using techniques that avoid scruffing or bearing down on cats. If something just doesn't "feel" right, don't think you're obligated to stay or to make an appointment for your kitty.

You should feel comfortable with the veterinarian when you meet. You and the veterinarian will be working together to keep your kitty healthy, so you should be able to develop a good rapport with this person. You should feel comfortable talking with your cat's veterinarian about any issue regarding kitty's health and welfare. And you should feel your veterinarian is someone who knows about and enjoys working with cats.

Many veterinary hospitals are members of the American Animal Hospital Association (AAHA) and are required to meet a standard of practice. If the hospital is a member, you will see that clearly displayed. (You can find AAHA-accredited veterinary hospitals online at www.healthy pet.com.)

Kitty's First Visit

Kitty's first examination should come within seventy-two hours of bringing her home. Most cat owners tend to rely on the veterinary checkup their cat received at the shelter or from the breeder's veterinarian. But even if kitty came from a breeder or shelter and was seen by their veterinarian, you will want to start out on the right foot with a veterinarian of your own. This is the time to do it—not when there's an emergency.

Wherever you get your cat, you should receive paperwork explaining which tests and vaccines kitty has received and when. This may include the manufacturer of the vaccine. If you have obtained your cat from a neighbor or friend, the same should apply. If they haven't taken kitty to the veterinarian, that's all the more reason to take your cat to the vet within seventy-two hours of obtaining her.

Consider bringing your new kitty by the vet clinic for a cheerful meet and greet before the regular appointment, so kitty can see that the staff are friendly and that she isn't always going to be poked or prodded whenever she visits. Bring a few tasty treats for the staff to give her.

Bring kitty to the veterinarian in a safe carrier with sides that don't sag in on her. Make it as comfortable as possible with a soft towel or cushion inside and a toy. You can also drape a towel over the front of the carrier so she won't be frightened. It will decrease visual arousal and give her a feeling of security. Take some time to get kitty acclimated to her carrier, as I described in chapter 3. Don't just put it away after the trip to the vet, awaiting the next trip to the vet. Keep it out with the door open and a treat and toy or two inside so she learns it's a nice, safe place to be.

When it's time for kitty's actual checkup, make sure the veterinarian gives her a complete examination and whatever vaccines are required. You will be keeping kitty indoors only, which means that she needs only some of the vaccinations available for cats.

I've outlined the latest recommendations for feline vaccinations in chapter 1. Please discuss this with your veterinarian. There was a time when cats were overvaccinated with everything available. This was not

Microchipping

Many cats and kittens arrive at their new owner's home already micro-chipped. A microchip is a teeny tiny conductor the size of a grain of rice that holds information—in this case a specific registration number assigned to your cat. It's inserted under kitty's skin via a hypodermic syringe. You then register that number in a database, along with your contact information, to protect your cat in case she gets lost.

If your kitty hasn't been microchipped, ask your veterinarian about it at the first visit. Many veterinarians do it at their office. If not, they can tell you where you can get your cat microchipped.

Be sure to fill out the accompanying form and register the micro-chip, because if you don't, the chip won't do your cat any good. The form will ask you to give the name and contact information of another person in addition to yourself. If you can't be reached when kitty gets loose and is found, someone you trust can be notified and kitty can be safely returned to you.

A microchip can save your cat's life if she gets out. Most shelters and veterinary offices have a scanner to check for a microchip, and you will soon be reunited with your pet.

A collar and a tag are also important, but cats should always wear breakaway collars that open if they snag on something. And that means the cat can easily lose the collar and the tag. Be sure the collar is comfortable but snug, so that no more than two of your fingers fit under the collar after it's put on. The most common mistake people make is putting a collar on too loose, which makes it much easier to possibly harm their cat or lose the collar and the tag. The microchip is an extra measure of protection for kitty and for you!

good for their health. But your cat does need to be vaccinated. There are people who are totally against vaccinations, even for their children, but they are taking a real health risk that can put the general public at risk as well.

The safest way to give vaccines is not all at once in a combo shot but one at a time over several visits. They should also be given at specific sites on the body: rabies vaccine in the right hind leg; panleukopenia in the right front; and, if indicated, feline leukemia virus vaccine in the left hind leg. Veterinarians use these sites so that if the cat has a reaction later, they know exactly which shot was given where.

Don't give your cat vaccines yourself, even if you can legally buy them in your state. They need to be properly stored or they lose their potency. Also, some cats develop a life-threatening allergic reaction, called anaphylaxis, to vaccinations, and you need to be at the vet's office if that happens. So if your cat is in for vaccines, stick around in the waiting room for about thirty minutes after the vaccination has been given. You don't want to be in traffic if kitty has an anaphylactic reaction. This is no reason not to vaccinate, though—these reactions are very rare.

During the examination, your veterinarian will check for parasites and common diseases found in cats. This visit is also a good time to discuss your kitty's nutritional needs, as well as dental care.

Routine Visits

Everyone knows we humans are supposed to visit the doctor once a year for a checkup. Once a year is great for cats, too, but twice a year is even better. Cats age more quickly than humans, and their health status can change more quickly as well. Certainly, when kitty is a senior you'll want to stay on top of any changes that may occur and catch little problems as soon as possible, before they can develop into something worse. It's far easier to treat and manage a little health problem than a major one.

Your veterinarian will examine your cat first, listen to her chest for any cardiac problems, and look in her mouth. The doctor will run a routine blood panel to establish what is normal for your cat, and then periodically recheck it to make sure there are no deviations. They'll listen to your cat's chest for any cardiac problems, and look in her mouth, and take her temperature.

A normal temperature for a cat is 100.5 to 102.5 degrees Fahrenheit. If kitty's not feeling well and you take her temperature at home,

Does Your Cat Need Health Insurance?

The decision to buy or not buy pet health insurance for your cat is purely personal. If there's some sort of catastrophic injury to your cat, it can certainly be helpful. For routine care, some policies are better than others. There are several companies selling pet insurance. If you do want to buy insurance, read each plan carefully to decide which is best for you and your cats. And be aware that some companies do not accept pets over a certain age when selling a new policy.

Another option is to open a separate bank account when you first get your kitty and add to it faithfully, just as if you were paying for an insurance policy. If you start saving when kitty is healthy, you'll have money for any unexpected emergencies or illnesses in the future.

anything higher may mean a trip to see the veterinarian. Feeling her ears or paw pads isn't enough; you need to know her internal temperature. Your veterinarian may or may not take her temperature if she's not been ill. A rectal thermometer can cause arousal, fear, and subsequent aggression in many cats. Some veterinarians use veterinary-specific ear thermometers..

If your cat is living indoors only, as I've discussed, then she will receive the necessary number of vaccinations. Your veterinarian will also weigh her. This is a good time to discuss her ideal weight and her diet.

Your veterinarian will palpate (feel with the hands) kitty's internal organs. Any abnormalities will be noted. If she is healthy, that will be noted, too.

They'll also check the eyes. Cats have a nictating membrane, which is commonly called the third eyelid. Normally, you don't see it. When it's visible (a cloudy membrane in the lower corner of the eyelid), it can be a sign that you have a sick kitty and should get her to her veterinarian as quickly as possible. Your veterinarian will probably find that she also has an elevated temperature. She may also look glassyeyed or have a glazed-over appearance. Keep in mind, though, that the third eyelid can also show when the cat is happy or contented and is squinting, and may also show if she's sleepy.

The vet will look in your cat's ears. You can ask your veterinarian to show you how to clean your kitty's ears. Some cats seem to produce an inordinate amount of ear wax, while others may have ear mites. To tell the difference, your veterinarian will clean kitty's ears and take the swabs and check under a microscope to see if there are mites. If that's the case, you will be shown how to put eardrops in kitty's ears. Cleaning your cat's ears is always a good idea, but it's important to do it the right way. So ask the vet to show you how.

Bring along a fresh stool sample, scooped that day from the litter box. Your veterinarian may want to discuss your cat's litter box habits, so be prepared to describe what you've observed in the box.

If there are several veterinarians in the practice, it's a good idea to have each of them see kitty at various visits so they will get an idea of what she's normally like. This way, if your chosen veterinarian isn't available when kitty is sick, you'll have a back-up veterinarian whom you like and who is also somewhat familiar with your cat.

The Perfect Client

While you are ensuring that you have the perfect veterinarian for your cat, be sure that you are the perfect client. Show up on time for appointments. If you need to reschedule, please try to give enough advance

Subtle Signs of Illness

Cats are very good at hiding pain and illness, so you must be alert to the slightest little warning signs. That means you need to become very familiar with what is normal for your kitty and what isn't.

According to the American Association of Feline Practitioners (AAFP), even something as subtle as changes in a cat's behavior or routine may be the first sign of illness. These changes might seem as if the cat is just being naughty, when in fact she feels terrible. The AAFP lists ten signs that can mean your cat is sick. If you see any of these, take kitty to the veterinarian.

1. Inappropriate elimination
2. Changes in her interactions with you—for example, increased affection, aloofness, or unexplained aggression—or changes in her interactions with other pets in the household
3. Changes in activity level—and that could mean becoming more active or less active
4. Changes in sleeping habits
5. Unexplained weight loss or gain
6. Changes in food and water consumption
7. Changes in grooming habits
8. Signs of stress, such as hiding
9. Changes in vocalization
10. Bad breath

notice so your veterinarian can give your appointment to someone else. Whenever your veterinarian prescribes a medication, be sure to give the entire course of treatment. Don't stop because kitty looks better or because she is difficult to medicate. You need to follow through on all instructions.

If you have questions, be sure to write them down so you don't forget them while you're in the office. Write down the answers, too!

Feline Spa Services

You are the provider of feline spa services. Cats are fastidious and will spend hours grooming themselves. The reason a cat's tongue feels rough when she licks you is that papillae on their tongue—little hooks that face toward the throat—enable your kitty to comb her own coat with her tongue. If you have more than one cat, you will often find them grooming each other. This social grooming is common.

In addition to kitty's daily self-grooming, your cat requires regular grooming from you. If you have a longhaired cat, this means daily brushing and combing. If you have a shorthaired cat, this means grooming at least twice a week, but daily is a good idea for them as well, since it will help prevent hairballs. It's also a nice, relaxing way to bond with your cat.

Sitting with your kitty and grooming her can be a very rewarding experience for both of you. She'll enjoy it if you make the experience enjoyable for her. You can start slowly with your comb or brush and gently work your way through her coat. Talk soothingly to her. It doesn't matter what you say as long as you talk quietly. Kitty will listen and enjoy the attention. Keep the first grooming sessions very short. If you start slowly and calmly, you will find that the experience becomes part of your daily routine. At the end of the grooming session, be sure to tell her how wonderful she looks, how good she is, and give her a special treat.

It's critical that you do this daily if you have a longhaired cat so she won't get matted. Mats are painful to cats because they pinch the skin. Mats that can't be separated will have to be cut out of kitty's coat, and

Romona Marek

Only 40 percent of cats are ambidextrous. The rest favor either the right or left paw.

you may need to have her coat cut down and start over if things have gotten so far out of hand that she's completely matted.

By grooming her daily, you are helping spread natural oils throughout her coat and keep the hair and skin healthy. You'll be preventing hairballs, too. And it gives you a chance to see if there are any lumps, bumps, scrapes, fleas, or ticks on her skin and get them treated as soon as possible.

Getting Your Cat Used to Grooming

Unless your cat has been introduced to comb, brush, and nail clippers in her first home, it will be up to you to make those introductions. Wait until kitty is in a relaxed mood, perhaps lying on your lap, then bring either the comb or brush on your lap and let her sniff it and touch it. Tell her what a good girl she is!

If she's accepting of it, you can hold it in your hand and gently put it closer to her. Take this in slow stages until she allows you to use the brush or comb in one hand and stroke her with the other, so it becomes pleasurable for her. Don't do it for more than a few seconds at first, slowly building up the time until she is completely accepting. Repeat the process with the other tool.

Nail clippers can be a little trickier. Some cats are fine with it, and some seem to be appalled by the idea. You are, in a sense, taking something

Kitty Whiskers

Your cat's whiskers are very sensitive, and it's important—critical in fact—that you do *not* cut or trim them. The whiskers are connected to a cat's nervous system. Kitty has about twenty-four whiskers, although some cats have more, and they are all moveable.

These extrasensitive hairs, called vibrissae, help her in myriad ways. She can detect the slightest breeze or movement with her whiskers, and receives "messages" from them about the size and shape of nearby objects, including prey. Her whiskers will tell her if a space is wide enough to get through. They also help kitty's sense of smell.

As I mentioned before, it's important that kitty have wide dishes and not deep food or water bowls because her whiskers can bump against the sides of a bowl, which will make it uncomfortable for kitty to eat. Don't wash kitty's whiskers, either. She'll take care of them herself, thank you very much!

Occasionally, you may see a whisker that has fallen out. Don't worry, kitty will grow another in its place.

from them—the tips of their nails. Choose your nail trimming tool carefully, based on what will work best for you. You can use nail clippers that resemble scissors but are made specifically to trim pets' nails. There's a guillotine type of clipper, and there are nail clippers made for humans. Some people prefer to use a Dremel tool or a nail grinder to file the nails down rather than clip them.

Whichever tool you choose, make yourself comfortable with it before you approach kitty with it. As with the brush and comb, be sure that she has an opportunity to see it, touch it, be near it. Let her get used to the sound of either the clippers or the Dremel before you attempt to do her nails. Take your time with this. Slow and steady wins the race.

If your kitty is savvy about clicker training (the training technique I'll describe in chapter 11), you can click and treat as she touches the equipment and each time she allows it to come closer and closer to her. You can also click and treat when she is calm while she listens to the clippers or the Dremel.

It will be much easier to give your kitty the spa treatment if she's comfortable with the equipment. Remember that even if you can only clip one nail at a time, it's better than none. Conditioning kitty to the equipment will result in a relaxed cat when you groom her.

Manicure and Pedicure

As part of your complete feline spa service, you will need to trim your cat's claws. You don't want your cat scratching someone or inadvertently hurting anyone. This is easy enough to do if she uses a human lap or a shoulder as a launching pad to get to another place. It won't be on purpose, but her claws could pinch or dig in for a moment. That can be easily avoided by trimming her nails.

The mani-pedi experience is not a whole lot of fun for some cats, although some of them love it and some simply don't mind. How your kitty reacts is anybody's guess, but you can have a big influence on that by how you start out (see the previous section). Hopefully, you will be able to make it a pleasant experience.

If you have a kitten, it's easy to start this routine early by gently touching her paws every day and slowly moving along to extending the claws and then trimming them. Be sure to take your time so it's a natural, relaxing experience for kitty.

Trimming claws is fairly straightforward. Use a special pair of clippers made for pets. Hold kitty's paw in one hand, the clippers in the other, and press gently on the underside of her paw at the toe pad. Her claws will automatically extend. Clip them just where they begin to curve. Easy!

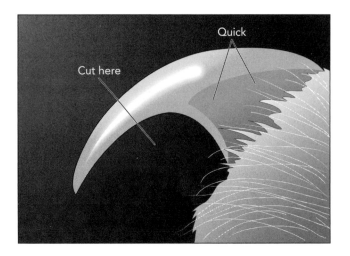

Be sure to avoid the quick (the blood vessel inside). If your cat has white nails, you'll be able to see the quick as a pink area within the nail. If she has black nails, be sure to cut right where the curve begins and no closer to the paw. If you accidentally nick the quick, it will hurt kitty, so please do be careful. It may bleed a bit, too. Put a dab of cornstarch on the nail to stop the bleeding. And stop for the day, because your cat has had enough.

Do each nail in turn, talking quietly to your kitty. Don't forget those dewclaw nails on her front paws. All nails count! Front paws are done? Now it's time for back paws. The easiest way to do this is to sit your cat up in your lap with her back leaning against you and her legs extended as if she were sitting like a human. Do the back nails exactly the same way.

Always end the nail trimming with a treat. If kitty doesn't enjoy having her nails trimmed, you may have to settle for doing one nail at each session until they're all done.

Fleas and Ticks

Your cat is far more likely to pick up these parasites if she goes outdoors. But even indoor cats can get them, because they hitchhike onto people and other animals to get inside. Grooming daily will give you a chance to look for flea dirt in her coat (it looks like little specks of salt and pepper). If you find it, you will want to bathe her first to kill the fleas, and then give your veterinarian a call and ask what product they recommend to treat the problem. New flea and tick preparations are nontoxic to mammals. They go on the cat once and protect for weeks. Not all are safe and effective for cats, though, so be sure to ask your veterinarian.

Fleas can have an incredibly long life and reproduce with a speed that would be the envy of any rabbit! They don't spend all of their time on the pet and can live and reproduce only too well in your carpets, furniture, and even the cracks between the floorboards. The vacuum cleaner will become an indispensable item. Vacuum often and well to remove any fleas and flea dirt. And be careful when you empty the vacuum cleaner bag or cup so that fleas don't escape back into your house!

If you allow your cat to go outdoors, she is far more likely to have ticks on her body. A tick will look like a brown spot, either crawling slowly through the coat or latched on to the skin—in which case the head will not be visible. Ticks carry all sorts of diseases that affect both your cat and human family members as well. These include Lyme disease, which, if allowed to progress, can be fatal. Ticks look for any warm-blooded individual, four legs or two, so take special care.

If you do find a tick, grasp hold of it firmly with a tweezer as close to the skin as possible and slowly pull it straight out. Dab the spot with antibiotic ointment and watch it carefully for a few days. If you think the head has broken off and is still in kitty's skin—or if you simply don't feel comfortable removing the tick—take your cat to the veterinarian as soon as you can.

To safely dispose of a tick, don't flush it down the toilet; the tick will survive the journey. Don't squish it between your fingers, either, because this will expose you to any disease the tick may be carrying. Put it in a jar with some alcohol, tightly close the lid, and carefully throw it away in a trash can with a cover.

Dental Care

Brushing your cat's teeth daily is important to kitty's overall health. Your veterinarian can show you the proper way to brush your cat's teeth. Even weekly brushing is better than nothing. Dirty teeth and bacteria buildup will cause health problems that can be avoided.

Use a flavored toothpaste made especially for cats. Your veterinarian will show you how to introduce first the toothpaste and then the toothbrush to your cat. This should be an enjoyable process for both you and kitty, so relax. If you're tense, your cat will know that something is up and think this process is not a good thing—when, in fact, it is a very good thing for her health. Whenever you clean kitty's teeth and examine teeth and gums at home, give her a dental treat as a reward. Your veterinarian will be able to recommend something made especially for cats. Some veterinary cat diets actually treat dental disease.

Use a toothpaste made for pets. This is very important. Not only can toothpaste for people make your cat sick, but it foams, which can be frightening for your cat. Put some of the proper toothpaste on a gauze or finger brush. Then go slowly, just a few teeth at a time. Continue if your cat enjoys it; if not, come back another time.

If not managed with proper preventive care, kitty's teeth should be professionally cleaned if they're very dirty. She might even need to have one or more teeth extracted. Your veterinarian will be able to determine the condition of your cat's teeth at her regular examination. They will look for any plaque or tartar that may have begun to gather on her teeth and check to see if her gums are receding.

Bad breath, drooling, a change in appetite, or picking up but then dropping food are the first clues of dental disease. The cat may not be able to close her mouth or may be pawing at her mouth, which could be indicative of tooth pain. If you see any of these signs, a trip to the veterinarian is in order so kitty can be examined and the source of the problem can be determined.

Do You Need to Bathe a Cat?

Since cats are such good self-groomers, it's seldom necessary to bathe a cat. In fact, many cats never need a bath. But some cats do.

Show cats are bathed weekly to keep them looking their beautiful best. Cats with skin problems may need bathing, and cats with fleas do, as well. If your cat has dry skin or an allergy, your veterinarian will have you use a special shampoo that will help with her coat or skin problem. (Dandruff can appear if your cat is stressed. If you know what is stressing her, try to alleviate the problem as much as possible. Pay attention to kitty. Play with her and be sure to brush her. She may appreciate some cuddle time, too.)

Sometimes a cat gets into something she shouldn't have and it's not safe to let her groom herself clean—or not prudent, because she'll make a mess around your house while she's grooming. Occasionally a cat just gets too greasy. And fat cats and older cats sometimes need help to stay clean.

Be sure to get all the bathing equipment ready before you start. Have everything on hand, so you can be quick and decisive once you start. Some cats, like Turkish Vans, actually like the water. But those cats are the exceptions, not the rule. You'll need shampoo made especially for pets (shampoos for humans dry the skin), or the therapeutic shampoo your veterinarian recommends. If your kitty has dry skin, you'll need a conditioner as well. If your kitty has greasy hair, the first soaping should be with a gentle dishwashing detergent such as Dawn to cut the grease.

Put a towel or an old (but clean!) window screen in the bottom of the sink so kitty can get a firm footing, fill the sink about three inches deep

Show cats like these Scottish Folds are bathed before a show to keep them looking fluffy and fabulous. Your house kitty will generally be able to take care of her own bathing needs.

with lukewarm water, and then stand your cat up in the sink. Use a cup to gently wet her, then apply the shampoo and work it through her coat.

Be careful to keep shampoo out of kitty's eyes and ears. Rinse the shampoo out thoroughly. If you use a conditioner, be sure to rinse that out thoroughly, too.

Wrap kitty in a fluffy towel and let her air-dry if it's warm enough in the house. You will need to blow dry and brush a longhaired cat. Be sure to keep the hair dryer at a low setting and move it around so you don't burn her delicate skin.

Senior Cats

Older cats are special treasures. A combination of genetics and proper care will help your kitty live a long, healthy, happy life. You may well have your kitty for twenty years, if you're lucky and you keep her indoors.

When kitty is about 10 years old, it's time to consider her a senior. Celebrate her birthday by taking her to the veterinarian for a senior wellness visit. This will establish baseline levels for her heart, lungs, blood work, and other health parameters. With the baselines established, it's much easier to catch any changes early on. By the time she's

11, you should be scheduling appointments twice a year with her veterinarian (if you're not already doing that). Six months in a cat's life might well be equivalent to three and a half years in a human's life, so a twice-annual exam routine makes sense.

Cats always appreciate routine and familiarity, and never so much as when they're seniors. Make things as easy and relaxing as possible for your special senior kitty.

Cats are masterful when it comes to masking illness. Sometimes they just get quiet or go off and hide. It's up to you to notice any changes and to be able to locate your kitty if she disappears. Don't assume anything. If your cat is sleeping more than usual, don't jump to the conclusion that it's old age. She may have an underlying problem. If you begin to see any changes in her habits, note them on the calendar. When you make an appointment with your veterinarian, you'll be able to document how long the problem has been going on.

Many problems may benefit from better nutrition. There are also therapeutic veterinary diets for conditions such as kidney disease, dental disease, arthritis, diabetes, and others.

You should watch for the signs of aging. Are your cat's eyes looking like they have a cloudy blue tinge? Have it checked out; it may not affect kitty's vision, but it's best to be sure. If your kitty does lose some or all of her vision, please don't move the furniture. She'll depend on the familiar. You may want to put a strip of carpet at each doorway to help her delineate one room from another.

Remember that she may not be able to groom herself as well when she's older. Make sure you give her regular spa sessions.

Cats can lose their hearing with age. You may or may not see any buildup on her ears associated with a change in hearing. If she has lost her hearing, remember that she can still feel vibrations. Don't scare her by approaching too quietly. Stamp your foot on the floor as you come into the room so she'll realize that you're there.

Because cats are so good at masking pain, arthritis is greatly under-diagnosed in cats. Your arthritic cat may not climb her cat tree or jump on or off furniture or climb up or down stairs. She may complain when you pick her up. You may notice that she's not grooming herself in some of those harder to reach places. Take her to her veterinarian to have these signs checked. There are foods, supplements, and medications that can help (they should always be given under the supervision of your veterinarian, of course). Meanwhile, you can make her as comfortable as possible and help facilitate access to the sofa, for example, by piling up pillows or buying a small ramp or set of steps. Kitty will need soft bedding so she can rest her achy joints. You can use foam rubber egg crate mattress cover material that makes humans more comfortable and put a washable cover over it.

If your kitty can no longer reach up and stretch out on a vertical scratching post, get her a horizontal one so she can still perform that necessary task.

Your cat may also begin to lose muscle mass, especially in her rear legs. Again, it's time to see the veterinarian. Some diabetic cats can also have trouble walking. Your veterinarian can make the diagnosis and get your cat started on a treatment plan.

Be sure that you continue to brush her teeth with toothpaste made especially for cats, and have your veterinarian see if she needs any teeth removed. She may have tooth pain and will feel so much more comfortable if a bad tooth is removed.

Cats usually consider a bath to be a nasty experience. Some who are accustomed to it, like show cats, tend to tolerate the process well, but as cats age, they find it more stressful. You can help kitty keep herself clean with combing, brushing, and using one of the newer disposable wet cloth products made for cats. Try to avoid a full bath. If you have to give her one, do it with her mental, as well as physical, health in mind. Be sure there's good footing. She can use her claws to grasp onto a bath mat or other soft material placed at the bottom of the sink or tub while you bathe her.

Watch for any changes in the amount of food and water she consumes each day. This can point to an underlying health or dental problem, and your veterinarian should see her as soon as possible.

Older cats sometimes have trouble getting to, or in and out of, their litter box. You can buy a large plastic container and cut one side down so there's a low entrance that's easier to access. Be sure the box you buy is large enough for her to move and turn around in comfortably. And when you're scooping the box, note any changes in her stool.

Kitty may not play as athletically as she once did, but that doesn't mean that she shouldn't play. Just like senior people, she needs a proper diet and exercise regime. Shorter, easier play periods will be most welcome in keeping her body and her mind active as she ages.

Engage her in simple games. She will still enjoy following a wand toy. Use one with a long strip of cloth attached to it and drag it along after you. She can move from room to room at her own speed, following the wiggly cloth. She'll be getting some exercise and keeping her mind engaged as well.

Treat- or food-ball toys, as I mentioned before, are a wonderful way to engage an older cat's mind and give her some exercise as she rolls the ball around to get it to dispense dry food or treats.

If kitty hasn't lost her hearing, you can play clicker training games to keep her engaged. That's a nonstrenuous way to exercise both her mind and body. If she has lost some, or all, of her hearing, you can use a flashlight to play clicker games (make the light click on and off as her signal that she's figured out the game). Or you can just give her some exercise playing with the light. (This, of course, is if she has her vision.) Remember to start the game with the light coming out of a specific spot and end it with the light returning to that spot, so she doesn't become upset looking for the light long after the game has ended. That will only cause her consternation.

When you pet a cat and run your hand over her hindquarters close to the tail, you'll probably notice her rear go up in a posture some people call an elevator butt. This is actually a reflexive reaction. As your cat gets older, petting her to elicit this reaction will give her a little exercise. Just be sure it doesn't stress or hurt her if she's arthritic. Check with your veterinarian first.

Exercise is as important for the aging cat as it is for the aging human. But please do watch for signs of kitty tiring easily or having problems breathing while playing. If you see either or both of those things, take her to your veterinarian right away, because it's indicative of disease. The sooner you treat a problem, the easier it will be to cure or manage it. And if it's nothing—well, better safe than sorry. It will ease your mind to have your veterinarian examine her, and you may just catch a problem before it becomes far worse and more difficult to treat.

Stress is also an issue for cats, and more so for the older ones. Try to keep everything as simple and stress-free as possible. You'll both feel better for it.

The relationship with your senior cat is a precious one, built over the long time you've shared together. You owe it to kitty (and yourself!) to make her life as happy, healthy, and long as possible—a good quality of life that you both delight in.

CHAPTER 8

SPECIAL FELINE HEALTH CONCERNS

W e wish that everyone we love, human or animal, were free of diseases and other health problems, but that's just not realistic. Every living creature has health problems at one time or another. As cat owners, we hope we never have to deal with any of these problems. But chances are that at least one of them may crop up during your kitty's lifetime. It never hurts to be aware of what might be.

The most common feline health problems seen by general practice veterinarians are dental disease, obesity, respiratory problems, kidney and bladder disease, and intestinal problems resulting in vomiting and/or diarrhea. All of these are treatable—as are most of the other diseases described in this chapter. Some can be cured and some can be managed quite well. But the sooner you start, the better for your cat. That's why it's so important that your cat get a veterinary checkup at least once a year. Twice yearly is preferable for senior cats, whose health status can change so quickly.

Cats are incredibly good at hiding when they're sick. They may be ill and not show any signs at all. This is another good reason to be sure to see your veterinarian regularly. And keep an eye out for kitty; if he disappears for an inordinate amount of time, he may be hiding because he isn't feeling well.

Feline Lower Urinary Tract Disease

Feline lower urinary tract disease (FLUTD) is the most common medical reason for cats urinating outside the litter box. That's why it's so important to take your cat to the veterinarian for a complete checkup before assuming that a litter box indiscretion is a behavior problem. FLUTD is a complex set of problems that can have many causes. Most cat owners and many veterinarians don't understand it very well. Let me try to untangle the mystery for you.

The lower urinary tract is made up of the urinary bladder, the bladder sphincters, and the urethra. A problem that affects any of these organs is classified as FLUTD.

Cystitis is part of the FLUTD complex. Any inflammation of the urinary bladder is called cystitis. Infection is rarely the cause of the inflammation. More commonly the specific cause is not known and the condition is called idiopathic cystitis. Idiopathic cystitis most commonly occurs in cats between the ages of 2 and 6, obese cats, and sedentary cats. Stress may also have a role to play. There seems to be a genetic component as well that makes a cat more susceptible to cystitis.

Symptoms of FLUTD include squatting and straining for a long time, going in and out of the litter box without eliminating, urinating frequently, passing bloody urine, urinating in odd places because the cat now associates the litter box with pain, excessively licking private parts, and crying out while urinating. Some cats may have only one or two of those signs or even none! With some of these symptoms, it's easy to see why people think their cat has a behavior problem when the problem is actually physical.

FLUTD can be caused by a number of things, including an obstructed urethra, which may be blocked by mucus, crystals, or urinary tract stones. (Know that a fully obstructed urethra can be a matter of life and death and must be treated as an emergency.) It can also be caused by the presence of stones or crystals with no obstruction, bacterial infection, or other conditions that irritate the bladder. It can even be caused by an unclean litter box, reduced physical activity, and stress. Among all these causes, bacterial infection is least likely in young cats.

Veterinarians now know that diet is a major factor in the development and control of FLUTD, so it's critical to follow your veterinarian's nutritional guidelines. For example, a dry diet combined with a less than optimum water intake can contribute to FLUTD. The American Animal Hospital Association (AAHA) and the American College of Veterinary Nutrition have recently collaborated on nutritional assessment guidelines for veterinarians, so be sure to ask your veterinarian about them.

The diagnosis is made using a variety of tests, including repeat urinalyses and imaging such as ultrasound and X-rays. In severe, chronic, and recurring cases, uroendoscopy may be used to evaluate the lower urinary tract. (A tiny tube is threaded up the urethra for visualization and biopsy.)

Urinalysis, including sediment evaluation, should be done regularly on affected cats, even if kitty appears to be normal. In most cases, veterinarians prefer to get the sample by cystocentesis, where, just like taking a blood sample, the urine is collected with a syringe. This prevents any contamination of the urine sample by matter in the urethra, the surface on which the urine is deposited, or the container. Ever try to catch a urine sample from a cat into a sterile container? I can't even imagine it! And it's pretty unlikely your kitty will take a container over to the litter box and collect a sample for you.

FLUTD has a 50 to 75 percent chance of reocurring in a cat. To prevent this, your cat may have to stay on a special veterinary diet, and kitty's urine will have to be checked every six months. These veterinary diets are useful if the cause of the problem is small stones or crystals in the lower urinary tract. Veterinary diets change the pH of the cat's urine, making it more acid or alkaline, depending on what type of mineral sediment is forming in the cat's urine (although elderly cats should *not* be fed an acidic diet). If the cat remains healthy for about nine months, your veterinarian might let you take the cat off the special diet. Again, your cat should be checked every six months to see if a switch back to the veterinary diet is indicated.

Your veterinarian may recommend a wet food diet or at least offering wet food because of its high water content. Also, make sure your cat has access to plenty of fresh, clean water. Be sure that kitty gets enough exercise each day and that she isn't stressed. And please remember to keep the litter box scrupulously clean!

Urinary Tract Stones

Cats are subject to developing urinary tract stones, called uroliths, and this may be more serious in males because they have a higher likelihood of developing an obstruction. Stones are hard, rocklike accumulations formed from mineral crystals and some mucuslike organic matter. They are very painful and can cause litter box aversion if the cat experiences pain when he's in the box trying to urinate.

Uroliths can be found in the bladder or the kidneys—although kidney stones are not as common in cats. Symptoms may include blood in the urine, frequent urination, and difficulty urinating. If you see any of these symptoms, please take your cat to his veterinarian as soon as possible, because this is an emergency. The problem can be mistaken for constipation, but don't take chances. The most common uroliths in cats are struvite (magnesium phosphate) and calcium oxalate. Special acidic diets will discourage the formation of struvite crystals and stones, but they may also encourage the formation of calcium oxalate uroliths. That's why it's important to discuss all diet changes with your veterinarian.

Struvite can appear in both males and females, but the highest incidence is in female cats. The highest risk is in females who are 1 or 2 years old. When struvite occurs in a cat less than 1 year old, a bacterial infection may be the culprit.

Calcium oxalate crystals and stones occur a little more often in males than in females. The risk of this type of urolith increases with age, so neutered male kitties who are between 10 and 15 years old have the bigger risk. It has also been noted that Burmese, Persian, and Himalayan breeds have a higher incidence of these uroliths. Some cats who have these uroliths have high blood calcium levels, as well.

Uroliths can cause either a partial or total obstruction of the urethra, so the cat can pass little or no urine. If a urolith blocks the cat's urethra, it can be a matter of life and death. Don't take chances—get your cat and head for the veterinary hospital immediately.

X-rays and ultrasound of the lower urinary tract are the best means of diagnosis. If regular X-rays are inconclusive, a bladder ultrasound may be the best means of diagnosis, because small stones may not show up any other way. (Interestingly, the only way to know what type of urolith a cat has is to remove it and send it off to be analyzed.)

A cat with a partial or total obstruction is often dehydrated, lethargic, and has electrolyte and acid-base imbalances. He also has more waste matter in the bloodstream. This can lead to heart and kidney dysfunction, bladder damage, and death if left untreated.

If kitty is dehydrated, he will need intravenous fluids. And to get urine flowing again, he'll need a catheter. Once the veterinarian has removed the obstructions surgically, a proper treatment plan can be developed. Kitty will be put on a special veterinary diet and will need regular follow-up care from the veterinarian. Note that antibiotics are used only if the veterinarian determines that the stones were caused by a bacterial infection.

If the cat has stones but is not entirely blocked, a special veterinary diet can frequently dissolve struvite stones, but it can take up to four months for the diet to dissolve the stones. Calcium oxalate uroliths cannot be dissolved and must be removed surgically. (It's sometimes possible to flush out smaller ones while the cat is sedated.)

Once a cat has had stones, he will be at risk for them to develop again. This can be prevented by feeding a special veterinary diet. There are several maintenance diets available to prevent each type of stone. Antibiotics are used only if the veterinarian determines that the stones were caused by bacterial infection. Generally, wet food is preferred because it has a higher water content than a dry diet—although there are some cats who enjoy drinking water and will do fine on a dry diet as long as they continue to drink enough water to compensate. This is another time when a water fountain can be helpful to encourage kitty to drink more.

Dental Disease

Dental disease can occur in cats of any age, and unless you take specific care of their oral health needs, it can begin to develop in adolescent and young adult cats. Dental disease can be painful and dangerous, and pathogens from diseased teeth can get into the bloodstream and cause a variety of serious health problems.

You will want to pay attention to kitty's gums. Cats aren't prone to cavities, but they are prone to developing plaque and gum disease—yes, just like us. And it's not uncommon to see kittens develop gingivitis (red gums) when they're anywhere from 6 to 9 months old.

Start gently checking your kitten's teeth and gums regularly, so he'll be used to it. Your veterinarian will check more thoroughly at each routine wellness visit. Start brushing your cat's teeth when he's young or new to the family, as well (if kitty is receptive at that time—start slowly!). Your veterinarian can show you how to do this.

If your veterinarian finds a buildup of plaque and tartar, it's time for a professional cleaning. There are special veterinary dental diets that can really help control plaque and tartar buildup, and you should ask your vet about them. But you will still need to schedule professional cleanings for your cat.

Tooth extractions are not uncommon in cats. Veterinarians see a lot of periodontal disease (tooth root infections and loss of bone attachment to the tooth). Cats with tooth resorptive lesions (loss of the tooth structure), which are very painful to the cat, also require extraction of the affected tooth. At the earliest stages, these lesions will look like small pits in the surface of the teeth. If they're not taken care of, over time they will allow bacteria into your cat's bloodstream.

Check a picky eater for dental problems by holding a cotton-tipped applicator on the suspected problem area. If the cat moves away with his jaw quivering, take him to the veterinarian as soon as possible, because his teeth hurt.

Cats can also have broken teeth. More often than not it's the tip of the tooth that is broken. Since both the pulp and the nerve inside the tooth extend to the tip, you can't afford to wait around to see what will happen. Kitty should go to the veterinarian's office as quickly as possible. Nearly all teeth in which the root is exposed will be extremely painful and susceptible to infection. Your cat needs either a root canal or a tooth removal as soon as possible.

Cleaning kitty's teeth is your best bet for a healthy mouth. When brushing teeth, it's important to brush at the gum line. And do ask your veterinarian about dental treats for kitty. They will help keep his teeth clean but are, of course, no replacement for dental care. They're just a nice addition to your cleaning tools.

Abscess

An abscess is an area of pus and debris that is surrounded by inflammation. The most common way cats get abscesses is from bites by other cats. Cats have an incredible amount of bacteria in their mouths. When they get into fights, there is always a risk of a bite, and that bite developing into an abscess.

While cat fights are possible in a multicat household, the greater risk is for outdoor or indoor-outdoor cats to fight with unfamiliar felines. It's just one more danger of the great outdoors.

An abscess from a bite usually forms under the skin because cat teeth cause puncture wounds that seal over quickly, trapping the bacteria inside. Within two or three days your kitty will not eat. He'll become lethargic, and there will be pus where the puncture occurred as the bacteria multiplies. The area will be swollen and painful when you touch it; you'll be able to smell it, too. Your cat may have swollen lymph nodes as well.

An abscess is an active infection. Unlike other types of infections, antibiotics alone will not take care of it. The abscess must be opened and drained by a veterinarian. The sooner your veterinarian cleans the wound and removes the dead tissue, the better.

Kitty will also need to be treated for the infection. That means a full course of antibiotics. Be sure to give your cat the antibiotics your veterinarian prescribes for the entire course of treatment. Some people stop treatment when their cat looks and feels better. But that gives the infection a chance to recur. So even if your cat is difficult to medicate, go the distance. Pain management is also needed for abscesses; be sure to ask for and follow your veterinarian's advice.

It is so much safer to keep your cat indoors where he isn't going to get into any territorial fights with stray cats. The old saying, "An ounce of prevention is worth a pound of cure," really holds true.

Diabetes

Obesity is a common predisposing factor for diabetes in cats. How well diabetes can be managed in a cat depends on the cat and if there is any other underlying disease. Most cases are manageable. Most cats have type II diabetes, which means their pancreas produces insulin but their body does not use it properly. Some of these cats will require insulin injections, but many can be managed with dietary modifications, weight management, and, sometimes, oral medications.

A high-protein, low-carbohydrate diet is recommended for diabetic cats. A number of cats who initially need insulin may be able to stop taking it over time with this kind of diet change and weight loss. Some cats will respond better to one type of insulin than another, but, unfortunately, the number of insulin types available for cats has decreased.

In cats whose diabetes is difficult to manage, your veterinarian will look for underlying infections (thyroid, urinary tract, dental disease, and others) and treat those. Or the veterinarian will determine if there is other underlying endocrine disease, such as acromegaly, which is excess production of growth hormone in an adult cat. It occurs in older cats and seems to be more common in male cats. The short-term prognosis for cats with this condition is good, and so is the long-term prognosis if it's diagnosed and treated.

Hyperadrenocorticism, more commonly known as Cushing's disease, is another endocrine illness that can cause the symptoms of diabetes. Cushing's disease is excessive production of cortisol by the adrenal glands. Symptoms in cats are increased thirst, increased urination, increased appetite, an enlarged abdomen, symmetrical hair loss, muscle wasting and weakness, decreased activity, and lethargy. This disease can also be caused by corticosteroids, in which case it's resolved when the medication is very gradually withdrawn to allow the adrenal glands to return to normal function.

Liver Disease

I've already discussed hepatic lipidosis in chapter 6, but there are other things that can affect the functioning of your cat's liver. Hepatitis is an inflammatory liver disease. The cat will be lethargic, he'll have a fever, he won't eat, and he will likely be vomiting. His feces will be gray and he may urinate excessively. If this disease advances, the light parts of his eyes and the membranes inside his ears and mouth will turn yellow. Hopefully, you'll have a diagnosis before kitty reaches that stage.

Get your cat to his veterinarian as soon as you begin to see any of these signs. Your veterinarian should immediately order blood and urine tests to check liver function and see how much damage has been done to kitty's liver. As mentioned, the pancreas is right next door, as are the intestines, and frequently there is inflammation of all three organs (called *triaditis*). Signs are inconsistent, and advanced lab work and other tests may be required to properly diagnose the presence and extent of any of these problems.

Another reason to keep kitty indoors is toxic liver disease. Your cat can encounter many toxins as he roams around the great outdoors. Lawn poisons, antifreeze, and all manner of chemicals sprayed on lawns and shrubs can be poisonous to your cat. Lilies are also very toxic to the liver. Immediate veterinary intervention is crucial. Look for kitty to have a very sore tummy and stop eating. He'll be lethargic, he'll urinate a large amount of orange urine, and he'll lose weight. Without swift treatment, he can die.

Tumors on the liver are another possibility. If a tumor is detected on the liver, a biopsy and an ultrasound will be done along with bloodwork to determine if the tumor is benign or malignant.

To a certain extent, the liver can regenerate when the disease process is halted. But it's up to you to keep an eye open for changes in kitty's behavior, eating habits, and elimination, and get him to the vet before things progress too far. Remember that cats are stoic. Run, do not walk, to your veterinarian with kitty in tow for an expert diagnosis and treatment. The sooner treatment is started, the better the outcome.

Allergies and Intolerances

Like us, cats can be allergic to things they touch, inhale, or ingest. Unlike us, the most common allergy symptoms they experience are itchiness and irritation of the skin.

The most common allergies are due to insect bites—most often fleas. Cats can also be allergic to household chemicals, plastics, insecticides, molds, trees, grasses, and pollens.

If your cat is itchy or is biting at his own skin, a visit to a veterinary dermatologist is in order. Allergies can be tough to diagnose, but the effort is worth it. A significant portion of cats referred to veterinary behaviorists for chewing on themselves turn out to have allergies.

Your veterinarian or veterinary dermatologist is best able to choose a course of treatment that will be safe for your cat and bring him relief from the allergy.

Cats can also be intolerant of or develop an intolerance to certain foods. Sometimes it's a specific protein source, such as beef, fish, or chicken. They can also be allergic to wheat gluten, corn, or other grains. Food intolerances more often cause vomiting and/or diarrhea, but they can also cause dermatologic signs. A special diet made of ingredients that the cat has not been previously exposed to can often relieve these symptoms.

Asthma

Feline asthma affects about one percent of all cats. It should be suspected if your cat has a cough or a wheeze or increased respiration rate or effort. If you see any of these signs, take your cat to your veterinarian—sooner rather than later.

Asthma in cats is a hypersensitivity to environmental allergens. It resembles bronchial asthma in humans. There may be a seasonal trigger.

The asthma causes bronchoconstriction, so the cough is really more of a wheeze. Some cats may have this chronic wheezing, while others might have severe respiratory distress, which is an emergency. A cat having trouble breathing may hunch his shoulders or lie with his chest to the floor and his mouth open. This requires *immediate* veterinary care.

Asthma is diagnosed with an examination that includes listening to the chest with a stethoscope, a complete examination, along with a history of signs and symptoms that you will provide. Chest X-rays are always indicated, but may need to be postponed depending on the severity of the condition when your cat first sees the veterinarian. It's important to differentiate asthma from bronchitis, pneumonia, heartworm, and lung cancer. Heartworms are endemic in almost all areas; they are spread by mosquitoes and in cats cause lung disease rather than heart disease. A cough caused by lung disease sounds exactly like a cough due to asthma or bronchitis. Every coughing cat should be tested for heartworm.

A bronchodilator is used to control asthma attacks in cats. That, combined with anti-inflammatory drugs (steroids), is generally used for long-term management. Anti-leukotrienes, which help people with asthma, have not been found to be effective in cats. However, research into the feline immune system is ongoing, and newer treatments may be on the horizon.

These medications are most effectively administered using an inhaler. There are now specially designed inhalers made just for cats. It's not difficult to teach a cat to calmly accept the inhaler mask.

Asthma is a chronic, recurring condition. It can be managed, not cured. If the cat is diagnosed early and treated aggressively, she can live a full life. Some cats are able to be on medication only when the seasonal allergen triggers their asthma or when attacks flare up. Others must be medicated throughout their lives. Secondhand smoke and feline obesity are two of the biggest complicators of feline asthma. Allergy testing by your veterinarian and minimizing exposure to allergens can be helpful.

Upper Respiratory Infection

Upper respiratory infections (URIs) in cats usually have a viral cause. They are relatively common and very contagious. They can rip through a shelter or cattery, causing serious disease especially in very young cats. Good sanitation and air circulation, and maintaining overall health, is important in any crowded cat situation.

Two major virus groups—herpesvirus and calicivirus—are responsible for almost 90 percent of all URIs in cats. Once a cat has caught the virus, it cannot be eradicated; all you can do is treat the symptoms. When the infection is no longer active, the cat will not have any symptoms but the virus will still be there. Periods of physical or emotional stress can reactivate it.

If your cat has signs of an upper respiratory infection, including runny or gummy eyes, sneezing, mucous in the nose, difficulty breathing, or loud breathing, isolate him from your other cats and take him to your veterinarian as soon as possible. When you discuss treatment, be sure to also discuss how you will protect your other cats from infection.

Your cat will need lots of supportive care to keep him well hydrated, well rested, and comfortable. Cats make a particularly thick form of mucus, and they can't blow their nose, so it can be difficult for them to get the mucus out of their nose. A cat with this problem won't eat because he can't smell the food. And if a cat stops eating for even three days, the situation can become life-threatening.

A warm room with a home vaporizer or a steamy bathroom can help. It may also help with mild asthma. The warm steam loosens mucus

---

What's the Alternative?

Think about acupuncture, chiropractic, or Tellington-Touch (T-Touch) alternative therapies for your cat. Each has been shown to work, often in concert with conventional medicine. Just be sure to work with a qualified practitioner if you choose one of these alternatives. There are also veterinarians practicing conventional medicine who also offer one or more of these alternatives in their practice.

secretions. You may also need to wipe your cat's nose, eyes, and mouth with moist cotton balls.

You can help shrink swollen nasal membranes using Little Noses nose drops for children. (But *always* check with your veterinarian before giving your cat any over-the-counter medication, including this one.) Raise the cat's head, put a drop on each nostril, and the cat will snort it in. Do that twice a day for three days, and use plain saline drops for three days. (You can get plain saline at your local drug store.) Then go back to the nose drops for three days. You alternate with saline because if you use decongestants too many days in a row, the cat may experience rebound congestion.

There are some antiviral medications that have been used in cats, with varying success. Ask your veterinarian about them. But generally, a virus must run its course, as it does in humans. Keep your little patient away from other kitties until he is well, and provide supportive care as directed by your veterinarian.

If there are signs of a secondary bacterial infection, your veterinarian may prescribe antibiotics. If there are signs of conjunctivitis (an eye infection), eye drops may also be prescribed.

Herpesvirus

As I've already mentioned, the herpesvirus group is one of the most common culprits in upper respiratory tract infections. The most common form is feline viral rhinotracheitis. A cat with an acute infection with this virus will be sneezing and congested, and one or both eyes will be tearing and inflamed. Affected cats may also have a sore throat, a cough, and a fever, and they won't want to eat or drink.

Feline viral rhinotracheitis will cause conjunctivitis (pinkeye), which can lead to corneal ulcers or keratitis (chronic dry eye). The virus in some cats will also cause a facial dermatitis that can look similar to a more severe facial allergic reaction. Some cats will transition from the acute phase into a chronic nasal and/or sinus infection with eye discharge and disease, sneezing, nasal discharge, and nasal snuffling or snorting.

Veterinarians diagnose herpesvirus by taking swabs from the surface of the conjunctiva (the membrane that covers the eyes) and the back of the throat.

There is no specific treatment for herpesvirus. You must give the cat supportive treatment, as I've described for URIs. Treatment may also include antibiotics for secondary infections, antibiotic and antiviral drugs for any eye problems, food and fluid support, and decongestant therapy if needed. Dr. Vicki Thayer, president of Winn Feline Foundation and past president of the American Association of Feline Practitioners,

Can My Cat Catch My Cold?

Although feline viral rhinotracheitis looks much like a human cold, it's not. Cats can catch cold from one another, but they can't catch them from us. And we can't catch their colds. The respiratory viruses that affect cats don't affect humans. The opposite is also true.

The only exception we know of so far is swine flu, also known as H1N1. In 2009, a handful of people infected with swine flu gave it to their cats. There were no reported cases of people catching it from a cat.

for example, recommends warm steam therapy. To do that, you can get the bathroom warm and steamy by running the shower for awhile, and then sit in the bathroom with your cat.

The amino acid L-lysine is used orally to help cats decrease virus replication. Recent studies do not seem to support its effectiveness, though it does not seem to hurt and may be beneficial in some cases. Probiotics may also offer some benefit. More recently, an antiviral drug called famciclovir seems to be able to control symptoms in a number of cats and may be a worthwhile addition to the treatment regimen.

Colitis

Colitis is an inflammation of the colon. It can come on suddenly or it can be an ongoing, chronic condition. Any number of things can cause it, including food allergy, bacteria, virus, parasites, trauma to the colon, or cancer.

The most obvious sign is bright red blood and/or mucus in your cat's stools, loose stools, and straining or trying frequently to defecate. If your cat has chronic colitis, you will likely see a concurrent weight loss.

You really do need to see your veterinarian right away. After a complete veterinary workup, which will likely include a colonoscopy, your veterinarian will recommend treatment that will probably include some dietary changes for your kitty. The cat will probably have to fast for twenty-four to forty-eight hours and then start eating a bland diet.

If your cat's colitis was caused by a parasite, he will get medication to kill the offending creature. Antibiotics and anti-inflammatory drugs are also part of treatment for this condition.

If the colitis was caused by an infection, it can be cured. If not, the disease can be managed. It's wise to keep a record on a calendar of any flare-ups, and take kitty to the veterinarian for periodic checkups.

Diarrhea

This isn't exactly a pretty topic, but we really do need to mention diarrhea in cats. A loose stool every once in a while is no cause for concern. Mild tummy upsets do come and go. But if it lasts for more than one day, you need to take your cat to the veterinarian.

I've already mentioned that bloody, mucousy, loose stools are indicative of certain illnesses, including colitis. If the stools are bloody, or black and kind of tarry, don't even wait the one day—take kitty to the vet. The same goes if kitty is dehydrated, has eaten something poisonous, or his gums are pale. If he's a kitten and hasn't had all of his vaccinations yet, take him to the vet. Take him to the veterinarian if he appears to be in pain, and certainly if he's also vomiting.

There are any number of causes for diarrhea, and it's best to let your veterinarian sort it out and discover whether the cause is in the large or small intestine, or if it is caused by nonintestinal conditions. Looking for intestinal parasites, and treatment and prevention, are important whenever there is an intestinal disorder. Whatever the cause, your veterinarian can diagnose the problem step by step and start appropriate treatment. Obviously, a cat with diarrhea isn't feeling well, so it's up to you to get him the care he needs to feel better.

Vomiting

Vomiting and cats are almost synonymous. Let's face it, if you have a cat you're used to hairballs (although those can be kept in check with regular grooming) and seeing kitty's entire meal regurgitated up on your once-lovely carpet after he has eaten too fast. Cats can vomit pretty easily and look quite happy afterward. They usually feel so much better after disgorging whatever it was they wanted to bring up and out of their system.

But not every vomiting episode is as benign as a hairball or a speed eater. Cats should normally be able to pass the hair they swallow while grooming all the way through their intestines and out in the feces. So if your cat is having a hairball more than once every few months, have him examined by your veterinarian to treat this problem early. Chronic vomiting from any cause can develop into more serious intestinal conditions, including cancer. Inflammatory bowel disease, for example, is frequently the precursor to gastrointestinal lymphoma.

Intestinal parasites and food intolerances that develop over time (rather than with a new food) are two more serious reasons for kitties to vomit. If your kitty is older, she may have inflammatory bowel disease.

Cat Scratch Fever

The *Bartonella* bacteria is the cause of cat scratch fever, a disease that is transmitted to humans through cat scratches and bites or contact with cat saliva on broken skin or the white of the eye. Of course, the cat must be infected with *Bartonella* bacteria to pass on the disease, which is also known as cat scratch disease.

In an infected person, lymph nodes near the site of the bite or scratch will swell within about two or three weeks following exposure. Other symptoms may include a bump or blister near the site of the bite or scratch, fatigue, fever, headache, and overall discomfort. Less common symptoms include draining lymph nodes, an enlarged spleen, loss of appetite, sore throat, and weight loss.

Cat scratch disease often goes undiagnosed, although the *bartonella heselae* IFA test is accurate in diagnosing the disease. Mild cases usually clear up on their own, but severe cases are usually treated with antibiotics. People who are immune-compromised will certainly need antibiotic treatment.

It's important to call your doctor if you have enlarged lymph nodes and have been exposed to a cat. Avoiding scratches and bites is certainly helped by learning to play properly with your cat. And remember that not every cat carries this disease. As with most illnesses, indoor-only cats are far less likely to be carriers.

And many other illnesses can cause your cat to vomit, including pancreatitis, infectious diseases, and hiatal hernias.

If your cat vomits more often than once a month or is showing other symptoms along with the vomiting, such as weight loss or lack of appetite, take your kitty to your veterinarian. The diagnosis can be tricky because vomiting is so common in cats and has a multitude of causes. The important thing to remember is that it's abnormal and should be checked out.

Hip Dysplasia

Hip dysplasia is a disease of the hip and joint. The hip is a ball and socket joint; the ball, or head, is at the top of the femur (the thighbone). The ball fits into the hip socket (the acetabulum), which is a depression in the pelvis. In a normal joint, the ball and socket fit closely together. In a cat with hip dysplasia, the socket is abnormally shallow or inflamed and the ball joint does not fit properly within it.

The large muscles of the hip and pelvis hold the ball and socket in place and help it move normally. No such luck in a cat with hip dysplasia; the abnormal socket enables the ball to move in and out of the joint rather than be held in place. This dislocation of the joint is called a *subluxation*. Hip dysplasia is painful, and some cats will show outward signs of that pain—although most will not. The condition also causes excessive wear and tear on the joint.

Veterinarians don't see a significant number of cats with hip dysplasia, but it's probably underdiagnosed. This is a more noticeable problem in dogs; because cats are small animals, the ones with hip dysplasia may not show outward signs that we recognize. A limping or stilted gait is extremely difficult to see in a cat. Hip dysplasia in cats is most commonly seen in the larger breeds, such as Persians, Maine Coon Cats, Norwegian Forest Cats, Devon Rex, and possibly Bengals. Hip dysplasia is not obvious at birth but develops as a kitten grows.

Because only a small number of clinical cases of hip dysplasia are reported, we're not really sure how prevalent it is. One study reported a 6.6 percent prevalence of hip dysplasia in a hospital population of cats and also found no statistical difference in the prevalence of hip dysplasia between domestic shorthair and pedigreed cats, and no difference between neutered and unneutered cats.

We do know that, as in dogs, hip dysplasia is inherited. It's a polygenetic trait, which means more than one gene is involved. In addition, either both parents must have it or must be carriers of the gene. Familial genetics probably help explain why, for example, Maine Coon Cats as a breed are reported as having a hip dysplasia prevalence of 18 percent, which is rather high for cats. Hip dysplasia is not obvious at birth; it is seen developing as the kitten grows.

Usually, treatment is aimed at protecting the joints using supplements such as glucosamine and chondroitin, and alleviating pain and the arthritis that inevitably develops in dysplastic joints. Total hip replacement has been done in cats, though not in large enough numbers to determine its benefit.

Spinal Problems

Most problems with the spine in cats occur as the result of some kind of trauma, such as a fall, an attack by a dog, or being hit by a car. The tail is part of a cat's spine, and unfortunately, trauma to the tail is not uncommon. Most often, the tail is caught or trapped while the cat is moving, damaging the tail at the point where it attaches to the body; this results in fractures or dislocation in that area. This kind of injury can lead to loss of the use of the tail, and in some instances, loss of feeling in the bladder and bowels. When this happens, the cat becomes incontinent.

Disk disease does occur in cats, though in much lower numbers than in dogs. More common is spinal osteopathy, which is arthritic changes in the spine. In cats with this disease, there is extra bone production in the spine, especially at the lumbosacral area where the back attaches to the pelvis. This problem is usually found in geriatric cats. In all cases of spinal disease, pain should be managed with the supervision of your veterinarian.

Hypertension

Quite simply, hypertension is high blood pressure. Sometimes the first (and only) sign is a cat who begins vocalizing more than usual. Most cats suffer secondary hypertension, which means the high blood pressure is due to another underlying disease. Often it's kidney disease or a tumor on the thyroid gland that is constricting the blood vessels and causing the blood pressure to rise. As in people, hypertension often affects other organs, such as the heart, kidney, nervous system, and eyes.

Your veterinarian can measure your cat's blood pressure using a special cuff made just for cats. If hypertension is suspected but your veterinary clinic doesn't have a feline blood pressure cuff, ask for a referral to a veterinary clinic that has one. Blood pressure over 150 mm is suspect in a calm patient.

Veterinarians recommend taking a blood pressure reading in all cats with kidney and thyroid disease, repeating the test if there is any question of a borderline value, and monitoring any changes.

The most common blood pressure medications used for cats are the same ones used for humans: ACE inhibitors and calcium channel blockers. There are several drugs in each class, and some are more effective than others. The choice of medication is largely dictated by what other underlying health problem the cat has.

Hypertrophic Cardiomyopathy

Hypertrophic cardiomyopathy (HCM) is the most common heart disease found in cats. In a cat with HCM, the heart muscle becomes thick and inelastic in some spots. As a result, it cannot expand and contract as it should, and the ability to circulate blood properly is affected.

Generally it's the left ventricle that's affected, and this often leads to elevated blood pressure in the upper chambers of the heart. This can cause a backward flow of blood. The cat will then have difficulty breathing, and the heart may fail. Sometimes, the poor circulation causes blood clots to lodge in the cat's rear legs, causing paralysis. Sometimes, the disease causes sudden death.

If the disease is diagnosed early, with medication and a low-salt diet many cats can live at least a few years. Some cats even live out a normal life span. But most do not. In fact, HCM may be the most common cause of death among indoor middle-aged cats.

HCM probably has a genetic component, but it's not always inherited. Some breeds are more susceptible to it than others. These include Maine Coon Cats, Ragdolls, British Shorthairs, American Shorthairs, and Devon Rexes. The disease tends to affect cats ages 1 to 5, but it has been detected in kittens and in cats as old as 10. The Winn Feline Foundation's Ricky Fund is supporting research into this disease.

Hyperesthesia

Hyperesthesia syndrome is an interesting disease that is difficult to treat. Affected cats will twitch the tail and/or back frequently and almost involuntarily. They will turn and bite or lick at their back or base of their tail, sometimes frantically. They may do this type of behavior and then race off across the room, stop, and repeat the same process. The biting may also be directed at others in the household. The pupils are often dilated.

Veterinarians don't know if this is a neurological, orthopedic, behavior, or dermatologic problem in cats. It's possibly a combination of several of these causes. There also seems to be a genetic component, since the problem is seen more often in Siamese, Burmese, Himalayan, and Abyssinian cats. Your veterinarian will need to do a thorough diagnostic workup to determine what is going on.

Any specific underlying problems will have to be addressed in treatment: pain medication for orthopedic problems; antiseizure medication for neurological disease; corticosteroids for skin disorders; and behavior medications combined with environmental enrichment for any behavioral triggers. Some veterinarians choose acupuncture as another form of therapy.

Idiopathic Peripheral Vestibular Disease

The vestibular apparatus is part of the inner ear and consists of three fluid-filled loops oriented in three different planes. As the cat moves his head, the fluid moves and stimulates nerve endings that tell him where he is in space, so that he can balance and right himself with respect to his environment. Problems with the vestibular apparatus cause dizziness, loss of balance, and disorientation.

For reasons that we don't really understand (and that's what *idiopathic* means), some cats suddenly develop signs of vestibular disease. Suggested causes include inflammation of the nerve endings, abnormal drainage of the fluid in the vestibular system, or a change in the consistency of the fluid. Whatever the cause, the results can be very distressing for both the cat and you.

Affected cats are usually older, typically 12 to 13 years of age, and there may be a higher incidence in late summer or fall. Typically the cat is unable to stand and falls repeatedly, is uncoordinated, and if he's still able to stand may circle or stagger to one side rather than move straight. If he falls, he may roll and flop on the ground. The head is tilted to one side (unless the vestibular system is affected on both sides), while the eyes move rapidly from one side to the other (more rapidly in one direction—this is called nystagmus), or sometimes up and down. The cat will feel as if he has a really, really bad case of sea sickness and may vomit and be uninterested in eating or drinking. Some cats get very vocal about expressing their distress.

While the symptoms can be extremely frightening and distressing for both cat and owner, the good news is that with good nursing the cat will recover fully, usually within two to six weeks. Sadly, many owners and some veterinarians miss the diagnosis and assume the cat has incurable neurological disease and opt for euthanasia.

While a cause can be sought for the vestibular diseases and a veterinarian should examine the cat to rule out other problems—for example, middle or inner ear infections, thiamine deficiency, metronidazole toxicity, head trauma, polyps, cancer in the middle ear—most of the time the condition can be diagnosed with reasonable certainty without extensive testing. And this is a wonderful diagnosis, because full recovery can be expected.

The cat should be placed in a well-padded bed; the bottom of a molded cat carrier works well. Intravenous or subcutaneous fluids can be helpful during the acute phase, because it is hard to get the cat to drink water and stay hydrated. Medication for nausea may be helpful too, and there are injectable medications so you don't have to pill a cat who likely won't be very cooperative.

Symptoms resolve gradually, but usually the cat shows marked improvement in two or three days. Be careful to restrict the cat's environment as he recovers so that he doesn't fall down stairs or off a high perch. It can take several weeks before the head tilt disappears and full mobility returns, but recovery should be complete.

Feline Infectious Peritonitis

A diagnosis of feline infectious peritonitis (FIP) is one of the worst things a cat owner can hear, because FIP is a complex and fatal disease. Its pathogenesis remains unclear and it may be difficult to diagnose, as well.

FIP is caused by feline enteric coronavirus, a common infection in both wild and domestic cats. Many cats with the coronavirus show no signs, but those who do generally have a mild respiratory illness that clears up on its own. But somehow, in less than 1 percent of cats who have been exposed to one of the many strains and species of the coronavirus, it mutates into the lethal FIP virus. The mutated virus seems to have an increased ability to infect immune cells; some cats may have a genetic predisposition for the mutated virus to attach and infect these immune cells. It is believed that crowding with other cats and stress can also predispose a cat to mutation and infection. It's also speculated that genetics play a role in which cats develop this disease.

Cats, like humans, have two main types of immune responses: humoral immunity, which involves producing antibodies; and cell-mediated immunity, which involves producing cells that kill pathogens in the body. Healthy cats with feline coronavirus will have normal elimination of the viral infection by both mechanisms. Cats with FIP will have a strong humoral immune response and an inadequate cell-mediated response. Cells called monocytes and macrophages, which are supposed to attack invaders, instead become infected. These infected cells migrate from blood vessels into areas around the blood vessels, causing local inflammatory responses. Damage to the blood vessels from this inflammation can lead to vascular permeability (blood vessel leakage). This causes fluid to build up in body cavities, which is known as the wet form of FIP. Or it can cause the immune system to form masses of immune cells in an attempt to "wall off" the infection. These masses (called *granulomas*) may collect in the organs, leading to the dry form of FIP.

The symptoms can vary, depending on the form and which organ system is affected. The most common symptoms are weight loss, fever, and loss of appetite. The fever often comes and goes and is not responsive to antibiotics.

It is easier to diagnose the wet form of the disease. Cats with the wet form will develop a straw-colored, thick or viscous fluid in the abdominal or chest cavity. If it's in the abdomen, the belly will get large while the rest of the body gets thinner from weight loss. The cat may have breathing difficulties due to fluid in the chest.

The dry form is more difficult to diagnose. There may be lymph node enlargement, kidney failure, liver involvement, uveitis (inflammation anywhere in the pigmented inside the lining of the eye), or neurological changes such as seizures or paralysis.

There is no known effective cure at this time. Most treatment is aimed at relieving the symptoms and making the cat more comfortable. Corticosteroids have been used to slow disease progression. Human and feline interferon have also been used to try to inhibit feline coronavirus replication. Studies have not proven their effectiveness. Currently, a new drug called polyprenyl, an immune stimulant, is being studied and may have some promise in the future as a treatment for FIP.

Feline Leukemia Virus

Feline leukemia virus (FeLV) is a retrovirus that is found worldwide. FeLV is associated with more cat diseases than any other infectious agent. The virus can be immunosuppressive, possibly making the cat susceptible to other infections or diseases as a result. The virus is the most important cause of cancer in cats. It can also cause degenerative conditions such as a severe non-regenerative anemia.

The virus is transmitted from cat to cat by infected saliva. This can mean cat bites, but sharing food and water bowls, and mutual grooming, can also transmit it. Kittens can acquire it from their mother before they are born, or from mama's milk.

Many cats can be infected with FeLV and be asymptomatic. Cats who are especially at risk are male cats who fight, those who go outdoors, and cats who have contact with other cats of unknown status. Veterinarians recommend retrovirus testing for all cats—even indoor cats—to know their status. Any positive tests should also be followed by retesting to confirm the positive result.

There is no specific treatment for FeLV infection. Your veterinarian will treat any underlying diseases and recommend good nutrition, decreased stress, and keeping the cat indoors. There are some therapies that have been tried experimentally. One is interferon and another newer one is lymphocyte T cell immunomodulator (LCTI). So far, no studies have confirmed their effectiveness.

Osteoarthritis

Osteoarthritis is a degenerative joint disease—basically the same arthritis we humans get. Amazing creatures that they are, cats compensate for orthopedic diseases, including this one. What this means is that it's tough to diagnose osteoarthritis in the cat, because the signs may be very subtle. Obviously, mobility and activity are affected by osteoarthritis, just as they are in people, and sometimes changes in these factors may be the only signs.

The shoulders, elbows, hips, and tarsal joints seem to be the most common areas in which cats are affected. Arthritis often appears in more than one joint. It may result in poor grooming because of an inability to comfortably reach certain parts of the body. It may also result in inappropriate elimination because of impaired mobility.

Osteoarthritis is most common in middle-aged and older kitties, just as it affects people in the same age groups. And, as it is in humans, arthritis in cats is both progressive and incurable.

Unfortunately, there aren't many therapeutic options. In dogs and in humans, the pain and inflammation of arthritis can be treated with non-steroidal anti-inflammatory drugs (NSAIDs). But those aren't an option for cats, who do not easily tolerate this class of drugs, since NSAIDs can only be used with extreme caution under the close supervision of a veterinarian.

The safest and most common options for cats, as of this writing, are therapeutic nutrition (also sometimes known as nutraceuticals) and rehabilitation therapy (which is discussed in chapter 9). Nutraceuticals may include glucosamine, chondroitin, and the fatty acids found in fish oils. These can be given as supplements, and are also part of some special veterinary diets formulated for cats with osteoarthritis.

I'd like to note here that nutraceuticals are not regulated by the Food and Drug Administration, although they do fall under the laws that regulate dietary supplements. The result is that you cannot always rely on the potency of the supplement you are buying. For example, if you buy a glucosamine and chondroitin supplement, while the amount of supplement may be accurate, the effectiveness of it is not guaranteed. Your veterinarian can suggest specific brands.

Cancer

We seem to hear more about cancer all the time. Perhaps it's because we know more about it now, or perhaps it's because it really is more prevalent than it used to be. Cats develop cancer less frequently than dogs, yet it causes almost 33 percent of feline deaths. Generally, cancer appears when the cat is older than 7 or 8 years of age. And, just as in people, there are many different types of cancer with different prognoses and outcomes.

Any organ or tissue may develop cancer. It may then spread to local lymph nodes, lungs, and other organs. There are more than one

Vaccine-Associated Sarcoma

Cats are genetically susceptible to developing gene mutations, which transition into sarcoma sites of chronic inflammation. That's what happens with vaccine-associated sarcomas.

The inflammatory response at vaccine sites has been presumed to be generated by inflammatory cells that react to the aluminum hydroxide adjuvant in some vaccines—notably those for rabies and feline leukemia. (An adjuvant is a pharmacological agent added to a vaccine to increase its effect. In other words, it boosts the action of the vaccine.)

However, researchers are no longer sure this is the case. These vaccines do cause some kind of inflammation at the vaccination site, leading to cancer in anywhere from 1 in 1,000 to 1 in 10,000 cats, but the adjuvant may not be the cause of the inflammation. Nonetheless, vaccine manufacturers have developed a recombinant DNA rabies vaccine that avoids the problem, and many veterinarians prefer to use this product.

hundred types of cancer that affect cats. The most common, in no particular order, are:

- Lymphoma, which most often attacks the intestines and bone marrow but may appear anywhere

- Skin tumors, including squamous cell carcinoma, basal cell carcinoma, and mast cell tumors

- Squamous cell carcinoma of the oral cavity and other head and neck tumors

- Mammary (breast) cancer

- Soft tissue sarcomas and carcinomas, including vaccine-associated sarcoma and others

Lymphoma is treated with chemotherapy, which can be successful. Happily, cats are amazing! They generally handle chemotherapy quite well and do not lose their fur. Squamous cell carcinoma and other carcinomas are treated with combination therapy using surgery, radiation therapy, and chemotherapy.

White cats exposed to the sun develop skin cancer, just as people do. Cats who live with smokers are at risk for developing lung disease and intestinal lymphoma; the carcinogens in the smoke cling to their fur, and the cats ingest it when they groom.

While there are many types of cancers that can be treated successfully and survival times have been greatly prolonged, the time comes when you must make a decision about continuing treatment. In other words, when is enough enough? Decisions about cats with cancer are very personal. They depend on the family's attachment to their kitty, their financial ability, treatment logistics, and how well the cat tolerates treatment. Overall, if the quality of life for the cat can be maintained with therapy, then the therapy is justified.

When a cat on therapy is declining, with signs such as pain, weight loss, loss of appetite, lethargy, nausea, vomiting, diarrhea, or difficulty breathing, then you must think about changing or discontinuing a therapy that is clearly not working. The key to any decision is quality of life. The cat has had enough when quality of life has diminished. The family must make the final call and allow the gift of euthanasia for their beloved cat when quality of life is lost.

Many cat lovers want their cat to die "naturally," with no intervention. However, that may be very difficult for the cat. In nature, a disabled cat would fail to catch food or be killed by predators. There is nothing natural about a cat who lingers and suffers at home.

This is a difficult situation. But you are your cat's protector. Euthanasia can provide a peaceful and painless passing. It will be more painful for you, but it is the final gift you can give a beloved kitty.

CHAPTER 9

EMERGENCIES AND SURGERY

C ats aren't immune from accidents, and falls can be darned dangerous. Here's another myth I can dispel: Cats do not always land on their feet! Their righting mechanism that enables them to turn in midair and be oriented to the ground certainly is a remarkable thing. A small fluid-filled organ inside the cat's ear is what enables her to right herself during a fall. The fluid shifts when the cat moves, so she always knows her body position. Also, cats have no collarbone, and the feline backbone has more mobility than is found in many animals. This skeletal structure helps cats absorb the impact of a fall.

But the righting mechanism doesn't work in a very short fall because cats don't have enough time to turn. And in a very long fall, landing on their feet will not keep them safe from injury because those tiny feet cannot take the impact of landing from a great height. If your cat falls out a window or off a high ledge or tree branch, she will likely break bones or even her neck. The farther she falls, the more bones she's likely to break. Balconies can be another source of trouble for kitty if she takes a flying leap off one or accidentally falls. Even if your cat falls a short distance, she can be injured.

Falls are one of the top reasons why cats end up in the emergency veterinary hospital. Car accidents are another. Cats can't read street signs. If your cat is allowed to roam outside, you're greatly increasing the likelihood that she'll end up in the hospital.

Poison!

Cats can be poisoned by any number of things that are found around the house, so it's up to you to be aware of what is dangerous and keep poisonous substances locked away from kitty. Also remember that anything that gets on a cat's coat will end up in her stomach when she grooms. So kitty can be poisoned by things she hasn't actually eaten. The ASPCA's Animal Poison Control Center (www.aspca.org/pet-care/poison-control/) has an extensive list of poisonous plants and other types of things that are poisonous to cats, as well as advice about what to do if your cat gets into any of them. (The specific link for plants that are poisonous and those that are not is www.aspca.org/pet-care/poison-control/plants.)

You'd be surprised how many plants are poisonous to cats. Lilies are especially toxic; even a small nibble of any part of a lily can cause kidney failure in a cat. Flowering plants outdoors may also be toxic to cats—not just your own plants but your neighbors' plants as well. Outdoor hazards are many, including cars and other animals, but most people don't consider the combo of curious kitty and lethal plant.

Among the most common poisonous substances are human medicines. Those that are quite safe for us humans can spell death for the cat. Aspirin and acetaminophen (Tylenol), which are toxic to cats, are two examples. I know it can be tempting to try to treat a sick cat with things you have in the medicine cabinet, especially when money is tight. But this just isn't safe and the cost can be your cat's health or even her life. You need to talk to your cat's veterinarian before you medicate your cat.

You'll need to be careful with medications prescribed for your cat, as well. Make sure you understand exactly when and how they are to be given. If you're not sure, don't hesitate to call your veterinarian and ask for clarification.

Be very careful with people food, too. It's okay to slip the cat a bit of cooked meat, but some foods can be lethal to cats and other pets. Onions, chocolate, grapes, raisins, avocado, and anything containing the artificial sweetener xylitol can be deadly. Cats tend to prefer the flavor of anything salty, so keep this in mind when you're setting out food that might harm your cat.

Of course, household cleaners need to be kept out of reach of your cat, just as you would keep a child from investigating and tasting them. Any heavy metals, such as lead, zinc, and mercury, must also be safely locked up. Lead paint was once a particularly common problem for children as well as for pets. Fortunately, most households no longer shed lead paint chips. Still, it pays to be careful, especially in older buildings. If you're sanding a surface painted with a lead-based paint, cats may ingest the lead just by walking across the floor and then grooming.

Cats purr at the same frequency as an idling diesel engine—about twenty-six cycles per second.

If you, or your neighbor, apply garden products such as fertilizers and insecticides to your lawn and kitty walks across the lawn, she will ingest these poisons when she grooms herself. Chemical spills are another problem. Antifreeze is especially problematic. Pets seem to be attracted to it and will lick any spills.

Rat and mouse poisons will kill your cat. Exactly what is meant to attract mice and rats to the poison will also attract kitty.

Flea and tick products made for dogs are often toxic to cats. Talk to your veterinarian when selecting a flea and tick product.

Medical Emergencies

It's important that you know what is normal for your own cat, including the color of her tongue and gums, her heart rate and weight, the way she looks, what and when she eats, and her behavior. And if you have a pedigreed cat, you have to know what's normal for that breed.

Cats mask their clinical signs so by the time you know the cat is sick, the cat is *very* sick. That's why it's so important to notice the little deviations from normal behavior. Any dramatic change in water consumption, for example, can be a tip-off to something serious.

Cats hide their illnesses because in the wild they are both predator and prey. If they appear vulnerable, a predator would eat them, so they have to appear strong.

The following are all reasons to get your cat to the veterinarian immediately. If it's after hours, go to an emergency clinic. There's no time to lose!

- Urinary tract blockages are not uncommon in male cats. You may see your cat straining to eliminate in the litter box, but even if you don't, a cat who is having trouble urinating makes a kind of meow that is different from any other feline vocalization—a kind of wail.

- Cats in most stages of heart disease don't show any obvious sign until there's a crisis. A cat in congestive heart failure will lie quietly and breathe rapidly and heavily.

- In some cats with types of heart disease, the chambers of the heart don't completely empty. A blood clot may form in the heart and sit like a time bomb. If a piece of the clot breaks off, it eventually lodges in a blood vessel, often in the rear leg. If your cat has a sudden rear leg problem, or cold rear legs, it's a cardiac emergency.

- Gastrointestinal obstructions occur when the cat swallows a foreign object or string. Regurgitating, where the food comes up undigested, can be a sign of obstruction.

- String or thread can also end up wrapped around the base of the cat's tongue. The cat won't eat, and may paw at her mouth.

- If your cat has any abdominal pain, she will look as if she's cramping up, or she may yelp when you pick her up. Seek emergency care. Since cats generally don't show their pain, if you can see it, the problem is quite serious.

- If the cat has any difficulty breathing, seek emergency care. Snuffling, congestion, and snoring are not emergencies (although they should be checked out). An emergency is increased effort to breathe or rapid breathing that is not caused by purring.

- If the cat is not eating and is not sociable, it's likely an emergency.

- Injured and sick cats hide. If you come home and can't find your cat, you may have an emergency. In addition, indoor cats will sometimes try to find their way outdoors to look for a place to die, even if they've never been outdoors before.

Nursing Your Sick Kitty

If your cat has an illness, you'll have to be her nurse. There's a lot you can do to help kitty recover. The first and most important thing is to make sure she takes all her medication. When you come home from the veterinarian's office, make sure you have all her medicines and understand exactly how much she is to take, how often, and for how many days. If you have any questions at all, or if your cat seems to be having a negative reaction to the medications, call your veterinarian right away.

When you're giving a cat any medication, it's important to be quick and calm about it. But that doesn't mean holding the cat down and trying to overpower her. Cats certainly can't be negatively motivated. Each cat has her own personality and you have to let that personality guide you when you are medicating her.

If your cat is the type who allows you to do pretty much anything to her, you're going to have a much easier time. Just remember not to hold your cat too tightly. Less cooperative cats will need to be restrained and medicated quickly. The goal is not to get the cat so upset that she becomes defensive and won't let you near her again with medication. Once you cross that line, it's unlikely you'll be able to go back. This is another time when learning to read your cat's body language is going to come in very handy.

Cats also get defensive when they have had enough handling. If your cat is feeling attacked, she will take it out on the person nearest to her, even if she loves that person. If you feel your cat has progressed to that stage, just pack it in. Your goal is to keep the cat calm, so just back off and medicate her a little later, when you've both calmed down.

Giving a Cat a Pill

The reason there are so many jokes about pilling cats is because, by and large, cats find ways to outsmart us in this area. These same creatures who keep swallowing string seem quite capable of finding ways not to swallow medication. Cats are also fussy about food, so while sticking a pill in some liverwurst will trick almost any dog, cats eat rather delicately and your kitty is far less likely to be fooled.

How can you possibly teach a cat to accept a pill? Start with a treat. Sit in front of the cat, show her the treat, touch her mouth, and use your fingers to stick in the treat. Do this quickly with several treats, then stick in the pill. Quickly follow up with another treat.

To help the pill go down, coat it with a thin coating of cream cheese or butter so the cat doesn't get the bitter taste of the pill itself. You want the coating to be tasty and slippery enough that she will swallow it. And always follow up with a treat to make sure your cat swallows the pill. This is important, because if it gets stuck in her throat it can lead to esophageal damage.

There are commercial products that are meant to be sticky and tasty so you can conceal a pill inside. Some cats love them—but not all. They're certainly worth trying. If your cat loves them, problem solved.

As for me and my cat, I was thrilled at the thought of hiding the pill in a special treat designed for that purpose. I tucked the tiny pill into the treat, put it down for my cat to find, and she swallowed it. Hooray! Then it was time for her second dose. I did the same thing. I again left her alone with it. When I returned to the room, I thought she had once again consumed the pill. Then I walked over and looked closely. The treat was gone but the pill itself was neatly broken in half and left in the exact spot where I had placed the special treat. I can take a hint.

The moral of this story is that you have to watch the cat very carefully when you pill her with a treat to make sure she eats the whole thing. And sometimes you have to pill a cat the old-fashioned way.

You'll have to pill her quickly, before she can escape, so get out everything you need before you get the cat. It's easiest if you have someone to help you by holding kitty still on a slippery surface, like the top of your washing machine, so she can't escape as easily. Have someone else hold her from behind her, with their hands on her front elbows, cradling her.

If there's no help available, get her into the corner of a small room, get down to her level and use the corner to keep her in place. You can also wrap a towel around her like a burrito so no one will be inadvertently bitten or scratched in the process.

With the pill in your right hand (left if you're left-handed), open her mouth with your left hand, using your middle finger to brace it open for a second. Put the pill in the center of her tongue, use your finger to slide it back, then quickly close her mouth and hold it closed for a second while you blow gently in her nose or massage her throat to encourage her to swallow. When you see her swallow, either give her some water in a syringe that you can get from your veterinarian or a little wet food in a dish to make sure that the pill isn't stuck in her throat. You may even want to flavor the water with some tuna juice (the liquid from canned tuna mixed in water) to make it more enticing for kitty to swallow.

Have a favorite treat ready so that she associates the experience with something pleasant. You can also give her a small amount of a favored food right after pilling. Do *not* pill her at mealtime, however, or she will associate food with something she doesn't like and may stop eating. Don't remove her from the litter box to pill her, either, or you'll create a litter box problem that you certainly don't want.

Here's a link to an excellent video on various ways of pilling a cat, from Cornell University's Feline Health Center: partnersah.vet.cornell.edu/Cat-Pilling/Entire-Video.

Be sure to cuddle and play with the cat at different times of the day so she doesn't begin to associate attention from you with medication. You want to keep your bond intact.

You may have better luck with liquid medication or a transdermal patch. This will depend on your cat, the medication, and your veterinarian.

Giving Liquid Medication

Some cats are more amenable to liquid medication. Have your veterinarian show you the techniques for administering liquid medication using an eyedropper or a syringe without the needle. But be realistic. Some cats aren't awfully happy with liquid medicine and will spit it out in an interesting spray that will redecorate your walls. And don't fight with your cat, because it won't help the relationship.

Have the syringe prepared and a treat ready. Shake the bottle and draw up the prescribed amount of medicine. You will be best served if you have someone to help you hold kitty while you medicate her. If you have no one to help, hold kitty in your left arm if you're right-handed (or vice versa) and wrap her in a towel as if it were a shawl for safety's sake.

Open her mouth by tilting her head back a bit so her mouth opens. Quickly place the tip of the syringe in the side of kitty's mouth and

---

No People Pills

Don't ever give your cat medication made for people, unless you are specifically directed by your veterinarian to use a specific over-the-counter medication in a specific dose. The consequences can be lethal. Remember, always consult your veterinarian—even if you know someone who has given their cat medications for people. Every cat is different. Over-the-counter medications for people could cost your cat her life.

depress the plunger smoothly and quickly until she's gotten part of the medication. While she's swallowing that, give her more of the medication. You may be able to give the entire dose at once if it's small; otherwise you'll have to repeat the steps until kitty has been given the entire dose.

If you're unsure if she's swallowed all of it, hold kitty's mouth closed and gently blow in her nose to get her to swallow, and then reward her with a treat. Be sure to wipe any sticky medicine off kitty's mouth using a damp towel or paper towel, rinse the syringe, and properly store the medication until the next dose is due.

Giving Injections

Believe it or not, often it's easier to inject medication than to give a cat a pill or liquid medication. All too often owners have discovered a pile of pills the cat has hidden after the owner thinks she has swallowed them. Be sure to have your veterinarian show you how to give injections, and make sure you understand whether they go under the skin or into the muscle.

If your cat is fairly easy to handle, put her in a situation where she's curious or distracted, so it takes her mind off what you're doing. Perhaps put her up on a table or the top of her cat tree. While she's considering her options, you can quickly inject the medication.

It's very handy to remember to pet the skin, shake it, make a noise somewhere else as a distraction, and then inject the medication. This is when standing the cat at the edge of the table and letting her look down is handy because you can sneak the injection in. Or you can hold the cat up so she thinks she's climbing the wall. You just want to distract her enough to do what you have to do. When you're done, let her play or have a treat.

More Nursing Tips

You'll need to encourage your sick kitty to eat, as well as keep her clean and warm while she's recovering. Be sure she has a comfortable, warm bed in an area where she likes to sleep. It should have a nice pad and be cozy and snuggly. Cats love to hide in small places and sleep, so a fuzzy, washable bed will probably be to kitty's liking. She may prefer to be on your bed with you. Help her get there if she needs assistance.

Spend time with her, even if you just sit in the room and read while she naps. Or talk quietly to her and gently pet her so she knows she's not alone and that she's loved. If she has a special toy that she might find comforting, put it near her. If she indicates that she doesn't want to be touched, respect her wishes. Watch her body language.

Make sure your cat eats (unless your veterinarian has specifically said she should not). Offer her small meals throughout the day. Gently warm the food to make it more enticing. You can also put some tuna juice on her food to encourage her to eat.

Cats are masters at hiding illness. Often just a subtle change in behavior will be your only clue that kitty is sick.

Be sure she has access to fresh water. If she won't drink, try putting an ice cube up to her nose and mouth. Licking an ice cube can help to slowly rehydrate her. It's a good idea to let kittens play with ice cubes so they'll know what it is and enjoy it when you need to use it. If kitty doesn't like plain ice cubes, try putting tuna juice in the water before you freeze it.

Make sure your cat can get to her litter box. You may need to move it near her resting place. If she's having trouble getting in and out, try a plastic cafeteria tray with just a little bit of litter.

She may need help with keeping herself clean. You can buy special wipes made for pets to gently clean her. There are other pet wipes made especially for eyes and ears. Don't do more than she can tolerate at any given time.

Cats and Surgery

Cats tend to be pretty resilient when it comes to surgery. The one exception is fat cats. The extra fat on a small chest makes it harder for cats to breathe. Fat cats must be monitored very carefully in a referral hospital where there is an anesthesiologist or a special anesthesia technician on hand during surgical procedures. So keeping your cat in shape is not only important for her health but will also help her if she requires surgery.

The most common surgery for all cats is spaying or neutering. There are also several others that I will briefly explain.

Surgeries are often performed to remove foreign bodies. This is especially likely in kittens. Kittens seem to ingest an incredible assortment of things. Once a cat begins to swallow, she cannot pull or spit out the object, so she keeps swallowing. Commonly found inside these curious kitties are string, thread, cat toys that have been torn apart, dental floss, and even earplugs! One veterinary surgeon reports that when you see a tiny little spring inside a kitten on an X-ray, it is almost invariably the pop-up timer on an oven stuffer roaster chicken. It cannot be stressed too much or too often that you must keep all trash tightly sealed so your curious kitten won't have access to things that are tempting to swallow.

Other common surgeries are for broken limbs. This is not nearly as common with cats who are kept indoors. However, jumping from a balcony the cat can break limbs or even her jaw. Cats who are hit by cars will require surgery for everything from broken legs to pelvic fractures, ruptured bladder, jaw fractures, and even a broken tail that was caught under a rolling tire.

Perineal urethrostomy is performed to correct an obstruction in the urethra. The surgery creates an opening in the urethra to allow urine to flow. It may be necessary for a male cat whose urethra is blocked because of stones or scarring.

Oral tumors and other cancers, including intestinal cancers, require surgery. Ear tumors also require surgery. You can't always eliminate cancer with surgery, but sometimes if the surgeon cuts deeply enough, they can remove all of the cancerous tissue. Cats missing a limb or even up to half their jaw still do quite well.

Kittens sometimes have nasal pharyngeal polyps, which are growths that block the whole nasal pharynx, beginning in the middle ear and all the way down the eustachian tubes. This causes upper respiratory infections. Opening up the bony casing of the middle ear resolves the problem, and these kittens do quite well almost immediately after surgery.

Why You Should Spay or Neuter Your Cat

Spaying and neutering are very important—and not just to help prevent the serious overpopulation of cats. Spaying or neutering when your cat is young, before sexual maturity, will prevent not only behavior problems but some cancers as well. Your female cat won't get mammary cancer if she's spayed early enough, nor will she get pyometra, a life-threatening infection of the uterus. Male cats will not get testicular cancer, nor will they be likely to spray or to roam.

Only responsible, ethical breeders who are breeding and showing to improve a specific breed should have intact cats. And even these cats are spayed and neutered after their show and breeding days are over.

Unspayed females will require surgery if they develop pyometra, which is an infection in the uterus. This infection can be fatal—another reason to have your cat spayed so you never have to risk her life this way.

Megacolon is a bowel disorder in which the colon is enlarged because the nerves in the colon aren't functioning as they should. Symptoms include chronic constipation. The cat usually has a colectomy, which is surgical removal of most of the colon. A cat can live without a colon just fine. The little bit that's left after the surgery can stretch out and can start to block years later if you don't always keep on top of it. Be sure your cat goes to the veterinarian yearly, and if constipation is a problem, more frequent trips to the veterinarian are in order and kitty can be put on a veterinary diet.

Enucleation (removing the eye) is the surgical treatment for chronic eye problems, untreatable glaucoma, infection, or cancer, as well as eye trauma.

A leg or the tail may be amputated due to trauma or cancer; such cats do wonderfully well. A cruciate tear is a rupture of the ligament of the knee. While this type of injury is more often associated with large dogs, it can happen to cats as well. It can be treated nonsurgically by confinement for at least six weeks. It can also be treated surgically by stabilizing the femur on the tibia or putting implants in the knee joint. Your veterinarian may refer you to an orthopedic surgeon.

Hip dislocations are almost always caused by trauma. Head and neck excision, which is removing the head and neck of the femur bone and then closing up the surrounding muscle and fat layer, is the standard surgery for the cat with a hip dislocation. Many cats will form a false joint in the hip and do well.

Bile duct obstruction is caused by biliary carcinoma, a common form of liver cancer. It will require a surgical procedure called a cholecystojejunostomy, which is a bile duct bypass.

Portosystemic shunts are another reason for surgery. Commonly called liver shunt, this condition can be either acquired or hereditary, although most liver shunts are congenital. It is an abnormal development of the blood vessels that drain the gastrointestinal tract. When there is a portosystemic shunt, the liver is bypassed and therefore unable to do its job detoxifying the cat's system. This disease tends to show up before one year of age. It's potentially fatal and is painful to the kitty. Symptoms include central nervous system disorders, poor growth, lack of appetite, vomiting, diarrhea, tremors, and more. This is, unfortunately, fairly common in Yorkshire Terriers but not often discussed in cats. It's not common but it does occur. The shunt is surgically tied off and the cat is put on a special veterinary diet.

Pleural effusion is not a common cause of respiratory difficulty in cats, but it can occur. It usually happens in middle-aged to older cats. A type of fluid gathers in the chest cavity, making breathing difficult.

Cats Need Their Meow

A surgery called devocalizing (or debarking when done to dogs) is sometimes done to literally remove a cat's voice. Thankfully, this cruel and unnecessary surgery is not as common among cat owners as it is among dog owners—but even one is one too many. If you don't want a cat who "talks," choose one who is quiet. It's really that simple.

Cats need their voice. They talk for social reasons, and also to tell you that they hurt and when they need something.

Please pay attention to your kitty when she talks; is she well? Take her to her veterinarian to see if there's a problem. Excessive vocalization can be a sign of thyroid problems, high blood pressure, cognitive dysfunction or other health problems.

If she's healthy, remember to interact with her more. Many people enjoy discussing the day's events with their feline companion, and vocalization time can then become a give and take. If you truly want a little less conversation, increase your cat's training time, hide things around the house for kitty to find, and enrich her environment in other ways. It's important to keep her mind occupied so she's not bored and letting you know about it. And be sure to relax and enjoy your kitty's companionship every day.

Surgery is required to remove some of the fluid from the chest cavity. This is called a chest tap and may not require general anesthesia, depending on the cat. The chest tap will allow the cat to breathe more easily. Some of the fluid that's removed will be analyzed by the veterinarian to see if there are abnormal cells present.

Patent ductus arteriosus (PDA) is a congenital heart defect more commonly found in dogs, although cats do get it. PDA is an abnormal connection between the left and right ventricles of the heart that shunts blood between the pulmonary arteries and the cat's descending aorta. Within twenty-four hours of birth, the shunt is supposed to close. If it doesn't, the kitten has PDA. Surgery will tie off the shunt and allow the blood to flow as it should.

Anesthesia

Before surgery, every cat should have baseline blood work done to determine the cat's condition and if there are any underlying problems that the veterinarian should know about that might cause complications. Older cats—ages 8 or 9 or more—should also have a screening

X-ray and more extensive blood work. This will confirm that all organs are operating properly, that there are no parasites present, and that there is no underlying kidney disease, diabetes, hypoglycemia, anemia, or similar disease that must be considered during and after surgery. If the veterinarian is looking for a mass or a foreign body, the cat will need X-rays or an ultrasound to guide the surgery.

The last step before the actual anesthesia is an IV catheter inserted into a vein. This will enable the veterinarian to administer any drugs the cat may need.

Anesthesia itself starts with a drug to put the cat under. Every veterinarian has a different anesthesia protocol. If you take your cat to a major teaching hospital or referral hospital, there will probably be a veterinary anesthesiologist or anesthesiologist technician who will mix an anesthesia "cocktail" for your cat.

Usually, smaller animal hospitals offer fewer choices. Cats can be sensitive to a lot of medicines and often don't go under easily. Your veterinarian can make the best choice for your cat, but feel free to discuss the choices with the vet.

One of the more popular and common drugs used to induce unconsciousness in cats is propofol. After that is administered, an endotracheal tube is inserted in the cat's mouth and down the trachea to keep the airway open. Then another anesthetic will be used to keep the cat under during the procedure. Anesthesia is most often administered as a gas because it can be precisely controlled in this form. Sevoflurane is often preferred.

How quickly the cat begins to regain consciousness after the surgery varies with the cat, her age, and her condition. Some are groggy for awhile and some come right out of it.

Going Home

The average postoperative stay is two to three days. Some cats can go home the same day as the surgery, others will be required to stay for a week. In point of fact, there is no set time for hospital release.

The length of time a cat stays in the hospital after surgery is often dictated by the type of procedure that was performed and what kind of follow-up care is needed. Everyone does better at home, including people. If your veterinarian feels comfortable and you do as well, then the cat may go home sooner.

Make sure you carefully follow all postoperative instructions for your cat, including those for medications.

Critical Care

A veterinary critical care unit is very much like the intensive care unit at a human hospital. You might be surprised at the similarities, especially if you visit a major teaching or referral hospital with your cat (although I hope you never have to!).

The critical care unit is open twenty-four hours a day, seven days a week, and the animals who are there are constantly monitored. Veterinarians and technicians are now trained and certified in critical care.

A cat may need to be in a critical care unit because of respiratory problems, congestive heart failure, a blockage, or a major trauma such as being hit by a car.

Often owners wonder if they can or should visit their cat while she is in a critical care unit. There are pros and cons, of course, and often your choices are limited by the hospital's policy. But these visits are reassuring for the owners as well as the cats. It's important to be calm and positive when you are visiting your critical care patient. If the cat isn't eating in the hospital, bring kitty's favorite food from home. She may only eat from your hand. This is certainly the time to pamper her.

Rehabilitation Therapy

While it might seem unlikely, cats can and do receive rehabilitation therapy. Rehabilitation therapy is what we call physical therapy in human medicine. This is a veterinary specialty, and you will need a referral. You might ask about it if your cat is overweight, has arthritis, has sustained an injury, was in a car accident, or has had a surgical procedure.

Rehabilitation therapy always starts with an evaluation by the veterinarian at the rehabilitation practice. The vet will review any X-rays or

MRIs, and medical records such as surgical reports. Then, a general plan is established for each cat's individual therapeutic needs. This includes how many visits per week will be needed and when the cat's physical condition will be reevaluated by the veterinarian, as well as the veterinarian's goals for that specific case.

Depending upon the individual cat's needs, therapy may include walking on an underwater treadmill to strengthen the cat's muscles or for weight loss. The underwater treadmill enables the cat to have a cardiovascular workout without any weight bearing. This may be especially important for the postsurgical animal.

Swimming is another part of some treatments. The cat wears a life-jacket at the beginning, but some can progress to swimming without the jacket. Swimming is used to increase range of motion, strengthen muscles, and help a cat lose weight. It also increases endurance. Cats can also be put on a small surfboard in the pool to help with core strengthening and overall balance.

Robin Fenton

This cat in rehab is swimming at Stirling Impressions Animal Rehabilitation Center of New England.

Muscles can be stimulated using electrical impulses. The impulses cause the muscles to contract, which increases blood flow and speeds healing in an animal who is less able to contract a muscle due to injury or a degenerative disorder.

Other forms of rehabilitative therapy include walking up ramps (steep incline and decline walking), walking over a cavaletti rail (a low rail placed close to the floor), walking through appropriately small obstacle courses, and walking on uneven surfaces—all under close supervision. Sometimes toys are incorporated in the therapy so, for example, a cat will reach up and stretch for one. A wobble board is also used for balance and to encourage the cat to put weight on a limb. Sometimes a physioball is used. Those are the big balls used in human physical therapy. The cat is placed on her chest on the ball and rolls from side to side to help with core strength.

Other therapies used for cats include massage, stretching, and range-of-motion exercises.

With all these therapies, work with cats begins slowly. They must be desensitized to the noise and motion of the machines. And it's no secret that most cats don't enjoy being in water, so with something like the treadmill, they would start with a dry treadmill and then gradually add water to a higher and higher level. The cat gets a break when she wants a break, and everything is done on the cat's terms. You can't force a cat to do anything, but they usually enjoy the therapy sessions once they get used to it.

Therapy usually begins with two sessions a week. Each session is about half an hour. The number of weeks varies.

Cats are much more active at home following therapy. And that means their quality of life is vastly improved by rehabilitation therapy.

Owners are shown how to do follow-up therapy at home and are sent home with a plan for exercise. The exercises are simple things that the owner can do easily, such as having the cat walk on a bed or follow a treat up a ramp.

CHAPTER 10

POPULAR CAT BREEDS

Cats come in a variety of shapes and sizes, coat lengths and colors. Mother Nature's paintbrush is put to creative use when it comes to cats. Cats also come in a variety of breeds. While most people opt for a moggie, or cat of unknown heritage, there are those who prefer to have a cat of a certain size, coat, and personality. And there are those who have both a moggie and a pedigreed cat at home. Whatever you are looking for—and this includes lifestyle and activity level—there is a cat for everyone who wants one.

I don't have room to talk about every breed of cat in this book, but I will be looking at some of the more popular breeds—with a dash of the somewhat lesser-known to add a little spice to the mix. Not all cat breeds are recognized by every pedigreed cat registry, but to get an idea of most of the current breeds, have a look at the web sites of the two largest registries: the Cat Fanciers Association (CFA, www.cfainc. org) and The International Cat Association (TICA, www.tica.org). If you have your heart set on a pedigreed cat, you can expect to get certain characteristics of that specific breed—so be sure you know what you're getting into and if that breed is a good match for your lifestyle and personality.

Keep in mind that when you buy a cat with registration papers, you should be able to see the kittens and their mother. Be sure to ask about the socialization the kittens have received, as well as those all-important questions about health and temperament. As with all living creatures, cats can have genetic problems that are hereditary. Once you've chosen a breed and located a breeder, ask the breeder what they are doing to eliminate those problems from their breeding program. This will help you make a more informed decision.

Also ask about how they raise their kittens. You want a kitten who has been thoroughly socialized and not just trained for cat shows. You want a kitten who will be adaptable because he has been exposed to a variety of objects, people, and circumstances early on. This should include people of all shapes and sizes, car rides, and an opportunity to play with other cats in the home, and age-appropriate toys. The kitten should also be accustomed to having his nails clipped, his coat brushed, and his teeth cleaned, and all of it should seem perfectly normal.

If you're getting an adult cat, then you will be able to see for yourself the cat's temperament and personality, although you can expect some changes after your cat has settled into his new home. Your relationship will grow daily, and your cat's personality will blossom. Don't forget to check with breed rescue groups for an adult. Many pedigreed cats have lost their home through no fault of their own and are looking for the second chance you could provide.

Abyssinian

The Abyssinian is an active cat who is curious about everything. This is a cat who appears to want to "go shopping," since everything is so interesting and, to the cat, demands to be seen and explored.

This is one of the oldest known cat breeds. The name comes from the place from which the first ones where exported to Britain, but it's not necessarily the place where the breed first appeared. There aren't

---

Is a Pedigreed Cat Always a Purebred?

That sounds like a trick question, doesn't it? But the answer is no.

A pedigreed cat is a cat who belongs to a certain breed and is registered as such, with a traceable family lineage. The cat is registered with a recognized registry, such as CFA or TICA.

A purebred cat is one whose family tree contains only cats of the same breed, for as far back as records exist. But in many cat breeds, outcrossings (mating two cats of different breeds) were permitted in the past, and some breeds still permit outcrossing today. Outcrossings may be necessary to establish certain characteristics of the breed or to maintain the health of a breed. So a cat with a pedigree might not always be a purebred cat.

The typical Abyssinian is always busy, and moves with a natural grace.

any written records to substantiate their origins, so it's a bit of a mystery. In any case, the Aby was developed into the cat we see today by British breeders. The breed arrived in North America from Britain in the early 1900s.

When an Aby chooses to sit still, he bears a remarkable resemblance to a piece of fine porcelain sculpture. The coat is ticked (agouti ticking, where each hair shaft has four to six bands of alternating color), which makes it appear to shimmer. There is a semilonghaired Abyssinian called the Somali, who is identical in all ways except the length of the coat.

The Abyssinian is a medium-size cat. Males weigh between eight and ten pounds, while females are between six and seven pounds. They come in a variety of colors. These intelligent and loyal creatures aren't lap cats, so if that's what you want, you won't find it here. But you will find an amusing, intelligent, affectionate, active companion.

American Shorthair

Long-lived and easygoing with dogs and gentle children, the American Shorthair's history likely traces back to the cats on the *Mayflower* who were on board to hunt rats. Loving and dear, they were as prized for their sweet manner as they were for their hunting skills. One American Shorthair was offered for sale at the second annual cat show at Madison Square Garden in New York for the then-princely sum of $2,500. The year: 1896. In today's money that would be an astronomical sum.

This is one of the earliest registered breeds in the United States. They were originally called Domestic Shorthair, but that name is now used for shorthaired cats of unknown parentage. Male American Shorthairs weigh between eleven and fifteen pounds, while the females weigh between eight and twelve pounds. They are a medium-size cat of medium bone.

These cats are recognized in an astonishing eighty different colors. Long-lived, their life span can be between fifteen and twenty years. The American Shorthair is a playful but not demanding companion, with the males supposedly more easygoing than the females. Some are lap cats, while some aren't. They are adaptable pets for either a family or a senior.

Bengal

This breed is a cross between the Asian Leopard Cat and a domestic cat. It's one of the most popular breeds recognized by TICA but is not recognized by CFA because of its wild ancestry. The Asian Leopard Cat is not a domesticated feline, and how many generations removed a Bengal is from his wild ancestor will definitely influence his behavior.

A huge mistake made by many who buy these cats is thinking that they're gorgeous and look wild (which is true) but are absolutely no different from a domestic cat. Bengals are particularly intelligent and active, and some people who get them for their looks find they don't have the energy to keep up with such an active companion, nor are they always prepared for a cat who can usually outthink them. These cats will dismantle household objects like a professional mechanic, and you will tire of their games long before they will. Be certain that sort of activity level and intelligence fits into your lifestyle before bringing a Bengal home.

Birman

Believed to be from Burma, where they are considered sacred, these beautiful longhaired cats have a fascinating legend surrounding them.

The Bengal is the only domestic cat that can have rosette markings, like the markings on leopards, jaguars, and ocelots.

Yellow-eyed, longhaired white cats were once the guardians of the temple of Lao-Tsun. The temple's golden goddess had deep blue eyes. The head priest, Mun-Ha, had one of these cats as his companion. When the temple was attacked, Mun-Ha was killed, and his cat, Sinh, at the moment of Mun-Ha's death, put his feet on his master's feet and faced the goddess. Sinh's fur suddenly turned a golden hue and his eyes turned the same blue as the goddess's. Sinh's face, legs, and tail turned the color of the earth, but his paws, where they touched the priest, remained white as a symbol of purity. All of the other cats in the temple turned the same colors. The legend says that after seven days, Sinh died and took Mun-Ha's soul to paradise. A lovely tale.

These cats do, indeed, have white paws and are marked with white on the legs called laces.

Around 1919, a pair of cats was shipped from Burma to France. The male didn't survive the trip, but the female, who arrived pregnant, did, and that is all we know of the beginning of the Birman breed. The whole breed was built on this foundation. The French cat registry recognized them in 1925, but after World War II only two of these cats remained in Europe. Outcrossings (breeding with similar cats of another breed) were allowed to reestablish the breed.

Large and stocky, Birmans are beautiful and endearing. Their silky hair doesn't mat, but they shed copiously. The coat colors are pointed, rather like the Siamese. Birmans are playful, but they're also very gentle, sweet, charming, and often rather comical.

British Shorthair

If the British Shorthair looks familiar, with its plush coat and chubby cheeks, it's because this breed was Lewis Carroll's inspiration for the Cheshire Cat in *Alice in Wonderland.* It's likely that this is Britain's oldest cat breed and is certainly one of the first breeds to be shown at cat shows.

Early on in the breed's development (around 1914 to 1918), Persians were crossed with the domesticated cats the Romans had brought from Egypt when they invaded Great Britain. The resulting shorthaired cats went into British Shorthair breeding programs, and the longhaired cats went into Persian breeding programs. The shorthairs were known as the British Blue until other colors were introduced.

These are very sweet cats but not lap sitters; they prefer to just be near you. Nor do they appreciate being picked up and carried around. They're quite capable of transporting themselves. They're also more cautious than most cats, preferring to check out the situation before leaping off into the abyss. These are quiet companions, so don't expect a lot of chatter.

This is a medium to large, muscular feline with that familiar Cheshire Cat smile. Be sure to comb this cat daily to remove dead hair before it can mat. The cat weighs from nine to eighteen pounds, and the weight should be pure muscle, not fat. British Shorthairs have a healthy appetite, so you'll need to be aware of this when managing your cat's food intake.

Burmese

This breed dates back to the early 1930s, when a doctor in San Francisco owned a female cat given to him by a sailor who had just returned from Asia. This single cat, Wong Mau, is also the cat behind the European Burmese, a different breed. Wong Mau and her progeny were bred selectively to Siamese cats, and the Burmese breed was established.

Often called bricks wrapped in silk because of their weight in comparison to their delicate appearance, Burmese come in several colors to appeal to any eye. Their short coat requires very little in the way of grooming. These are intelligent cats who love children and will learn to get along with the family dog.

The kittens are quite lively, and as adults they are charming companions who are never far from their human family members. Males are generally sweeter than females, preferring to cuddle, while the female is in the middle of everything as a full participant until she relaxes on the nearest available lap. This is a medium-size, sturdy cat.

Chartreux

The smiling blue cat from France, with a robust body and small, dainty legs and feet, is an absolute charmer. The Chartreux has a "silent meow," but will speak up if there's something to complain about. When he does speak, the voice is a high, small squeak, which is rather amusing coming from such a robust body. Basically, it's rather like living with Marcel Marceau in a cat suit.

This is another breed whose origins are surrounded by legend. Allegedly, these cats lived with the Carthusian monks in France and may even have shared a bit of their Chartreuse liquor. They may also have been named for the Spanish wool of the same name, since it's alleged that their coat is wooly. (I think the coat on this double-coated breed looks and feels more like chenille and appears to shimmer.) The double coat requires grooming to get out dead hair. Cleaning their ears is also a good idea, since they can develop earwax—as many other cats do.

This is a natural breed who was mentioned as far back as the sixteenth century. The Chartreux's eyes are round and the color ranges from gold to copper. In some countries they are shown with the British Shorthair, but this is a different breed and is recognized as such in the United States and elsewhere.

The Chartreux learns quite quickly and will follow you around, respond to his name, play fetch, sit on cue, and do a variety of other behaviors.

The writer Colette, who wrote, among other things, *Gigi*, owned a Chartreux. She isn't alone. Other writers today are also Chartreux owners, including me.

Cornish Rex and Devon Rex

These are two separate breeds that look somewhat alike and are shown separately at cat shows. Rex cats are rather interesting to look at. They have very short hair and small, elegant bodies, and bear a striking resemblance to Egyptian statues.

The coat of the Cornish Rex is short and wavy and feels like that of a lamb. The back arches like that of a Greyhound. These cats are very affectionate and playful, usually into their senior years. They love to play fetch and will even use their paws to toss small objects. Like all cats, they shed, although their hair isn't usually as easily spread around as that of other cats.

The Devon Rex was first seen in Britain when a cat gave birth to one kitten with curly hair. Devon Rexes have large ears, a pixie face, and are utterly adorable, bright little friends. They are active, playful, and, like Superman, think they can "leap tall buildings in a single bound." Since their coat isn't particularly insulating, they tend to look for heat, so finding the cat anyplace warm isn't unusual. Snuggling with their owner is optimum for this medium-size cat.

Maine Coon Cat

Probably the largest of the domestic cats, Maine Coon Cats are a popular companion. Native to the United States, they are prized for their talents as mousers. These longhaired cats love both children and dogs, which tends to make them sought-after family pets. They come in a range of colors and patterns. Males can weight from thirteen to eighteen pounds, while females weigh in somewhere between nine and thirteen pounds. They *look* large.

The official cat of the state of Maine, this is one of the oldest established breeds in North America. One of the myths surrounding them is that they were developed from a mating between a cat and a raccoon. This rather bizarre thought is nothing more than a flight of fancy.

Maine Coons like to be near their family members, enjoy playing games of fetch, and never seem to outgrow their kittenhood.

Norwegian Forest Cat

The Norwegian Forest Cat's roots are said to go back to the days when they explored the world with the Vikings. The cats protected the stores of grain both on land and at sea. Some of the cats were believed to have been left behind in North America.

They developed in harsh climates, and their spectacular water-resistant coat helps them withstand the weather. The coat is rich and warm in winter, and the undercoat sheds in summer, enabling these cats to be more comfortable in warmer weather. The coat comes in a wide range of colors, and for a longhaired cat requires less grooming than other longhaired breeds.

Maine Coon Cats are the first pedigreed cats native to the United States. The breed is more than a century old.

These cats nearly became extinct and were put into a special breeding program in Norway. It was in the 1970s that King Olaf named them the Official Cat of Norway. The first Norwegian Forest Cats were imported into the United States in 1979.

This is a cat of substantial size, but the size does vary a bit by lines. If these cats are well socialized from kittenhood, they are the most loving of family members. Affectionately known as Wegies (pronounced WEE-jees), they're extremely sweet, laid-back, and very playful.

Oriental Shorthair

One look at the Oriental Shorthair and you just know they're related to Siamese. However, they come in a wider range of colors and patterns. In fact, this breed comes in a mind-boggling more than 300 colors and patterns. Originating in Britain during the 1950s, they made their way to the United States in the 1970s, where they have gained a devoted following.

They also have a personality that nearly defies description. These felines are such little clowns that it's impossible not to love them, even when they're getting into mischief that might otherwise drive you to distraction. Sleek and slim, graceful and elegant, the Oriental Shorthair is never very far from the humans of his choosing. These cats love to play while also discussing the affairs of the day.

Despite this cat's slim body and long legs, it is a muscular breed—all the better for flying around the room, from mantelpiece to chair to cat tree and back.

Persian

This is the number-one breed in popularity. These cats probably predate their alleged origins in Persia, from which their name is taken. Famous for their long, luxurious coat and their sweet personality, these are fairly laid-back cats. They are brachycephalic, meaning that they have a short nose and are subject to runny eyes and breathing problems, much like Pekingese and Pug dogs. The long coat requires daily combing to maintain its appearance and prevent mats. Owners must pay careful attention to coat care.

Longhaired cats were secreted between the jewels and spices in Persian caravans and eventually smuggled into Europe. These were the cats upon which the breed was developed.

These cats prefer a quiet home but can adapt to a more active one with time, patience, and love. They're not given to climbing and jumping, preferring to have their feet on the ground while their humans worship at their little paws. In fact, their favorite activity would appear to be posing like fashion models. Their coat comes in so many colors that the breed has been divided into seven color divisions at cat shows. And for those who are wondering why the Himalayan isn't listed separately here, it's because it is a pointed, blue-eyed Persian.

These are gentle cats, sweet and loving, and are best suited to gentle owners. Persians are medium to large with muscular bodies and shorter legs. Their large, copper-color eyes are very expressive.

For those who love the Persian but don't want the grooming, there is the Exotic Shorthair, which is, essentially, a shorthaired Persian cat.

Ragdoll

Semilonghaired, large, and gentle, Ragdolls would seem to live up to their name. Altered males weigh between fifteen and twenty pounds. while the females weigh ten to fifteen pounds. This breed was begun by Ann Baker in California in the 1960s. Other breeders eventually broke away and further developed the breed. The coat, which comes in four color patterns, sheds with the seasons and requires daily combing so mats don't form. These cats have lovely blue eyes.

These cats are so people-oriented that they will be the first to greet you at the door when you come home, will follow you around, spend lots of time cuddling with you, and, of course, will sleep with you. Well-mannered little darlings, they prefer to have their feet on the floor and their people within eyesight.

They are incredibly good with children, frequently allowing themselves to be carried around like, well, rag dolls—some even allowing themselves to be dressed up in clothing. These cats are quiet and not given to jumping.

Russian Blue

Another breed whose beginnings are swathed in legend, Russian Blues are believed to have originated in the Archangel Isles in northern Russia. The plush coat has been compared to that of a beaver or a seal, and it's said these cats were once trapped for those coats. Then again, it's also alleged that they were descended from the royal cats of the Russian czars. They are also thought to have been pets of Queen Victoria.

The coat of this medium cat is a bluish gray tipped in silver, so it appears to glisten. Russian Blues were first shown at the Crystal Palace in London in 1875, when they were called the Archangel Cat and competed in a class for all blue cats. These cats were imported into the United States around 1900, but they weren't developed as a breed in the United States until after World War II and didn't see a rise in popularity until the 1960s.

These cats are very intelligent and enjoy interacting with their owners but are equally capable of entertaining themselves. They would rather survey a situation before getting involved. They have a very sweet demeanor and are fairly quiet, although if you talk to them they will respond. They're pretty adept at figuring out how to open things like doors and jars, so you should probably be sure your home is kitty-proofed before you bring home a Russian Blue. They also learn a large number of words, so there's no getting away with anything as far as this cat is concerned. Russian Blues don't require much in the way of grooming. Comb them, pet them, love them.

Scottish Fold

The Scottish Fold gets its name from its ears, which fold down when the cats are just a few days old. Not all of them have ears that fold, so you will see straight-eared Folds—but not in the show ring. Both varieties will appear in a litter. The ones with straight ears still make lovely pets.

The first Scottish Fold was seen at a farm by a shepherd, William Ross, in 1961. Ross asked the owners if he could have one of the

Every Scottish Fold today can trace their ancestry back to the original solid white longhaired female, Susie.

kittens, and it was from this kitten that he developed the breed. The folded ear is a spontaneous mutation of one gene. The fold will appear at between eighteen and twenty-four days of age, if it is going to happen at all.

To expand the gene pool, outcrosses were allowed to American Shorthairs and British Shorthairs, among others, but the cat doesn't resemble any of these, having its own unique look. Some say these cats look like pixies, while others think they resemble owls. They come in a variety of colors.

These intelligent, medium-size cats are sweet and hardy and make lovely pets. Their small voice is as gentle to the ear as the cat is to his people.

Siamese

Another extremely popular breed, the Siamese, or Meezer, as it is affectionately called by its fans, is familiar to anyone who has seen the Disney animated film *Lady and the Tramp*. And they pretty much live up to the lyrics of that film's "Siamese Cat Song": "We are Siamese if you please/We are Siamese if you don't please."

Known for being slim, elegant, and talkative, Siamese will want to discuss absolutely everything with you, including their place in running the household. Lithe and agile, their long, slim, tubular body seems made for propelling them through the air as they go in search of new adventures. For all of their activity, though, they are people oriented.

The Siamese may well be the oldest of all cat breeds. Officially exported from Siam (now Thailand) in the late 1800s, the first Siamese cat to enter Britain was a gift from the ambassador of Siam to a British ambassador. These cats quickly found their way into British cat shows, and American shows shortly thereafter.

They are primarily white, but are known for their points of color on the face, ears, tail, and feet. Each point shade has its own name. The Seal Point Siamese is probably the best known and was also the first to arrive. The coat is a rich, creamy white, and the points are very dark brown, nearly black. There are also Blue Points, Chocolate Points, and Lilac Points. Obviously, there's a color palette for every discriminating Siamese lover.

Siamese adore their humans, talking to them, sitting in their laps, sleeping with them, truly a "Whither thou goest" feline companion. They love children and other pets. Their deep blue almond-shaped eyes are sure to grab your attention.

The Siamese in the show ring are extremely sleek. The old-fashioned look of the Siamese, with a less angular head and a slightly heavy body type, is not considered a Siamese these days by true aficionados, but these cats are wonderful pets and some prefer the more traditional look.

The Balinese is a longhaired Siamese.

Siberian

A natural cat and the national cat of Russia, Siberian cats have been around for about a thousand years. First imported into the United States in 1990, this breed is still considered somewhat rare. This is a semilong-haired, strong, large cat whose coat will thicken in cold weather—as befits their homeland.

These cats have very strong hindquarters, enabling them to jump exceptionally well, rather like a ballet dancer doing a *grand jeté*. They are known to be very intelligent, and if they can't accomplish something the first time, they will work out a way to do it.

Siberians are very loyal, often selecting one family member as "theirs" or electing to cozy up to the people who like dogs—they seem to be favored by "dog people" because Siberians are quick to greet their humans at the door and love to follow them around the house. They don't let something as silly as a door get in between them and the object of their affection—they're smart enough to open that door and beat a path to their beloved human. There's precious little they can't figure out, so you'll want to be on your toes if you decide to bring a Siberian into your home and heart.

They purr, chirp, and otherwise entertain you with a full description of the events of the day. They mature slowly, so prepare for your Siberian to reach maturity at around 5 years old.

Singapura

This is probably the very smallest of the pedigreed cats. Its name is derived from Singapore, its country of origin (*Singapura* is *Singapore* in Malaysian). The coat color is a combination of ticked and dark brown that is native to Southeast Asia. The eyes are hazel or green or even yellow. Kittens are so small that if one is not familiar with the breed, one might wonder if there was some abnormality in the kitten. There isn't. They're just, well, small! When fully grown, males weigh between six and eight pounds while females weigh between five and six pounds.

Singapuras were brought to the United States in the early 1970s by Hal and Tommy Meadow when they returned home from Singapore. Health and temperament were important to the breeders who worked to establish breed type (the unique characteristics of the breed) in the United States.

These cats are outgoing, curious, and perpetually underfoot. They adore people and want to be with them at every possible opportunity. They are also mischief personified but will look at you quite innocently even when caught in the act. "No, it can't be me, it's that invisible cat doing all those naughty things! Do you want to believe your eyes or me?" they seem to be saying.

Despite their diminutive size, they are powerful little cats who combine that with litheness to create one adorable dynamo. Life with a Singapura is not going to be dull.

Sphynx

The Sphynx, a hairless cat, bears an uncanny resemblance to the movie character E.T. In fact, the first one to be shown was named after the film.

In Toronto in 1966, a domestic cat gave birth to a hairless kitten. It was a natural mutation, although the gene for hairlessness is considered a defect by veterinary dermatologists. It's an anomaly, certainly, and the breed has been built upon this anomaly, with breeders breeding hairless cats to normal cats, then back to hairless cats for about forty years. Their goal was to keep the cats genetically sound so they would have few health problems.

Some of the cats, like hairless dogs, will have a fine line of hair down their back. They look rather wrinkled, sort of like prunes with four legs and a tail.

It should be noted that just because they have no hair doesn't mean you do no grooming. The skin requires special care, including baths, and, as with many cats, they will need their ears cleaned. As with hairless dogs, the skin feels warm to the touch and somewhat like chamois, probably due to the downy hair they retain.

In cold weather, if you feel cold indoors, so will your Sphynx, which is something to note if you're taking your cat to the veterinarian in a carrier. Get your Sphynx a sweater to wear when it's cold indoors or if you're taking him somewhere. He will likely be all the more inclined to seek your body warmth, so expect extra cuddles.

These cats, whose name is probably derived from the Egyptian sculpture they resemble, are of a medium size and considerable strength, so while they may appear delicate, looks can be deceiving. They're smart, curious, friendly, and funny, seemingly setting up a situation to make you laugh, rather like a stand-up comic.

Despite any claims you may hear, these are not hypoallergenic cats. Because they are hairless there may be less of an allergic reaction, but the allergen in cats comes from the skin, not the hair. If someone has allergies, they should spend some time with a Sphynx long before bringing one home.

Tonkinese

It's impossible not to feel compelled to stare at these exquisite cats. Their aqua eyes are alluring and look as if they were painted by an artist. The breed comes in a variety of colors, each based on mink to set off those exquisite eyes. The combination of Burmese and Siamese cats that went into creating this breed brought the rich traits of both to the breed. It should be noted that the solid-colored cats have chartreuse eyes, which are also quite captivating.

A medium-size, muscular cat, with males weighing between eight and twelve pounds and females ranging from six to eight pounds, the Tonkinese, or Tonk to his friends, is intelligent, funny, and friendly, an utterly charming companion. Not just a lap sitter, the Tonk will be glad to go for a ride on your shoulder, whether or not you want a four-legged hitchhiker as you move through your home.

Like the Burmese, the Tonkinse trace their origins back to Wong Mau, a cat who came to California in the 1930s.

If these cats were human they might be part of the Wallenda family of aerialists, performing acrobatic stunts from the highest spot in your house. The Tonk will run to the door to greet your visitors, playing social host. Needless to say, with such an intelligent and friendly cat, you're going to have to catproof your home as if you were childproofing it.

Moggie or Mixed Breed

Mixed-breed cats are wonderful pets. They can be the best of all worlds if they are raised properly and loved. They come in a wide range of colors, sizes, shapes, personalities, and activity levels. Of course, none of this is as predictable as it is with a pedigreed cat. But they are each wonderful in their own way.

If you would like to show off your moggie, you can do so at cat shows in the Household Pets category. They are commonly designated as either Domestic Shorthair (DSH) or Domestic Longhair (DLH).

There are a few things that need to be said about these wonderful companions. It doesn't matter whether you got your cat from a neighbor, a friend, or a shelter, all cats deserve love, gentle handling, veterinary care, to be kept indoors, not to be declawed, and to be given environmental enrichment to make their lives as full and interesting as possible.

Cats in the Household Pets classes are judged on condition, beauty, and show presence.

Let's talk a little bit about colors and patterns. There are the well-known tabbies, who come in a variety of shades. Tabby is the most common pattern in domestic cats. Then there are tuxedo cats—the black-and-white kitties—who are primarily black and often have amusing patches of white. Primarily white cats with colored or patterned patches have van markings.

Calico cats are not a breed but a specific color pattern. A calico must have black, white, and orange (also known as red) in his coat. All three colors must be present. Primarily, these cats are female because the genetics responsible for this color pattern is a sex-linked trait. It's really that simple. A black background with random spots of red is called a tortoiseshell pattern, also known as a tortie. This pattern is also sex-linked.

And finally, there are solid-colored cats. The one surrounded by superstition is the black cat. Who knows why? Sadly, though, black cats are the object of abuse, especially around Halloween. In fact, many shelters and rescue groups specifically prohibit the adoption of black cats in October, since some people want them for less than savory reasons during Halloween. Black cats are also less likely to be adopted from a shelter. You may want to consider a black cat if one is available; he can bring love and laughter to your life.

To get into all the colors and patterns in which all cats appear would probably require a genetics book. For our purposes, a cat is a cat and each is beautiful and wonderful in his own right. The mixed-breed cat you choose will give you a lifetime of love. Open your heart and your home to a kitty and watch the love flourish.

CHAPTER 11

CATAPULTING INTO ACTIVITIES

N ow that we've dispelled the myth of cats as independent loners, we can move on to far more important things: all the fun and wonderful activities you and your cat can do together. Doing things together means you'll both have a wonderful learning experience and a closer bond. And we're about to dispel another myth. For some unknown reason, most people are convinced that cats can't be trained. In fact, nothing could be further from the truth. Cats are incredibly smart and learn quite quickly. What they can't figure out on their own, they can often pick up from watching others—cats, humans, even dogs. In other words, they see someone else doing something, and they try it too. Think copycat!

The day you bring your new kitty home is the time to start training. Yes, you can and should start right away; every interaction you have with your cat is a training experience, so you may as well start off on the right foot (paw?). If you think you can train only dogs, you need to think again. Cats are trained the same way dogs are: using praise and rewards to show them what you want them to do. It's easy, it's fun, and every member of the family can be involved.

For those skeptics still shaking your heads, let me point out that your cat, unless she's deaf, runs to the kitchen at the sound of the can opener. Why? You've trained her, whether you realize it or not, to associate that sound with dinner being set down for her. You may as well use training to your advantage and hers, and teach her other skills.

Start Training

The first thing you'll teach kitty to do is recognize her name. This is important, because when she knows her name, you can use it to get her attention and even to have her come to you. You do this by offering little treats or bringing out a toy for her to play with when she comes. She should know that coming when called is a pleasant experience. This will work to your benefit, not only in your relationship with your kitty, but also if you ever have to find her in a hurry. In an emergency, this could be a lifesaver; for example, you may need her to come to you if you have to evacuate the house.

Name recognition also allows you to experiment with motivators. In other words, you can find what motivates your kitty to do things for and with you. This is important, because you will want to teach your cat to do more than respond to her name.

Teaching your cat her name is pretty easy to do. Use her name whenever you speak to her, and be sure to pair it with something nice—pet her, call her to you, give her a treat or a toy. She'll quickly learn that her name means something wonderful is about to happen. When she does, she'll pay attention when you say her name. Praise her lavishly when she responds. Once she's paying attention to you by looking at you and coming to you, you have the foundation for more training.

Click!

You may choose to train using a clicker—although it's certainly not a requirement. This is a little hand-held toy that makes a click sound

Sue Janson

A cat's heart beats twice as fast as a human heart—110 to 140 beats per minute.

when you press it. Clicker training was developed as a way to work with marine mammals because, let's face it, you can't put a collar on a dolphin. Animal behaviorist Karen Pryor, among others, popularized it for animal training when she used it to train marine mammals at Sea Life Park in Hawaii.

Clicker training uses the principles of operant conditioning, which was originally studied by B. F. Skinner. Operant conditioning is a behavior modification technique by which each positive response is rewarded. The cat is the one who makes good things happen by figuring out what you want her to do and doing it. Each time she does, you reward her. And each time she gets a reward, she's more likely to do the behavior again.

The sound of the clicker marks the moment the cat does exactly the right thing. The clicker cuts through the language barrier because, unlike the human voice, it makes a consistent sound that the cat always recognizes as being associated with training.

Some people can't use a clicker because it requires some coordination and excellent timing. If that's the case, you can use a word—"Yes!"—to mark the moment your cat does the right thing, or you can click your tongue.

You will pair the click with the treat. The treat is called a reinforcer. That means it reinforces the message that kitty has done the right thing. Teach your cat that a click means a treat is coming. Set up a training session no more than five minutes long in which you simply click and treat consecutively without saying anything. You may want to do this before mealtime so your cat is hungry, and then you can just feed her meal this way in tiny bits. Or you may choose to give her another healthy tidbit at a different time of day.

Make sure you're picking food your cat really loves and a time of day that works best for you. If your kitty isn't motivated by food, you'll need to find some other reinforcer. You may find that your cat would prefer access to a screened-in porch or sitting on your lap or playing with a certain toy. Some cats just want to make you happy and will do something just because of the interaction with you. It's your job to experiment and find out what your cat enjoys doing. You should watch your cat to learn her body language and discover what she really enjoys. Whatever motivates your cat will be your reinforcer.

Clicker training emphasizes rewarding the positive. As a training technique, it is so much easier and nicer than trying to force an animal to do something. It helps enhance the human-animal bond rather than strain and possibly break it, the way a relationship built on negatives can.

Touch a Target

The next step is to teach your cat to focus her attention on a particular spot. This is called targeting. Using a target stick makes it easier to show kitty what you want her to do and where you want her to go. A target stick is a pointer that shows your kitty where you want her to direct her attention. You can also use your finger, or even a pen.

The first thing you want to do with the target is teach kitty to touch her nose to the target stick. Food is a really good motivator for most cats, so you can use healthy treats for training sessions. (Healthy treats are those that provide some nutrition, not just sugar, salt, and flavor chemicals. Reading labels is as important for treats as it is for cat food.)

This is also an excellent time to try out various cat foods, which you can use as training treats. This way, you'll find it much easier to get your kitty to eat different foods when she's an adult. If your kitty likes to be brushed or combed, you can use that as a motivator, and through these interactions she will learn to enjoy it even more.

You can use a target to begin teaching your cat to come when you say her name. Here's how.

1. Touching something with the nose is a typical cat behavior, so you can either use the plain target stick or the first time you use it, dip the end of it in some wet cat food or something else that smells tempting to your cat.

2. As soon as kitty touches her nose to the tip of the target stick, click your clicker and give her a treat (or let her lick the food off the stick).

3. When she is doing this reliably several times, stop and put the target stick away. Training sessions should be short.

4. Next time (and it can be later the same day), take out the stick and remind her of what she learned last time. Present it, say her name, and click and treat and praise her when she touches it. Repeat several times. This training session is over.

5. For the next training session, you can begin to use the target stick to move your cat from place to place. Present the stick a small distance from her, say her name, and click and treat when she comes over to touch it.

6. Once she learns to touch a target stick or your finger, you can get her to move from place to place. In other words, you can hold the target where you want her to go and she'll go there. That might include jumping over a small hurdle, through a hoop, or from one

chair to another, touching her nose to the target stick with each move.

7. Always give her a click and a treat when her nose touches the target stick.

What Else Can You Teach?

Training is good for so many things! After you've trained your cat to follow a target, the next step is to train her to go into her carrier on cue. Start by making the carrier a fun place to be. Put in a nice bed or fluffy towel to snuggle into, add a toy or two, and give her a treat while she's in there.

Use your target stick to point to the carrier entrance. When kitty gets to it, click and treat. Slowly, on successive tries, move the target stick farther and farther into the carrier, clicking and rewarding with each small increment.

Once she's going in reliably, close the door for short periods of time and then carry her around the house in the carrier. Take her for short rides in the car, too. Don't just take her to the veterinarian or she'll come to dislike car trips. Keep her guessing about where you'll get out of the car. It will also help if you are moving and need to transport kitty in a very safe way to your new home.

Place training, or training your kitty to go to her mat or another chosen place, is also very handy. It can be used to keep your cat off counters, keep her from darting out the door, or keep her from winding between your legs on stairs—which isn't awfully cute if someone trips and falls.

To teach kitty to go to a mat, use your target stick, and click and treat each time she goes to the mat. At first she may just touch the mat with her paw. That's good for a click and a treat. You want to build the behavior in small steps. Eventually, don't click and treat until she is standing with all four paws on the mat.

When she's going to the mat fairly reliably, you can add the word "mat" or any other verbal cue you want, so kitty associates the mat with the word. Just be sure to use the same word every time. To see this training in action, point your internet browser to an award-winning training video made by Certified Cat Behavior Consultant Jacqueline Mason Munera. It shows how she taught a kitten to go to a mat instead of attacking ankles: www.youtube.com/watch?v=jrGj246t57Y.

The training skills I've outlined here are good throughout your kitty's lifetime. Everything else you teach her is frosting on an already sweet cake.

Kitten Kindergarten

Kersti Seksel, an Australian veterinarian with a specialty in behavior, originally developed kitten kindergarten classes, and they are now popping up all over the United States. The idea behind kitten kindergarten is to socialize kittens, teach their owners, and get the kittens to see a veterinarian, since most don't see a veterinarian as often as dogs do.

Kitten kindergarten is for kittens between 8 and 14 weeks of age who have already been seen by a veterinarian to make sure they're healthy. At a typical class, each kitten will be socialized to unfamiliar places, sights, smells, her carrier, the experience of traveling in the car for a fun event, and being held by other people in a game of pass the kitty.

Cat owners will learn the proper way to groom their kitty, including dental care and nail clipping. Owners will also learn what is normal for a cat, both physically and behaviorally. There will be an introduction to clicker training, and a discussion of litter boxes and scratching posts. And kitty will likely learn a trick or two, like giving a high-five or sitting on cue.

Of course, you do have to take the proper precautions for infection control, because the kittens have not yet been fully vaccinated. A well-run kitten kindergarten class will have instructions for all participants on how to do that.

Be cautious of 8-week-old kittens interacting with those who are 14 weeks old, since they are at different developmental stages and will play differently. There is also a size difference that will affect the interactions. You can, however, have supervised visits with older friendly adult cats, and those can be very positive interactions.

Training and Pet-to-Pet Issues

Most people make the mistake of integrating their pets too quickly. Rushing a new cat into the family is seldom successful; you need careful introductions over an extended period of time. Even dogs need time to adjust to each other, and cats aren't dogs. They are not creatures who like to "marry in haste, repent at leisure." In fact, two cats who don't know each other are likely to be downright unfriendly. A little time spent doing the right thing in the beginning can save you a lot of time trying to undo a problem later. This is where both patience and training can pay off handsomely.

In chapter 4 I discussed how to slowly and carefully introduce a new cat into your household. If things didn't go as smoothly as you hoped and you now have a problem, you can use training to help resolve it.

Start by feeding your newcomer and your resident cat on opposite sides of a closed door. Mealtime is a comfortable, happy event for cats, just as it is for us. The cats are likely more relaxed and interested in their meal, which means that the smell of someone new will be more comfortable under these circumstances and will be associated with good things.

You can give the cats an alternate behavior to perform instead of fighting. This is a good time to introduce "look"—a behavior that can make a huge difference. Basically, the "look" cue means each cat looks at the other cat while maintaining a calm demeanor. Or you can teach each cat to look at you. Just make sure you use a distinct and different word as a cue for each behavior.

Teaching your cat to be able to look at your other cat (or dog) without reacting is a form of desensitization—which is habituating kitty to something or someone so that individual or thing becomes familiar. Right now, your cat is reacting the way she normally would in the presence of another animal. You haven't told her what reaction you want, so she is making her own choices. When you teach the "look" cue, you are making the choice instead: I want you to look at the other animal and remain calm.

Here's how you do it.

1. Sit on the floor with your cat so you're at the same level to start. If you can't get down on the floor, you can do this while sitting down in a chair.

2. You have already taught kitty that a click means she's doing something right and a treat is coming. Now, each time her eyes go to the other animal while she's calm, click and treat. Mark this before she has a chance to do anything you don't want.

3. You start building this behavior in small increments. Kitty is rewarded for remaining calm just for a few seconds. Gradually, kitty will look for longer periods.

4. Add the cue word "look" after kitty has looked quietly about half a dozen times, so kitty can associate the word with the action. This is called putting the behavior on cue.

In one five- or ten-minute session, your cat can get the hang of calmly looking toward the other animal and getting rewarded for that. Start from way across the room. Gradually, the cat may be closer to the other cat or dog or look a little longer.

Slowly add distractions. Have the interactions happen in different areas of the house, and move forward only when everyone is very relaxed. Make the situation just a tiny bit more distracting, then keep practicing at that level until everyone is relaxed again. Keep moving forward in very tiny increments. Remember to go very, very slowly, waiting until you are sure all pets are relaxed before raising the bar. Be sure each one knows her name and to come when called, so that you can call one cat away if you see that either is the least bit stressed.

The time this takes varies, of course, depending on the individual pets. It can take a couple of weeks or it may take several months before the new cat is integrated into the household. Slower is better, so that you are sure that everyone is calm and accepting. What you are doing is teaching impulse control.

It's tough to train two animals at the same time, so it's a good idea to teach your resident cat or dog some basic training before you bring the new cat home. Then you can train the new cat while she's in her separate room, so they both know the "look" skill when you start introducing them.

Let's Have Some Fun!

Teaching cats of all ages to do fun behaviors (including tricks) is very important because most housecats are smart and bored. Cats are superb predators, and since they don't have to hunt for their food, they don't have much to do. A cat who is anxious or is a bully or is destroying things is usually just a bored, frustrated cat. Give her something to do and you'll see her behavior improve.

Cats also want to do things with you. They're not loners; in fact, they crave interaction. When you're training together, it will strengthen your bond.

You train a cat to do a trick the same way you train her to target your finger. Think about what you'd like your cat to do. Start with something simple, like shake paw or high-five. When you get the hang of training—and your cat gets the hang of learning—you can progress to complex tricks. Cats can learn to roll over and play dead or jump through hoops. Some people teach kitty a cute stance or to jump up on a chair or sit up on their haunches like a meercat. Others teach their cat to put a ball through a hoop or play a child's piano or open a door.

If you need ideas, you can even look at a dog trick book—because cats can do all the same tricks. You may want your cat to jump through your arms or ride on your shoulder. You could teach her to "go shopping" by pushing along a tiny doll's shopping cart. The sky's the limit. You can do as much as your imagination allows. The more tricks you teach, the more interesting it is for kitty—and you.

Princess Kitty, who was owned and loved by Karen Payne of Florida, wasn't a member of any particular breed, but she became an extremely famous cat. Karen lovingly taught her to do such a wide variety of behaviors and tricks that Princess Kitty ended up on television and in the movies. Karen made a video of her training techniques that is still available at www.princesskitty.com.

When you're training your own princess, start small with one skill and one session and build on it. For example, it can be very useful to teach your cat to sit on cue. Dogs aren't the only ones who can do this. For this very simple trick, we're going to use a bit of lure and reward training along with the clicker. We will eliminate the lure very quickly.

The lure will be one of your kitty's favorite treats. Have the clicker in one hand and the treat in the other. Let kitty smell the treat and slowly bring it up over her head and back, so it causes kitty to look up but not jump up. Looking up will cause kitty's rear end to go down. As soon as her rear hits the floor, click and give her the treat.

Don't use the word *sit* until she's done this successfully about half a dozen times, and only reward her when she sits. Pretty soon you can tell her to sit and she will, then you'll reward her with a tasty treat. And won't your friends be surprised when they see what your cat can do!

A cat isn't just a cat. A cat is a wonderful, loving, intelligent companion and a family member. Remember that what you get out of the relationship

Tricky Fun

Now that you've taught your kitty to do amazing tricks like playing a child's piano, jumping through a hoop or your arms, and riding on a skateboard, you can amuse your friends at home or help with fundraisers for shelters (as long as the facility is clean and safe) by putting on a little show that you and your kitty have created.

Once you've taught your cat to respond on cue, you can put whatever words you want to the trick and make it funny or instructional for your audience—or both! For example, if you've taught your kitty to play dead you can introduce the trick by saying to kitty, "What would happen if you raided the garbage can?" and then give her a hand signal for play dead. It's a good lesson for your audience, because the garbage can be dangerous for cats. But it's a painless way for them to learn.

will depend upon what you put into it. Open your heart up and let the love shine through.

Harness Training

Do you want to take your cat for a walk so she has an opportunity to safely experience the great outdoors? You can. But you can't just snap a leash and harness on her. After all, wearing a harness and a leash is a brand-new experience for her. Here's how to train your kitty so she enjoys the experience.

The first thing you will need to do is buy her a properly fitting harness. You should be able to get a finger under it, but she shouldn't be able to slip out of it. You may, instead, opt for a walking jacket. Do not use a collar and leash for walking kitty. You could easily injure her and she could easily slip out of the collar—and either way it's an accident waiting to happen.

When you bring the harness or walking jacket home, put it down for kitty to sniff. When she shows interest, click and treat. Let her get used to it like this for a couple of days before you put it on her for the first time.

When you first put it on her, do it at mealtime so she's happily distracted and associates the new item with something good. Let her wear

Claire Clayton

Cats can safely enjoy the great outdoors with a harness attached to an owner.

it for a few minutes, eating all the while, and increase the time she wears it each day.

After several days, add the leash and let her drag it around for a few minutes. Keep an eye on her so she doesn't get the leash caught on anything in the house. After a couple of days of this, pick up the end of the leash and walk around the house with her. Let her lead the way.

Practice this until she's comfortable with it, and always remember to give her a click and treat for positive behavior. Add a cue word. You can use "heel," "walk," or another word that's only used for walks on a harness and leash. Do *not* attempt to take her outdoors until she's accustomed to the harness or walking jacket and leash.

When you finally take kitty out, do it when there aren't a lot of people or pets outside so she doesn't have many distractions at first and her walks are positive experiences. Let her walk at her own pace and explore. She's not going to heel like a dog, but she will be sniffing, looking at, and otherwise exploring her surroundings. This is, after all, *her* walk. Make it a fun and enjoyable experience.

Cat Agility

If you think agility is only for dogs, guess what? Cats love this sport. Cat agility is a timed run under, over, and through an obstacle course. The obstacles include jumps and hoops, and one object set up for the cat to sit and stay for a set amount of time during the run. The owner runs beside the cat, giving her instructions and encouragement along the way.

Any naturally athletic and quick cat will want to do agility. Among the breeds that do well are the Abyssinian, Japanese Bobtail, Maine Coon Cat, Turkish Angora, and Bengal. Mixed-breed cats also do very well in agility. An award-wining agility cat named Black Jack, owned by Carroll Muck, accrued 1,131 points in competition—which is quite an accomplishment. Cat agility competitions are held at shows put on by both CFA and TICA, so there's ample opportunity to watch and participate.

The cats are in an enclosed agility area at cat shows, so they're not running loose in the show hall; it's all very safe. A cat agility course is run counterclockwise. The standard course consists of ten obstacles. There are stairs (three steps up, a twenty-two-inch-wide top, and three steps down), two jumps (one over a four-inch bar and one over a two-inch bar), an open tunnel (unlike the one in canine agility that collapses), a hoop that is six inches off the ground, a set of weave poles (four vertical poles set two feet apart that the cat must weave in and out of), two jumps (ten-inch and fourteen-inch), one last tunnel, and one last hoop.

A timer is running from the moment the cat's paw touches the first step until a paw comes down through the last hoop.

Generally, people handle their own cats in the agility ring, although other people can be recruited if the owner isn't agile enough to run the course with the cat. It's not a big course, mind you, but the handler must stay ahead of the cat and keep an eye on the obstacles at the same time to guide kitty through the course.

Agility is also something well-mannered, responsible children can do with their cats. It's a fine idea to get them involved in a sport that's fun, encourages good sportsmanship, and teaches them kindness and responsibility to animals as well as builds the bond between them. You and your family will also meet a lot of wonderful, like-minded people along the way, making friends within the cat agility community.

Cats are trained at home, of course. This is a great way to channel the energy of an especially playful cat who likes to follow toys that you drag. These are cats and kittens who enjoy spending time playing with you and will jump and leap and run. Obstacles are set up and usually the cat is lured through them using a piece of food or a toy. You can use anything as an obstacle at home; for example, kitty can go under a chair or a table and over a box. Just be sure that kittens aren't being asked to jump too high while they're still young and growing.

The key thing with agility competitions is to make sure your cat is comfortable performing outside your home. She needs to know she's safe whenever she's with you, no matter where she is. This is where socialization comes in, along with fun trips with you, including rides in the car that don't end in a trip to the vet or to see a groomer. Your calm behavior will help kitty feel calm wherever she is. You might take her to visit a friend's home, where she will be safe but can explore a new place. My cat has accompanied me on a ferry, stayed in hotels, and has even been known to go to the accountant's office with me. In fact, I think the accountant is disappointed when I don't bring my cat along, because right after saying hello he asks me where she is.

There are basic and advanced levels of agility competition. How far you and your cat advance will depend on your kitty—and you. As long as you're both having fun, there's no reason to stop, even if you're not winning prizes. Cats are extremely intelligent and learn quickly. They cooperate with those they love, so to them, this is just another wonderful way of interacting. They don't care about the ribbons and trophies. And their fans just love it! Watching the fun cats and their owners have in agility inspires others to try something new with their own cat.

International Cat Agility (ICAT) is the official organization for cat agility. It has a wonderful web site, chock-a-block full of great information. You'll find the web site address in appendix B.

Whether you enter official competitions is up to you, of course. Even if you don't, training for agility is a great way to give your cat's brain and body a workout.

Therapy Cats

Therapy dogs have gotten a lot of good press—and deservedly so—but many cats enjoy doing therapy work as well. Not every cat is right for this activity, just as not every dog is right for it, but if your cat is one who enjoys therapy work, it's very rewarding for both kitty and you.

Cats who are calm and gentle and aren't easily startled are best for therapy work, since they will be sitting on laps and must be gentle with elderly people and not scratch their fragile skin. Therapy cats can't be startled by wheelchairs, canes, or walkers.

Therapy cats visit hospitals and facilities for seniors. The cat will sit on top of a blanket or towel on a person's lap during a visit. Some cats wear a flexible figure-eight harness and leash, which is a good safety measure. There are other places you can visit, as well, including classrooms for special needs children. Autistic children, for example, often benefit from the interaction with an animal. With the children sitting on the floor, they can interact with the cat. Transitional housing for women

Quiet cats who like to plop in laps are the best candidates for therapy work.

with children who have been in abusive situations is also a candidate for a pet therapy visit. Cat-facilitated therapy is for people who need some extra help in physical therapy; to restore range of motion, you may help them pet or brush the cat.

Cats can help children who have been afraid of animals, mentally challenged people, and physically challenged individuals. You can show them how to put their forefinger out and let the cat sniff it during the initial greeting. Just putting a soft, cuddly cat up against a stroke victim so they can feel the heat coming through the animal's body can be helpful.

These cats bring something magical to the people they visit. Elderly people who haven't talked in a long time will begin to talk, perhaps reminiscing about the cat they had when they were young or making soft conversation, just talking to the cat. Troubled children who are afraid to talk to people will often confide in a cat, helping make that initial breakthrough on their road to healing.

Your cat must pass a test in order to become a registered therapy or pet partner cat. The Delta Society is a national organization that teaches people how to train their pets, and gives the required tests. There are classes and there is also a home study available at their web site (which you will find listed in appendix B). The Delta Society provides benefits to their registered Pet Partners teams, including liability insurance when volunteering.

The kind of work most cats do is called pet partners by the Delta Society, since therapy work is now mostly used to describe working pets who have been trained to help their owners cope with a specific problem, such as posttraumatic stress syndrome or certain fears.

A therapy or pet partner cat will require an examination by a veterinarian and must be up to date on vaccines, especially rabies. An evaluator from the Pet Partner Program will then evaluate the cat and her person as a potential Pet Partners team. The test is somewhat similar to

Live-in Love

Visits aren't the only way in which cats can help people. Some cats live at nursing homes and rehab facilities. Chantilly Nettles, a Chartreux bred by Nancy Dionne in Idaho and owned by Sandra and Jamie Nettles in Phoenix, Arizona, works at Deer Valley Counseling. She spends her time greeting people, interacting, and, of course, napping. There is something special about the presence of a cat.

the test for dogs, although cats are not required to sit and stay on command.

Among the skills a cat must demonstrate before being accepted into a therapy program are accepting examination by a stranger, clumsy petting, high-pitched voices, clumsy movement, clenched hand petting, a restraining hug, staggering movements, and angry yelling. Needless to say, your cat cannot be afraid of walkers, canes, loud noises, or shouting. The animal must be calm throughout all of this. Another test is being bumped from behind. You will carry your cat in either a basket or a blanket or towel, and, while you're walking as you would in a facility you would be visiting, someone will come up and bump into you from behind. This is a test for both you and the cat. Being crowded and petted by several people is tested as well. The evaluator will also give the cat a treat to see if kitty becomes excited or aggressive or will gently take the treat.

If your kitty is one who is suited to therapy cat visits, you will be sharing a very special gift with others in need. Just pay attention to your cat and know when she's had enough. Each cat is an individual, of course, and while some can't get enough of the interaction, petting, and attention, others will lose their enthusiasm after a period of time, perhaps a year. However long your cat is willing, it will be a very special time for you both.

APPENDIX A

SHOPPING FOR YOUR CAT

You really should put together a kitty "layette" before you bring your new cat or kitten home. You'll need the basics: food and water dishes, cat tree, scratching post, litter boxes and litter, comb, brush, a toy or two to start, and a cat bed. Needless to say, your collection of cat accoutrements will grow exponentially. Somehow, it's hard to stop buying kitty toys, furniture, and accessories. There are even some great items for cat owners. Ahhh, so many goodies!

There is a happy medium, and you'll find yours. Meanwhile, here are some suggestions. Remember when buying cat furniture that you are making an investment. Cheaper may not be sturdy enough or last long enough, so shop carefully.

Cat Trees and Beds

Arubacat has some great handmade cat trees that are solid and secure, with no worry of kitty tipping anything over. They also have scratching posts of various sizes and shapes. **www.arubacat.com**

Armakat carries a nice assortment of sturdy cat trees and cat beds at good prices. **www.armarkat.com**

When kitties get older, it's helpful for some to have stairs next to the bed and other furniture to help them climb up to you. A ramp can also help. Check out Steps for Pets. **www.stepsforpets.com**

The Refined Feline has some very interesting cat trees and shelves. If you live in a small apartment or just feel like splurging on something really striking, check out the cat trees. Even if you can't afford to buy anything, well . . . a cat can look at a queen! **www.therefinedfeline .com**

Another expensive but interesting site for cat furniture, including sculptured cat trees, is Angelical Cat Company. The company even has cat jigsaw puzzles and mailboxes, so it's worth spending some time surfing around. Their themed cat furniture has to be seen to be believed. Some of it is wonderfully whimsical and would certainly be great conversation pieces, as well as practical additions to your cat's home. **www .angelicalcat.com**

A nice twist on cat furniture that looks like furniture is the Bookcase Climber, Bed & Litter Cabinet, available from Cats Play. This particular piece of cat furniture, made by furniture maker Sauder, Woodworking Company, looks like a very attractive bookcase/wall unit. **http://cats play.com/pausbook.php3**

The Cattress Mattress company makes CatAWhack, a product designed to satisfy kitty's desire to scratch, no matter what her favorite surface is. It's a combo bed and scratching station, offering an unfinished wood frame, a scratching pad that can be adjusted based on whether kitty prefers a horizontal or a vertical scratch, a washable mattress for the sleep area, and several toys. **http://cattressmattress.com**

Dinnerware

If your cat is older and arthritic or tends to vomit up her meals, she might appreciate an elevated dinner bowl. When it's this elegant, it's hard to call it a food dish. With their classical design and lovely pedestals that never tip, these dishes not only serve a practical purpose, but will look extremely nice in your home as well. They're handmade on Vancouver Island. **www.classycatdishes.com**

Carriers

If you want to carry your kitty in a safe, durable carrier, a canvas SturdiBag from SturdiProducts is an excellent choice. It fits under the seat of the plane without collapsing on kitty and has a comfy, washable pad and a back pocket where you can carry some food or a paperback book or anything else that might be useful on your trip. Their CarGo for transporting one or two kitties in your car is another great carrier. It comes in a variety of colors or patterns and is simple to assemble. SturdiProducts has other handy products, too. All of them are made in the USA. Find their products in some pet supply stores and online. **www .sturdiproducts.com**

Cat Toys

Cats really do seem to love boxes and paper bags. They're rather like little kids who prefer the box the gift came in and play with that instead of the gift. Capitalizing on that is Catty Stacks boxes you can stack, with appropriate openings for kitty to climb in and out. They also make nice hidey-holes when kitty wants to get away from it all. **www.cathouse system.com**

Kong Company is primarily known for making great dog toys, but they have a wonderful line of cat toys as well. Their products will help keep kitty occupied and happy and can be found in many retail outlets or on the company's web site. **www.kongcompany.com**

If your cat has the catnip gene, you can buy catnip buds in a bag, catnip bubbles, catnip spray, and catnip toys in various pet supply stores. Try Dr. Daniels' for catnip toys and watch your kitty's ecstatic reaction. Just remember that catnip is a treat. Remove it before she has a chance to go completely bonkers playing with it. **www.drdaniels.com**

Collars, Harnesses, and Walking Jackets

Looking for a collar for your kitty? Lupine has a great assortment of breakaway collars that are guaranteed to last for the life of your pet. They come in a wide range of attractive fabrics. The company also makes cat harnesses and leashes. You can find them at various retailers or online. **www.lupinepet.com**

Premier products offers a safe walking harness along with a bungee leash in case kitty decides to dart forward. They also have some wonderful treat-dispenser toys to help kitty use her hunting and play skills and get some exercise while she's getting her treats or dry food. **www .premier.com**

If you'd prefer a walking jacket, one of the places you can find it is MetPet. Some cats find a jacket more comfortable than a harness. The jacket has more uses than just taking your cat for a walk, too. It is very handy when you're traveling, for example, clearing security at the airport, because kitty is less likely to slip out of your grasp when she's in her walking jacket. **www.MetPet.com**

Another source for walking jackets is Joykatz. They hand sew the jackets in a variety of fabrics and patterns. Very smart looking! **www .joykatz.net/walkingjackets.htm**

And here's a third source for your shopping pleasure: HDW Enterprises. In fact, we can probably expect to see more walking jackets available as the idea catches on. **www.hdw-inc.com/walkingjackets.htm**

Cat Enclosures

If you want your cat to experience the outdoors without the dangers, or you live in a small apartment with a balcony and want to safely allow kitty to enjoy the outdoors, the solution is a cat enclosure. Most require some assembly and must be set up in a permanent place. But one company, Kritter Kommunity, has created a portable, collapsible enclosure that you can fold up and store when not in use or take with you if you travel. Kritter Kondos are also sold at various online and retail stores. **www.kritterkommunity.com**

Stress Relief

If your kitty is stressed at home or while traveling, or if there's tension in your home among kitties, Feliway can be a very helpful product. You won't know whether it will work for your kitty unless you try. To learn more, visit their web site. Their products are sold at a wide range of pet supply outlets. **www.feliway.com**

If You Can't Get Out to Shop

If hauling home bags of cat food and litter is a problem, or if you are disabled and are faced with a logistical problem getting these large items home, one solution is to order online. Pet Food Direct has a very wide range of brands and will ship directly to your home. **www.pet fooddirect.com**

Just for You

Red Tango makes a variety of great accessories and clothing featuring a retro kitty. The products are found in various stores and some are available online from the artist's very amusing web site. **www.tangoland .com**

If only all the Red Tango products were at the company site! The laptop, iPod, and cell phone covers are hard to find, but I've tracked them down. On the main page, choose Art from the list on the left. Then you'll find the Red Tango icon. **www.musicskins.com**

Who can resist a cute T-shirt? Especially if it has at least one cat on it and it's funny. Cats on T-Shirts is full of fun T-shirts for cat lovers. **www .cats-on-tshirts.com**

Cat Lover T-shirts are the creation of well-known cartoonist Stephanie Piro. Her sense of humor and knowledge of cats and their people comes through in her cartoons, some of which have found their way onto T-shirts. Stephanie offers wholesale rates for shelter fundraisers. **www.stephaniepiro.com/StripTs.htm**

Action Cat is a web site devoted to free, mostly animated, cat e-cards. They're cute, clever, fun, and don't look like the average e-cards. If you're looking for a great e-card to send to a cat-loving friend for virtually any occasion, check it out. **www.actioncat.com**

If you love cat art and are looking for something really lovely, check out the work of Catman Drew. Drew Strouble's Feline Fine Art is worth seeing. He claims to have the largest one-man cat art gallery in the world. You can also purchase his work on puzzles, mugs, calendars, mouse pads, and more. Drew's Art for the Animals Foundations supports cat rescues and shelters. **www.catmandrew.com**

The Official Simon Teakettle Virtual MEWsical Society may be just your cup of catnip tea. The brainchild of Barbara Florio Graham, a writer based in Canada, this site features some amazing virtual theater productions. See for yourself. (In the interest of full disclosure, it should be noted that my cat, Aimee, is a member.) **www.simonteakettle.com/ musical.society.htm**

APPENDIX B

USEFUL RESOURCES

Finding the right resources is critical. There's a lot of information out there, but not all of it is good information. Just because something is in a book or on the Internet doesn't mean you can trust it. You need to be able to find sources you can trust. I've done some of the digging for you. The resources here are ones I know won't steer you wrong.

Web Sites

The American Animal Hospital Association

This is the organization to which many veterinary practices belong. They go through a certification process during which the hospital is evaluated on more than 800 standards that must be met. A portion of the web site is set aside for pet owners, and it has great health information. **aahanet.org/OtherSites/healthypet.aspx**

The American Association of Feline Practitioners

This is the association of veterinarians who are board-certified in feline medicine. They may be working in a multispecies animal hospital or in one dedicated solely to cats, but in either case their special area of interest and expertise is feline medicine. At this site you can, among other things, search for cat health topics, and even search out a feline practitioner in your area. **www.catvets.com**

The American Veterinary Medical Association

A portion of their web site is dedicated to pet owners. It has download-able brochures, disaster preparedness information, information on pet food recalls and more. **www.avma.org/animal_health/default.asp**

ASPCA

The American Society for the Prevention of Cruelty to Animals has a wonderfully useful web site. The ASPCA has the distinction of being the first humane organization in the Western Hemisphere, having been founded in 1866 by Henry Burgh. Today, they remain dedicated to their mission. Among their services is their well-known Poison Control Center; the web site has a very comprehensive list of poisonous and safe plants. (It's a good idea to keep the Poison Control Center phone number handy: (888) 426-4435. Note that they charge for the help you will get on the phone call, and it's not inexpensive, but in an emergency it's good to have in addition to your own veterinarian's number. The charge includes follow-up with your veterinarian.) **www.aspca.org**

CATalyst Council

The CATalyst Council reaches out to the public, shelters, veterinarians, local governments, welfare organizations, and others in an effort to ensure that cats receive proper health care and attention. It also has an e-newsletter. **www.catalystcouncil.org**

Cat Repellants

Why would you want to keep cats away? We know how much kitties enjoy snoozing on windowsills and looking out the window. But if you have strays in your neighborhood, or neighbors who let their cat roam, this can become a territorial problem for your indoor cat. To keep stray cats away from your windows safely and humanely, try the suggestions on this web site. **www.cat-repellant.info**

Clicker Training

Clicker training is wonderful; it's fun, it's easy, and the entire family can do it. One of the best resources is Karen Pryor's web site, where you will find helpful articles, a clicker training community, and clicker train-ing items for sale. **www.clickertraining.com**

Cornell Feline Health Center

Cornell University College of Veterinary Medicine is renowned for, among other things, its wonderful feline health web site that's devoted to cat health and behavior. The Cornell Feline Health Center was the "baby" of the late, great Jim Richards, DVM. His work continues today, as does the wonderful website. **www.vet.cornell.edu/fhc/**

The Delta Society

Great information here about their Pet Partner Program for therapy animals, as well as other initiatives. **www.deltasociety.org**

Feline Asthma with Fritz the Brave

The brainchild and life's work of the late cat writer Kathryn Hopper, this site was begun because her Siamese cat, Fritz, was diagnosed with asthma and she felt there was not enough information available for pet owners whose cats had received the same diagnosis. Kathryn contacted the leading experts in the field, including the esteemed Dr. Phil Padrid, to bring the best possible information to cat owners. The site is still relevant, useful, and helpful. **www.fritzthebrave.com**

ICAT

Agility isn't just for dogs. Now you and your kitty can have fun exercising both body and mind. ICAT is the official organization for cat agility. They have a good deal of helpful information, including upcoming competitions, on their web site. **www.catagility.com**

Indoor Cat Initiative

The Ohio State University's School of Veterinary Medicine has a wonderful web site with great information about keeping cats indoors, what indoor cats needs, what stresses them, and more. **www.vet.ohio-state .edu/indoorcat.htm**

Winn Feline Foundation

This wonderful nonprofit organization, founded in 1968, is devoted to funding studies to improve cat health. They have a lot of good information at their web site, including a free cat health library. **www.winnfeline health.org**

"I put down my book, *The Meaning of Zen*, and see the cat smiling into her fur as she delicately combs it with her rough pink tongue. 'Cat, I would lend you this book to study but it appears you have already read it.' She looks up and gives me her full gaze. 'Don't be ridiculous,' she purrs, 'I wrote it.'" —Dilys Laing

Finding an Animal Behaviorist

The American College of Veterinary Behaviorists lists board-certified veterinary behaviorists—veterinarians with a specialty in behavior. The number of board-certified veterinary behaviorists is small but, hopefully, growing. **www.dacvb.org**

The American Veterinary Society of Animal Behavior is a membership-only organization of veterinarians and persons holding a PhD in animal behavior or a related field. (You'll also find some good cat behavior articles on their web site.) **www.avsabonline.org**

The International Association of Animal Behavior Consultants is a group of dedicated behavior consultants who will work with you and your veterinarian. There is a need for them because there are so few board-certified veterinary behaviorists and applied animal behaviorists. Certified behavior consultants must meet rigorous qualification criteria and maintain their certification by meeting continuing education requirements. **www.iaabc.org**

Helpful Books

Cat vs. Cat by Pam Johnson-Bennett (Penguin, 2004).

> This book is devoted to helping you keep the peace if you have more than one cat. Pam is the chair of the Cat Division of the International Association of Animal Behavior Consultants. She knows cats well and provides a lot of solid information in this book.

Cat Owner's Home Veterinary Handbook, 3rd edition by Debra M. Eldredge DVM, Delbert G. Carlson DVM, Liisa D. Carlson DVM, and James M. Giffin MD (Howell Book House, 2008).

> This is a classic health book that belongs on every cat owner's bookshelf. It's both comprehensive and easy to read.

Encyclopedia of Cat Breeds by J. Anne Helgren (Barron's Educational Series, 1997).

> This is a wonderful resource on all popular cat breeds. It's another that cat lovers will enjoy having at home.

Getting Started: Clicker Training for Cats by Karen Pryor (Sunshine Books, 2003).

> This is a basic book to help start you and your kitty off on the right paw. Training is fun and easy for the whole family, and your cat will thank you for that extra helping of fun and interaction.

INDEX

ABOUT THE AUTHOR

Darlene Arden is an award-winning writer and a Certified Animal Behavior Consultant. She lectures widely on wellness for pets, on topics including behavior, training, and nutrition. She is also an experienced television producer/host, a lively guest expert on various radio and television programs, and a popular and much acclaimed speaker.

Veronique Schejtman

Darlene and Aimee

Darlene is a founding member of the International Association of Animal Behavior Consultants, a former director of the Cat Writers' Association, one of the few layperson members of the American Association of Human-Animal Bond Veterinarians, and a member of Boston Authors Club. Among her numerous awards are the CWA Muse Medallion and the Massachusetts Society for the Prevention of Cruelty to Animals/ American Humane Education Society's Media Award for veterinary writing and animal welfare.

In her "spare time," Darlene is a volunteer cat behavior consultant for Pets for Life in New York City.

You can visit Darlene Arden on her web site: www.darlenearden. com.

Twitter: twitter.com/petxpert

Facebook: www.facebook.com/#!/pages/Darlene-Arden/ 38527843746?ref = ts